KU-079-805

Contributors

Catherine Bailey, Freelance Consultant.

John Bank, Lecturer in Industrial Relations, Cranfield School of Management.

John Beresford, Lecturer in Statistics, Civil Service College, Sunningdale.

David Butcher, Lecturer in Organizational Behaviour, Cranfield School of Management.

Paul Dainty, Tutor in Human Resources, European School of Management Studies.

Jacqueline Drake, Lecturer in Organizational Behaviour, Cranfield School of Management.

Roger Jones, Lecturer in Industrial Relations, Cranfield School of Management.

Andrew P. Kakabadse, Professor of Management Development, Cranfield School of Management.

Ron Ludlow, Lecturer in Organizational Behaviour, Cranfield School of Management.

Tim Norman, Manager, Bank of America.

Fergus Panton, Consultant in Human Resource Management.

Shaun Tyson, Senior Lecturer in Personnel Management, Cranfield School of Management.

Paul Willman, Lecturer in Organizational Behaviour, London Business School.

Acknowledgements

We would like to acknowledge the contribution made by the hundreds of managers who have helped to shape these cases by their comments, when the cases have been taught in class. We are grateful for the help of Tony Kipperberger and Jean Bartlett in writing the Henry Smart, Grayle Engineering and Guy Roberts cases. We would also like to thank the people depicted here, or whose situations are described. Without them we can truly say there would not have been a book.

The cases in this book are drawn from a number of sources and any resemblance to existing companies is entirely coincidental.

Sections of the Box Makers case appear in *Working in Organisations* by A. Kakabadse, R. Ludlow and S. Vinnicombe, published by Gower 1987. The Epicurus Leisure Group, Archon Engineering and Thomas Nestor cases were quoted in *Evaluating the Personnel Function* by S. Tyson and A. Fell, published by Hutchinson 1986. We are grateful for permission to publish them here. The New York Times has kindly given permission for the reproduction of Appendix 2 of the Greenfields case.

Finally, we would like to thank Dorothy Rogers and Mairi Bryce for their patience and their typing skills.

Shaun Tyson
Andrew Kakabadse

Introduction

SHAUN TYSON

In this book are collected twenty-seven case studies which are designed to expand the reader's knowledge of managing people in organizations. The term 'human resources management' is intended to convey the value of managing people as other scarce resources are managed, so that care and attention may be given to the acquisition, utilization, motivation and development of employees. Managers now recognize how finite the quantities of energy, enthusiasm, and creativity are among their employees, and appreciate how the achievement of organizational objectives is dependent on their employees' abilities. When technology and financial resources are evenly matched between competing organizations the advantage rests with the organization whose employees possess superior experience, knowledge and skill. Hence success or failure in business turns on how human resources are managed. Our chief reason for compiling these case studies was our belief in the importance of this managerial task.

The case for cases

The case study or case history is an ideal vehicle for extending our understanding of organizational behaviour. From the contingency theory of organizations we know that behaviour in organizations is contingent upon a range of factors such as the organization's history, its markets, its preferred management style, the industrial relations traditions which prevail and the many cultural and technological influences which are specific to that particular organization, at that period of time.[1] Case studies may be used to expose the complexities of behaviour, and to provide a context for the study of social action.

Case studies encapsulate experiences, they allow for the singular circumstance, and grant readers the opportunity to select ideas and techniques, and to compare these with their own experience. Although there are different styles of learning, whatever the preferred approach, most managers place a premium on experience in their own development. This seems to be because when we are able to see, feel, and hear, we understand for ourselves. The way learning occurs through experience is described by Kolb.[2]

There is no doubt stories can trigger a response not found in other forms of teaching. Stories may be seen as one form of experiential learning, since they encourage us to see in our everyday experience of the world a deeper reality with which we may come into touch, and through our reflection on the message behind the story, we come to learn more about ourselves.

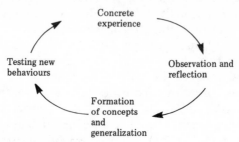

Figure 1 *Kolb's learning cycle*

This diagram demonstrates the role of experience in learning where we generalize from our experience, and experiment with new ideas, as a consequence of what we have learned. The 'feedback' we receive from significant others tells us whether the experimental behaviour was successful, so we may then modify our future behaviours, taking this into account. We may conclude that some generalization from our experience seems to be necessary in order to learn.

The crucial distinction between the case study and other methods is that with the case study method the reader draws specific ideas, or understandings, from a particular context which can then be compared with broader theoretical generalizations. This follows the pattern of our normal method of learning by moving from the particular experience to the broader generalization. Case studies may engage the consciousness of the reader at both the emotional and the intellectual level. In the human resources field an appeal to feelings is entirely appropriate, since the reader's identification with the characters or situations adds an emotional charge to the comparison between the written word and personal experience. This gives a powerful impetus to the learning process: it heightens an awareness of the issues as they were faced by the characters in the case study and from this empathetic experience comes a personal commitment to the acquisition of new learning.

This is not a new device for imparting wisdom and understanding. The case study is a story, and stories have always been used as a way of teaching. Parables are common in most religions, and we know from the *New Testament* that Christ used stories extensively in His teaching to reveal truths about ourselves. Stories, like *Aesop's Fables* or folk tales usually have a moral to impart. Good and evil, death and renewal are represented symbolically for example, and the power stories exercise over our minds has even led to the conclusion by Carl Jung that there are universal archetypes to which our subconscious minds respond when these basic human stories are told. Jung argues that myths and fairytales contain motifs which are found in all cultures.

'These typical images and associations are what I call archetypal ideas. The more vivid they are, the more they will be coloured by particularly strong feeling tones. They impress, influence and fascinate us.'[3]

Following these notions, Eric Berne saw stories and fairytales forming an important part of a child's understanding of the world, and hence conditioning its destiny.[4] Whether we accept these psychoanalytic arguments, or the religious view of stories as purveyors of truth about the self, found for example in the insistence within Zen that we should reflect on our experience of life intuitively rather than logically, there is no doubt stories can trigger a response not found in other forms of teaching. Stories turn myths into legends, and offer truths which may be interpreted at several levels of reality.

Organizational realities also may be found on different levels. Stories about organizational heroes help to create the organization's culture, and stories of success and failure are part of the socialization process, as they help to sustain values. The repetition of favoured stories is one way in which organizational continuity is maintained. The tradition on which we draw when using case studies is as old as teaching itself, and is a powerful ingredient in everyday learning from experience.

Selecting cases for teaching purposes

The cases in this book all seek to establish important teaching points about the management of human resources. Teaching notes are published separately which give an outline of how each case could be taught. However, in selecting which case is appropriate, teachers should be open to the possibility of using cases in a number of different ways. The guiding principle on which case study to use is dependent on the teaching purpose. The different purposes for which cases may be used can be seen from the following typology.[5] This typology was developed after many years of teaching cases, and writing them.

A typology of cases

Type and description

Areas which are suitable

Organization/environment interaction
Set at organization level, they pose problems of strategy, present broad business problems, and show the interrelationship of different functions.

- Corporate planning.
- Policy issues.
- Organization design.
- Management of change.

Illustrative of behaviour
Cases which illustrate a range of behaviours, or problems to which the student responds, typically by discovering alternative courses of action.

All 'operational' techniques in the areas of personnel management, and interpersonal skills.

Sequential
Core material, supplemented with extra briefs, are used to describe particular problems. Usually set at the organization level, these cases can be operated on a long time scale. The key issues are concerned with the type of information, and how the extra brief supplements or modifies the core material.

The working of policy. Given policy objectives, how can particular problems be solved e.g. negotiation strategy.

Type and description	**Areas which are suitable**
Role play	
Cases in which the basic information on the situation is supplemented by the students, who act out the roles of the people described. These cases most frequently demonstrate *process*. The focus is on the treatment by the students, rather than on the material itself.	Interpersonal skills areas especially: discipline ⎱ appraisal ⎰ interviews selection counselling negotiating persuasion conflict resolution (e.g. third party interventions) running meetings leadership skills
Solution based	
Cases for which there is a correct answer, where a particular solution is sought. This may be presented as a forced choice to the students, between alternatives, or in a more open ended way.	Knowledge of techniques, procedures, methods, best practice.
Reader's attitudes	
Cases where all that is sought from the student is a reaction to a problem. The focus is then on his/her attitude when faced with the situation described.	Interpersonal skills area. All interviews, and stressful situations.

Clearly it would be possible to classify some cases under several of the headings above, since their subject matter and treatment gives them a versatile use. Teachers may wish to set different questions from those at the end of the case, for example to ask students to put forward a series of solutions based on an analysis of the different options, or to comment on the skills employed by the participants in the case so far, and to say what they would do, perhaps role playing the characters. Attitudinal questions may be tackled by asking students to say what they feel about a problem or situation.

For those cases described as 'sequential' there are a series of 'add ons' available in the teaching notes which take the reader through a sequence, adding new information following each answer.

The structure of the book

Because case studies are such an effective way of bringing experience into the classroom, we have collected these cases especially for students of management, whether on diploma or degree courses, and for practising managers who may be delegates on management training courses. The cases developed here at Cranfield reflect our long tradition of using case studies as a teaching method on our MBA programmes. They are all based on actual events and companies, although in most cases it has been necessary to disguise the names as the material was not in the public domain. The cases have been arranged under four headings:

1 Interpersonal behaviour

The cases here cover leadership, motivation, interpersonal conflict, appraisal, group behaviour, and 'politics' in organizations.

2 Strategic management

These are cases which examine broad issues which show how strategy and business plans have to be considered from a behavioural perspective. They examine organization structure and design, consultancy interventions during the process of change, and the relationship between corporate planning and human resource planning.

3 Personnel planning and systems

Under this heading we feature cases on manpower planning, the structure of the personnel role, job evaluation and salary administration, management development and recruitment policy.

4 Employee relations

These cases cover management control systems, the manipulation of payment systems, trade union structure, employee relations strategy, quality circles, and employee involvement.

The following table is intended to assist with the selection of cases, according to the teaching purpose, as set out in the typology, and the subject matter of the case.

Working on case studies

Producing worthwhile answers to case studies is dependent on how the task is dealt with as a process, as much as any knowledge of the content of the case. If working on cases in groups, the process skills practised are similar to those used in a normal management meeting. There is much to be learned by working in groups on case studies, therefore – including the skills of chairing meetings, listening, questioning, checking for understanding and summarizing. These basic communication skills will help in the discussion of the case.

There are also problem solving skills to be deployed. A five-fold framework for problem solving gives structure to the discussion:

1 *Problem definition.* The question here is how do we know there is a problem? It is usually beneficial to spend time on this stage, so that all possible angles are explored.
2 *Analysis.* Here we are concerned with causes. Monocausal explanations of human affairs are seldom adequate. There may be many interlocking causes. It is sometimes useful to consider what is both a necessary and a sufficient condition for something to have happened, but a search for one final cause is not likely to be helpful. There are some simple techniques in analysis, such as listing the strengths, weaknesses, opportunities and threats to an organization (a SWOT analysis). Strengths and weaknesses are usually internal, opportunities and threats, external to the organization.
3 *Generating solutions.* The main danger here is the possibility of becoming attached to a particular solution or offering solutions too soon, before the analysis of the problem is complete. Techniques, such as brain storming, are often a good way of being creative in the generation of solutions. Recording *all* the ideas is important, and not evaluating them until the end against agreed criteria. It is often beneficial to examine the arguments for and against a particular proposal.
4 *Evaluating solutions.* Solutions need to address the problem, and to be workable. Sometimes a range of solutions may be offered, the choice being dependent on how the people in the case might react. In many case studies, there are no 'solutions' as such, and what is sought is the reader's opinion or reaction. If this is the position, then the opinion should be backed by factual evidence from the case.
5 *Presenting/implementing solutions.* When evaluating solutions the question of how would the solution be implemented should be addressed. It may be appropriate to set out a strategy for implementation, and to incorporate this in the answer. Presentation of answers is an important skill to practise: the skills of persuasion, of presentation can all be exercised, either individually or as a group.

Table showing teaching purpose and subject of each case in the book

	Interpersonal behaviour	Strategic management	Personnel planning/systems	Employee relations
Organization/ environment interaction	The Industrial Development Authority Grayle Engineering	The Box Makers Public Welfare Agency Epicurus Leisure Group Syntax Corp. Olde England Taverns	Pallas Electronics Archon Engineering Thomas Nestor Recruiting a sales force	BIFU Greenfield Industrial
Illustrative of behaviour	Henry Smart The Giro Group Grayle Engineering The Industrial Development Authority Kleine Plastics Secure Systems Guy Roberts	The Box Makers Celtic Woollen Co. Syntax Corp. Public Welfare Agency Olde England Taverns Fosbar Electronics	Archon Engineering	East Midland Electronic Case of piecework bargaining Suspending quality circles

Sequential	Kleine Plastics	Syntax Corp. Public Welfare Agency		
Role play	Henry Smart Peter Johnson Maurice Bradley	Celtic Woollen Co.		
Solution based	Henry Smart Guy Roberts The Industrial Development Authority Grayle Engineering	Celtic Woollen Co. Epicurus Leisure Group Public Welfare Agency Olde England Taverns Fosbar Electronics	Pallas Electronics Lysander Products Thomas Nestor Recruiting a sales force Archon Engineering	Suspending quality circles East Midland Electronic Case of piecework bargaining Greenfield Industrial
Readers' attitudes	Henry Smart Guy Roberts Secure Systems Kleine Plastics Youth Training Scheme	Celtic Woollen Co. Syntax Corp. Public Welfare Agency Olde England Taverns	Archon Engineering	East Midland Electronic Case of piecework bargaining Suspending quality circles

References

1 F. Fiedler, *A Theory of Leadership Effectiveness* (McGraw-Hill, New York, 1967).
2 D. A. Kolb *et al.*, *Organisational Psychology: An Experiential Approach.* (Prentice-Hall 1971).
3 C. G. Jung, *Collected Works* volume 10, paragraph 847 (Princeton University Press 1967).
4 E. Berne, *What do you say after you say hello?* (Corgi 1975), p. 39.
5 S. Tyson, 'The case study as one way of learning', *Banking and Financial Training*, vol. 1, no. 2 (1985).

PART ONE

Interpersonal Behaviour

Human interaction is a vital area of study in the fields of management and organization study. The manner in which human beings relate to each other influences the application and quality of performance by which people do their work. The values, drives, expectations and skills of each person are strong determinants of the commitment people apply to the tasks and activities they undertake. This effect is considerably multiplied when more than one person is involved in the completion of work. The interesting mix of perceptions, motivation and skills leads to outcomes which at times are unexpected and in certain circumstances undesired. It takes considerable understanding and application effectively to attend to the interpersonal behaviour issues of the work place.

We attempt to provide such breadth and depth of insight and approaches to solving the interpersonal problems of the workplace. The topics of personal values and needs, motivation, interpersonal perceptions and skills, criteria for performance, effective and ineffective communication, and management style, are encompassed in this section.

Secure systems examines the subject of motivation. The drives and expectations of one person are explored, and the reader is asked to provide possible solutions to a commonplace human issue.

The theme of motivation is continued in the case of *The Giro Group*, but taken from an organizational perspective, The Giro Group is portrayed as experiencing changes which have an impact on the levels of motivation of its employees. Identifying the nature of the motivational problems and possible solutions to these problems are the tasks required in the case.

One important influence on the motivation of subordinates is the behaviour of the superior. Such is the underlying issue in the case of *Kleine Plastics (Part 1)*, which describes a situation of managerial succession in a family owned and managed company. The case is sequential and Parts 2, 3 and 4 are to be found in the teaching guide manual.

In contrast the case of *Henry Smart* explores how people develop perceptions of each other, and how such views influence the manner in which work is conducted.

Generating perceptions of others by the impact of their conversation and

1

behaviour on us, is the theme of *Peter Johnson*, a role play exercise applied in a job appraisal situation. Likewise, the case of *Maurice Bradley* adopts a similar theme and style of teaching. Both cases describe somewhat different interpersonal tensions, and unlike other cases, the participants are required to act out, rather than discuss, approaches to problem solving.

The case of the *Industrial Development Authority* examines the complications of interpersonal behaviour during periods of fundamental organization changes. The threats and opportunities as perceived by each of the key managers in the case, and the manner in which they attempt to address complex issues, highlights the need for a realistic but professional approach to change management.

The terms 'realistic' and 'professional' do not just refer to skills, but also to the attitudes and values held by each individual. The case of *Guy Roberts* examines personal and group (shared) values and norms. Undoubtedly, one interesting reaction is yours, the reader, for it is rare that cases of corruption are discussed so openly in an educational forum.

Values, drives, needs, styles and skills are all elements requiring analysis in the case of *Grayle Engineering Limited*, where the focus is on identifying and evaluating managerial effectiveness. The intermittent and interruptive nature of managerial work is described in a company servicing the needs of one client (Ministry of Defence) who requires high standards of service. The internal coordination and organization issues in Grayle, demands that managers perform to high standards in order to provide an adequate service.

The Youth Training Scheme covers the topic of communication and the problems that can naturally arise when adequate communication has not taken place. Again the reader is asked to identify the communication barriers that exist in the case, and find ways of overcoming such problems.

ONE

Secure Systems

RON LUDLOW

Bill Johnson looked round his office, which he shared with Leslie Jones, and announced:

'God, this is really crummy, isn't it! How can they expect us to work well in a place like this?'

'You seemed quite happy with it a few months ago, Bill,' replied Leslie. 'In fact, you never seemed to notice the squalor at all!'

The office was twelve feet by eight feet, had no outside window, two desks which were piled high with files and papers, one filing cabinet which was full to overflowing, two rickety chairs, and a collection of papers in cardboard boxes. It was lit by a single 100 watt overhead light, unshaded, and a small grease-stained rug covered part of the dirty lino floor.

Bill had joined Secure Systems ten months ago. He had come from a major software house and had been excited to join a fast growing computer security company with an impressive image in the market.

'With the Data Protection Act coming into operation this year, lots of organizations are starting to get very worried about the security of their computer systems, Bill,' explained Rod Thomas, the Managing Director, after Bill had had his successful selection interview. 'One particular client, Gremlin Geotronics, does an awful lot of work for the Ministry of Defence, and for them, of course, security is the name of the game. I'd like you to start here by going over Gremlin's systems, making recommendations to their board, and implementing the new high-security systems in line with their requirements.'

This was quite a feather in Bill's cap, his creative genius was being recognized. At his previous job he had shown innovative ability, but the company was quite bureaucratized, and he had felt stifled in that sort of climate. Certainly, he had had a good salary – Secure Systems weren't paying him any more – a pleasant office and good secretarial back-up, but he felt restricted and he had steadily got more frustrated. The chance to move to Secure Systems was just what he had been waiting for.

Over the next eight months he put his heart and soul into the Gremlin project. Most of that time he had worked at Gremlin Geotronics sites anyway, only coming back to his office for a few weeks at a time to revise and consolidate systems designs and to catch up with his mail. He had struck up a friendship with Leslie Jones, a computer analyst who shared his office, and who had a dry, sardonic sense of humour. Leslie made Bill feel slightly uncomfortable at times.

'Bet you never thought you'd have to share a little box like this when you came here, eh, Bill?' Leslie remarked ironically as Bill shifted one box of printouts to get at some papers below it. 'Beats me why you put up with it: after all, I'm only one of the juniors here, not like you. You must be on at least £5000 a year more than me.'

Bill flustered 'Well, it's the challenge, Leslie. This project is so fascinating and it's posing all sorts of problems that I like to solve. I think also that some of the new ideas I've got are transferable, in that we'll be able to use them as a basis for work in other companies. Come on, Leslie, it's the work which turns me on, not where I do it!'

After eight months the Gremlin Geotronics project was finished, and Bill Johnson was mostly office-based for the next two months. There was no immediate project to follow the Gremlin one, and Bill got locked into a standard office routine, dealing with small jobs as they turned up, and trying to do some development work in his spare time. Leslie's mannerisms and cynical, cutting humour began to get on his nerves. With time on his hands, Bill started to take notice of his surroundings.

Questions

1 What are Bill Johnson's work needs and values?
2 At what motivational levels is he working:
  (a) Before Secure Systems?
  (b) During the first ten months at Secure Systems?
  (c) Now?
3 What possible actions can be taken to improve his motivation now?

TWO

The Giro Group

PAUL DAINTY

The sudden sound of voices in the corridor made Larry jump. He looked at his watch. It was after 8 p.m. and he cursed for having to work late again. But despite the long hours and the pressure, he enjoyed the job, and it was important. He was working on a policy document which was to be considered at the Directors' meeting tomorrow. He had been looking at the financing of three heavy engineering factories within the Group, and had to make recommendations on their long-term viability. He had come to the conclusion that they were too much of a burden on the company and should be closed. He knew that others would have a say in the decision, and marketing would probably argue against him, but his recommendations were usually accepted.

He recognized one of the voices – Ted Patterson from the Personnel Department. He had had some real arguments with Ted over the last eighteen months. Ever since his department had been given the major responsibility for finding ways of saving money, he had come in conflict with Ted. 'It was understandable in some ways,' he thought. Many of his cost-cutting suggestions had implications for manpower. After the company had been a model employer for over twenty years, a lot of what the company was doing now probably seemed unpalatable to Ted. Especially as Ted had been with the company for so long, and had been responsible for getting a reasonably good remuneration package for managers, and for getting the idea of management development accepted within the company.

He paused for a moment and thought back to last year when he had argued that the workforce, including managers, should take a cut in pay, and that most developmental activities should cease. Their friendship had been severely strained as a result. 'But it had to be done; these were tough times. Few people in finance, or on the board for that matter, could see the cost effectiveness of the kind of development programmes Ted was advocating. They seemed to be expensive with fairly vague outcomes. Moreover, the overall pay reduction of 5 per cent seemed to have been accepted by managers in most departments. The Managing Director had gone to a lot of trouble communicating why the cut was necessary, but it seemed to have been worth it.'

Ted put his head round the door. 'Thought you might like to be rescued from your jail. Coming down the pub?'

Larry looked at his watch again. 'Why not! But just give me two minutes while I put these files on Marjory's desk.'

As he walked down the corridor he noticed that John Holmes was still working. Although about the same age as Larry, John had been with the company much longer. He was also much less qualified. He had no formal accounting qualifications, although he always talked of getting round to doing something about it. 'That was typical of John,' thought Larry, slightly annoyed. Although he usually seemed to produce his work on time, he seemed to lack real 'go'. He wondered how well John was coping in reality. Tony Sadler's comments about John indicated that he didn't rate him highly either. 'Too quiet,' thought Larry, 'and I've tried to put a bit of life into him, but it hasn't seemed to work.' He thought how he probably knew John least of anybody in his division.

He put the files on Marjory's desk and returned to his office. As he walked in he noticed Ted looking over the report he had just finished.

'You know that recommendation could mean another 800 redundancies. That's nearly a fifth of the workforce.'

'Yes Ted, I know, but the company cannot afford these engineering works.'

'And what about the implications for Head Office. It could affect some of the people here, especially those who deal with the centralized functions such as personnel, finance and marketing.'

'Yes I'd thought about that – but it could mean that some people might have a bit of a breathing space for a time. That could be a good thing, especially as some seem to have difficulty in coping with the pressure. Sometimes these deadlines we keep having to meet, even get me down.'

'Come on Larry, are you kidding? If your Director knows that there are people around with less work to do he will want to do something about it.'

'Hmm. I suppose when I come to think about it, Ted, I'm the same way. I can't really go around paring costs throughout the Group, and then ignore the opportunities here.'

'But it won't affect management staff. You know our policy about getting rid of managers, Larry.'

'Yes, I know we have tried to maintain our management structure. Like you, I feel that gives some stability to the company, especially having older men like Tony Sadler around. I know we have a few problems with Tony, but as you know, I think the company needs people with his experience. Even so, as I keep saying, these are tough times.'

John Holmes heard Larry Kearns and Ted Patterson walk down the corridor towards the lift. They broke his concentration and he sat back. He felt good. He had worked hard today and this gave him satisfaction. He was sure his effort was appreciated within the company, and this also made him feel good. He liked to have the day-to-day financial responsibility for the Group's engineering factories. It gave him the chance to work quietly, with his own small team of staff.

He knew that the job was not one of the most attractive in Head Office. It did not have the status of, say, working in the policy making section, but he liked it. He knew the job and he felt secure doing it. 'Anyway,' he thought, 'once you got into areas like policy making you started getting into arguments.' He disliked that sort of thing, and he wasn't that concerned about getting to the top. He liked to get on with his work rather than be sidetracked with petty disagreements and people playing politics. But there were a few problems lately that were getting him down. He was working longer hours than he did normally and he was having trouble motivating his staff. He had ten people under him and he felt that they were becoming despondent. He put it down to the general feeling of uncertainty within the company. He would have liked to have talked to someone about it, but did not really get much of a chance, and was not really sure who to approach. 'Anyway things would improve when the company was back on its feet,' he thought.

He put his files away and locked his cabinet. As he switched out the light he saw Andrew Low waiting for the lift. He liked Andrew, who was a bright, pleasant man in his late twenties. He, Andrew and Tony Sadler all worked in the same division providing various financial services to the operating companies within the Group. Andrew had responsibility for a small number of component firms. The responsibility was not as great as his own, and Andrew was slightly below him in seniority, although both reported to the same boss. Andrew had been with the company about three years now, was well qualified, seemed to run his section well and was ambitious. 'What a contrast he was to Tony,' he thought. Tony was responsible for a group of companies equivalent to his own, and he and Tony had similar status. Tony and Andrew, however, were like chalk and cheese. Tony had been with the company many years. He was an 'old school' type of manager who emphasized his status and had an air of authority, but his section always seemed to be in a shambles. He had heard some of Tony's staff complaining that Tony came in late and never seemed to be there when he was wanted. 'Funny how Larry never seemed to interfere,' he thought.

He caught Andrew up. 'You're working late John.'

'Yes, just a few things to tidy up.'

They got into the lift together. Two girls from the typing pool who had been working late were already in the lift. Andrew caught the end of their conversation.

'Have you heard, they are laying off twenty more clerical staff.'

'No! Who's going this time?'

'I don't know, but you never hear of any managers being made redundant.'

The girls quickly changed the subject as Andrew and John got into the lift. Their comments triggered off something inside Andrew. 'No they hadn't made any managers redundant,' he thought. 'But you never seemed to know where you were. The redundancy rumour probably wasn't true but you never knew what to believe'. All the chopping and changing over the last eighteen months had left him exasperated. He didn't know where he was, and he didn't think those at the top of the company did either.

The lift came to a stop and jolted him back to the present. He heard himself say goodnight to John and was hit by the bitter night chill. He was off to the Harvester's Arms. He usually played table tennis on a Tuesday, but as there was no match tonight he had agreed to go for a drink with one of the other team members.

As he walked into the pub he noticed Arnold seated with two drinks in front of him. Arnold waved.

'Got you one.' Arnold shouted. 'How are you?'

Andrew sat down and unbuttoned his coat. He looked tense. 'I am fed up Arnold. I have been in this job since I joined the company and there does not seem to be any prospect of moving higher. I work like hell but it does not seem to make any difference. And as far as getting any more money goes, well you can forget it.'

'But I thought you were coping all right, and you have never been particularly concerned about money before. Anyway you cannot expect too much in a company that has lost nearly a quarter of the workforce over a year and a half.'

'Perhaps that's the problem. It does not seem to matter how hard I work. Oh, I suppose I can live with the money situation, and the perks aren't too bad, but I resent it when others just seem to plod away and they don't seem bothered. Tony in my division is like that. Oh, I don't mind him that much, but it's the fact that he and others like him are going to be in the job for years. They won't leave because they are settled here and would find it difficult to get a job outside anyway. What do you do when a company is looking to get rid of jobs rather than create them? It's even difficult to get moved to another section. You know, I don't feel I am developing at all.'

'What about Terry Carpenter. He's in your department, isn't he? I heard he was thinking of getting a new job. There would be a vacancy there. Ok, it would not be a promotion for you, but it would be a change.'

'Yes, I would quite like to do his job. The kind of financial analysis he is doing would be interesting and broaden my experience a bit.'

The conversation was broken by a loud voice from behind them. 'Hello Andrew. We don't often see you in here.'

Andrew turned towards the voices. Larry Kearns and Ted Patterson were looking over at him.

'Do you want a drink?'

'Join you in a minute, Larry,' Andrew replied. He was stalling. He noticed Tony was with them, and he wanted to cool down a bit before he went over. Especially as Tony was laughing.

Tony was ribbing Ted about the 'development' programme he had gone on once. The course had not gone as well as expected, and Tony had always used this to excuse himself from going on any other courses. Ted believed that these silly comments of Tony's had had an influence on Larry. 'We are the survivors,' he could hear Tony saying, 'What can they teach us on a course that we have not already experienced.'

Ted did not want to get into any more wrangles over development. He became too annoyed when the topic was raised nowadays, and just wanted to let it drop. Tony was a good friend, but he had some set ways and attitudes, and he always seemed to be putting the knife into something or somebody. Both he and Larry had given up trying to change him.

Ted felt relief as Andrew joined them and the conversation changed to football and assessments of the latest England squad.

Friday mornings always seemed to bring bad news for Ted. He put the phone down. So the board had accepted Larry's recommendations on the engineering firms. Larry had let him read the report thoroughly, but he had difficulty in fully understanding the financial reasoning of all the proposals. He had half expected what would happen and resigned himself to it. But he still felt he had a duty to maintain the management structure at Head Office. As some of the changes would affect Larry's department he felt he should go and discuss them with him.

'So what do you think we should do Ted?' Larry asked after they had been discussing the implications for an hour. 'It looks as if John Holmes' section will have to go, but what about John?'

'Well you know how I feel about pushing managers out,' Ted said.

'Yes, but this might be the right time. You know I'm not happy with John. He does not seem to pull his weight. He rarely works late and he has been having problems with his staff for some months. He produces the work all right, but he hardly ever shows any initiative.'

'I think that would be too harsh on him. I accept the section has to be closed down, but what about moving him into Terry Carpenter's job. That will become vacant in a month's time when he leaves us. Ok, so its a slightly lower status, but he could do that job, and it might give him time to look round for another. We could keep him on the same pay. That would not be a problem.'

'Ok, Ted let's do that. Come back to me tomorrow and we will discuss the details before I approach my director. But I think I will have a word with John as soon as possible.'

Ted turned to leave when he remembered the other issue. 'Oh Larry, what about this move to end the free management lunches and integrate all the dining halls? I'd like to know how the Managing Director is going to announce that. The managers won't like losing their perks.'

'Oh don't worry about that Ted. It will be just done quietly. Pointless making a fuss about something like this. After accepting a pay cut, managers are hardly going to get upset about losing a few free meals.'

The next day Andrew met John going down to the dining area. Andrew was annoyed again about the fact that old stagers like Tony were causing problems. His staff had been helping out Tony's staff for the second time that week, and he was sure that it was Tony's inability to cope with the load himself as much as his staff. But he always seemed to find an excuse or bluff his way through. Tony could talk the hind legs off Larry, and that was something. 'In some ways John was just as bad,' he thought. He felt he could do either of their jobs given the chance. But although a bit insipid, John was still probably willing to change, unlike Tony, who was a complacent old mule. However, despite his annoyance with these two, he was feeling a little bit chirpy. He had heard about Terry Carpenter's resignation, and was waiting for the job to be advertised internally. 'At least that's something to look forward to,' he thought.

He looked at John. 'You are looking pleased with yourself, John,' Andrew remarked.

'Yes I am a bit'. John always felt good when he had put in a solid morning's work. But it was the unexpected meeting that he was to have with Larry this afternoon, which had made him feel good. 'Larry must have been told about how I sorted out that tricky personal problem of one of the lads on my section. Ted had heard, and said he was going to mention it to Larry. Nice to have some recognition,' he thought. But John said nothing to Andrew. It did not feel right to him to brag about his little achievements at work.

Questions

1 Assess what you think are the current motivational problems in the company, and what will they be in the future?
2 What are the management development issues that you can identify:
  (a) For the company
  (b) For the individuals themselves.

Cases in Human Resource Management

Appendix 1 Head Office organization chart: the Giro Group
Parts relevant to the case.

Managing Director

Group Services Director | Technical Director | Finance Director | Marketing Director | Personnel Director

Division A General Manager (Larry Kearns)

Division B General Manager

Division A General Manager (Ted Patterson)

Division B General Manager

Section 1 Section Manager (John Holmes) (10 Staff)

Section 2 Section Manager (Tony Sadler) (15 Staff)

Section 3 Section Manager (Andrew Low) (6 Staff)

Section 1 Section Manager

Section 2 Section Manager

Section 3 Section Manager

Section 4 Section Manager (Terry Carpenter) (4 Staff)

Section 5 Section Manager

Section 6 Section Manager

12

THREE

Kleine Plastics

―――――

RON LUDLOW

Part 1

Kleine Plastics was a small company, which produced a wide range of household plasticware and was based in the East Midlands town of Oxminster. Established in 1960, it was wholly owned by the Kleine family and from the beginning had been managed by Joseph Kleine, a dynamic, yet charismatic, man of sixty. Joseph had a reputation for sound technical knowledge combined with the ability to motivate his workforce. He made a tour of inspection of the factory twice a day and in this way he was always aware of what was going on, both on the factory floor and in the offices. He was quick to praise the workers when he felt they had done a good job, and equally quick to remonstrate with them over careless or inefficient work.

In point of fact, Joseph Kleine had few occasions to discipline his staff and he proudly believed that this was because he had chosen a reliable and trustworthy group of managers to support him. The company, which employed some 200 people, was divided into six departments: design, production, sales, purchasing, warehouse and administration. Each departmental head had a lot of experience and ability in his own field and their average length of service with the company was fifteen years. Joseph felt completely confident that he could delegate work to them and they enjoyed a relative degree of autonomy, knowing they could turn to Joseph for help and advice should they need it.

Over the years, a rapport had developed between Joseph and his managers, based on mutual personal and technical respect. Similarly, a good working atmosphere existed within the departments, each manager having the respect of his staff. Because Joseph believed in plain speaking, he dealt with any disagreement between the managers by sitting down with them and thrashing the problem out on the spot. 'Politics is for Westminster. I'll have none of it at Kleine's,' was one of his favourite sayings.

Kleine Plastics had grown from small beginnings in the early 1960s to a turnover of over half a million pounds by 1970, with most of its products being sold in the East Midlands. However, like many small companies it was hit very hard by the recession in the construction industry in the early 1970s, and looked for markets further afield and commenced exporting in 1974. With the turnup of the construction industry in the late 1970s, however, the company marched boldly forward due mostly to the dynamism of its founder, Joseph Kleine, and showed steady growth in the early 1980s. Turnover increased from £2 million in 1980 to £7½ million by 1984, with net profit after tax increasing from £90K to £630K in 1984. 1985 showed every sign of being yet another profitable year, and Joseph Kleine felt that at last his company was making its mark on the market, both at home and overseas.

In October 1985, the company received an order to supply black plastic water tanks to East Africa. The original contact for this order had come to Kleine's via a personal friend of Joseph's, who worked for the World Health Organization. Although the initial tooling costs were high, Joseph considered the investment worthwhile, for the potential long-term benefit to the company was considerable. The water tanks would contain a supply of fresh drinking water for refugees and Joseph reflected, with some sadness, that somewhere in the world there would always be refugees, made homeless by either war or want. What Africa needed today, India might well need tomorrow.

As Joseph watched the installation of the new moulding machine which would produce the water tanks, he was struck by the irony of the situation, whereby a small company in England could be made more profitable by the destitution of East Africa. He reflected on the pictures of starving children in Ethiopia, which had appeared frequently on television. As he did so, he thought of David, his twenty-four-year-old son. Far from starving, David was actually rather overweight.

Yet, Joseph was enormously proud of his son. Bright, but not brilliant, David Kleine had obtained a BA degree in economics from Acton Polytechnic, followed by a diploma in management studies. Although Joseph had had little formal education, he had always encouraged David to study, in the firm belief that tomorrow's managers would need a sound academic background in order to cope with the increasingly sophisticated business world. He was very impressed with David's qualifications and felt sure that he would one day take over as Managing Director of Kleine Plastics. In fact, David was already employed by the company and was presently working on cash-flow forecasts and patent investigation. Joseph had received good reports of David's work from the Company Accountant, Alan Foulkes, who considered that David had an aptitude for detailed administrative work of this nature.

Walking back to his office, Joseph decided that now was the time to take his wife on a long-promised holiday. He had always said that when he could afford to take time off from the company, he would take her on a three-month cruise to the Far East. Now the pipe-dream looked as though it could shortly become reality. Business was thriving, David was showing himself to be capable and responsible – would there ever be a better time to take that well-earned break? Reaching for the telephone, he booked the holiday.

Before leaving that evening, he went to see Alan Foulkes. He smiled with pleasure as he told Alan that he had finally booked the cruise and explained that, while he was away, he intended to put David in charge of running the company. However, while he wanted his son to gain experience, he realized that he would need help and support and therefore asked Alan to keep an eye on him and provide guidance where necessary. He then sought out all his other departmental managers, told them his plans and asked for their full cooperation and support. Finally, he spoke to David. He told him that he was pleased with his work, emphasizing his progress during the past months. Then, he told him about the forthcoming cruise and explained that he felt that David would be well able to take over the day-to-day supervision of the company in his absence, with the guidance of Alan Foulkes and the full support of the other managers.

The next morning, Joseph called all his managers to the board room. 'As you all know, I rarely call meetings,' he began. 'That's not my way of doing things. However, I feel that on this occasion, a meeting is called for. I have already seen you individually and told you about my holiday. Well, this morning, I would like to formally introduce my son to you as my deputy for the next three months. We all know that this company practically runs itself. That is because you are all so good at your jobs. In fact, I don't suppose you will notice that I have gone. However, someone has to sign the letters! That someone will now be David, and I would once again ask you all to give him the support you have always given me.' On the last Sunday in November, Joseph and his wife left for the Far East.

On Monday, 2nd December, David Kleine installed himself behind his father's desk. His first action as deputy Managing Director was to telephone Alan Foulkes and ask him to bring in the job costing sheets for the last six months. Next, he phoned Victor Keane, the Sales Manager, and asked for the monthly sales records for the past two years, broken down by region and by product. Finally, he called Ian Breed, the Production Manager, for a complete summary of production schedules for the last three months and plans for the next six weeks. As the various pieces of information reached him, he worked closely on the figures, closeting himself in his office all week. Before leaving the office on Friday evening, he dictated a memo to his father's secretary, asking all department heads to meet him in the board room first thing on Monday morning. The memo did not contain any Agenda for the meeting.

Questions

1 How is David likely to handle this meeting?
2 What issues are likely to be raised by David at the meeting?
3 Will the senior managers be enthusiastic/not enthusiastic about tackling these issues?

FOUR

Henry Smart

RON LUDLOW

Henry Smart, aged forty-eight, stood at the window of his first-floor office, situated in the centre of Southsea, and surveyed the busy scene below. Since the death of his father, in 1951, he had been one of two partners in Smart & Co., one of Southsea's most respected Estate Agents. Henry was responsible for the day-to-day running of the business. His partner, John Newbold, aged fifty-five, handled the firm's financial matters.

Set up in 1936 by his father, Henry Smart Snr, the company specialized in handling properties at the 'executive' end of the market. Since joining the firm in 1938, Henry had specialized in this work, becoming a partner in 1946 after serving in the Army during the War.

However, it was now 1961, and times were changing. The centre of nearby Portsmouth, badly bombed during the war, was being redeveloped. Premium office blocks were already rising to replace the former Victorian buildings, and more were planned. At nearby Havant, a huge industrial estate was in the course of erection.

Henry was well aware of the market potential and was determined to see that Smart & Co. shared in this growth. With the agreement of his partner, he had therefore taken the decision, some six months earlier, to expand business operations into the sale and leasing of commercial properties.

In order to facilitate this move, he had invited his nephew, Alec Smart, to join the company. Alec was twenty-six and had worked for eight years in a firm of Estate Agents in London, which specialized in handling commercial properties. A qualified valuer and surveyor, he was well used to the 'cut and thrust' of property dealing in post-war London, and enjoyed mixing socially with property developers and directors of large building firms, in order to get business. Unmarried and ambitious, Alec worked assiduously, both in and out of office hours, to gain experience and improve his position in the company.

When his uncle's offer of employment reached him, he was not slow to see the chances it offered. Not only was he being asked to set up and run a commercial department for the firm, but he was also well aware that his uncle had no children of his own, to follow him into the business.

Within three months of joining Smart & Co., Alec had made his mark. He joined the local golf club and Round Table, in order to make contacts. He made it his business to know the social habits of the top men and women involved with the commercial development in the area. He made sure that, whenever possible, he frequented the same clubs, belonged to the same associations, and drank in the same bars as they did.

As a result of this, Smart & Co. was given contracts to lease a premium office block in the centre of Portsmouth, and several industrial units at Havant. During the following two months, he had found clients for most of these properties and was busy negotiating a further contract, which included several freehold properties. Company turnover had increased by 25 per cent and it appeared that Henry had been right in his policy decision and in his choice of the man for the job.

However, as Henry stared out of the window, his face bore a frown. In spite of Alec's obvious success, there were certain qualities about him that disturbed Henry. He was aggressive. Henry realized that a certain amount of aggression was necessary in order to achieve business, and that he himself had always possessed this quality. However, he was alarmed at his nephew's inability to temper his aggression within the office. Alec had already alienated his four fellow negotiators, who dealt mainly with the domestic market, and had also upset the office administrator, Marilyn, who had been with the company for fifteen years.

Marilyn complained that Alec persistently spent long periods out of the office, and on his return would demand that his work should be given priority over all other business. He had even taken to by-passing her completely, on occasions, going straight to one of the three typists and insisting that his work be done immediately. This disrupted the system, as it meant that other negotiators' work had to be laid aside. Marilyn frequently had to placate an angry negotiator who was shouting at an overworked, overstressed typist. She also had to suffer his reprimand for her own inability to effectively delegate the workload.

She felt the situation was fast becoming untenable, and considered Alec to be a selfish, thoughtless, young man. Her obvious dislike of him could not be mistaken, even though she had to admit that he would often buy a box of chocolates for a typist who had done an urgent job for him. She did not deny his ability and realized that he might well become a partner in the future, but made it clear that, in her opinion, this would not be wise – unless Alec could be persuaded to accept, and work within, the established office system.

Henry respected Marilyn, and relied upon her as an administrator. He also valued the loyalty and ability of his negotiators, and had received complaints from them about Alec's 'cavalier attitude.' Indeed, one of them had been so upset that he threatened to resign unless something was done about Alec.

Henry had decided to consult his partner on the subject. John said he was aware of the friction Alec caused within the office, but it could not be denied that the company had benefited financially since he joined and, for that reason alone, cautioned Henry in his dealings with his nephew.

Henry had therefore taken a paternalistic line when confronting his nephew the previous month. He had stressed that the firm was like a family, whose loyalties stretched both upwards towards the partners and sideways to each other. Mutual respect was the key to success.

He also expressed concern at Alec's use of the recently appointed junior negotiator, who was being trained by one of the domestic property negotiators. Alec had recently started sending this young man out with prospective commercial clients on 'accompanied viewings', saying that he needed an assistant to help out with the minor aspects of his work. This had caused further dissension among the other negotiators.

Alec's immediate reaction to this was one of protestation. Had he not been successful in getting a substantial amount of commercial business for the firm? Did he not work extremely hard, both in and out of office hours? He pointed out the difference between the commercial and domestic property market, saying that it took more energy and 'pushiness' to get commercial business.

His views of his fellow negotiators were far from flattering. He considered that they were slow, only dealing with clients who came to the company. They made no effort to go out and get business. He also considered that the junior negotiator was not receiving adequate training, and was being used as an office junior. Under Alec's supervision, he was responding well and learning fast.

He was equally critical of Marilyn, saying that she adhered rigidly to the 'system' but that this system did not meet the needs of commercial work. He found that direct approach to the typists worked well. They did his work efficiently and willingly.

He felt that the others complained about him because they were jealous of his success. However, he felt that perhaps this was not a bad thing, as it might 'shake things up' and act as a catalyst for their self-improvement.

Henry responded by reassuring Alec of his personal appreciation of his efforts and achievements. However, he urged him to try and conform, for the sake of harmony within the company.

Alec appeared to be mollified. He rose to leave, excusing himself by saying that he had an urgent appointment with a client, for which he was already five minutes late.

For a while it seemed as though Henry's talk had had some positive effect on Alec. He spent more time in the office, and deferred to the other negotiators before assigning work to the junior, and to Marilyn over administrative matters. However, Henry was disturbed to notice that during the past week, Alec had slipped back once again into his old ways. Murmurs of discontent were again rising within the company.

Turning from the window, Henry sat down at his desk. He knew he had a dilemma on his hands. He liked his nephew, seeing much of himself in him. Moreover, he had to agree with John, that Alec's input into company profitability was substantial. He was also extremely popular with clients, who saw him as a man to be trusted and who could be relied upon to deal with their business in a fast and effective way.

Yet Alec, the asset, was also Alec, the liability. His isolationist approach within the office was so disrupting that it could not be tolerated.

Henry knew that if he did not take positive action soon, he would lose at least one, and possibly more, of his loyal and able staff. On the other hand, if he demanded that his nephew should adhere strictly to the system, Alec might feel frustrated, demotivated, and leave the firm. Henry's long-term plans for his nephew's succession to a partnership would be wrecked on the rock of the established system.

Questions

1 How do Henry and Marilyn perceive Alec? Why?
2 How does Alec perceive Henry and Marilyn? Why?
3 What actions could Henry Smart take to improve the situation? If no action is taken, what are the likely consequences?

4 Assume Henry decides to ask Alec to change his office behaviour. List all the possible strategies/goals to be agreed in future meetings between Henry and Alec.

FIVE

Peter Johnson

DAVID BUTCHER AND CATHERINE BAILEY

Peter Johnson: General brief

Peter Johnson   Envelope factory manager

Personal

Aged 37. Married with one child (boy 7).

Education

Educated at Hawarden Grammar School and Deeside College of Further Education. Has an HNC in Mechanical and Production Engineering.

Career

Joined Trident Aviation Ltd as an assistant methods engineer in 1968 and moved through a series of promotions – methods engineer, material controller to manufacturing controller. Left Trident a year ago on being made redundant, and took up present appointment as envelope factory manager with Premier Manufacturing and Supplies Ltd.

As envelope factory manager Peter Johnson has overall responsibility for the envelope factory which has a staff of 63 employees and three separate production lines.

See Appendix 1.

Appraiser's brief
(Appraiser: Ken Firth, Production Director)

Premier Manufacturing and Supplies Ltd is a major manufacturer of stationery and office accessories. Traditionally it has had a stable market share although more recently the market has become more competitive and the company has come under pressure to define its marketing strategy more clearly. Premier has a skilled workforce and a low labour turnover. It is the largest employer in the area. The Premier culture has something of old fashioned benevolent paternalism about it.

You are forty-three years of age and have been with Premier for fifteen years and Production Director for the past four years. Before your appointment to director level you were the manager of the envelope factory, having been promoted to that position from the post of work study officer which is where you began your career with the company. A large part of your time is spent liaising at director level, particularly with the Marketing Director, with whom relations are difficult because in your view he is trying to subordinate the Production Department to Marketing, saying that the key to the firm's future lies in giving paramount attention to the marketing function. You try to let your factory managers have a free hand in running their units and although you are in frequent contact by phone with them your face to face contact is largely limited to the monthly departmental management team meetings and your weekly visits to each factory. You find these visits vital for retaining a feel for what is happening in the production units and it is very useful to walk around the factories and chat to the shop floor employees, many of whom you know well because they have been there for years – in fact as envelope factory manager you managed a number of them directly for several years.

Your three factory managers are all effective in their jobs and in general you are happy with the way in which the production units are operating. Two of the factory managers are long serving employees of the company whilst the third, Peter Johnson, the envelope factory manager, has only been with Premier one year. In many respects he is very competent in the job and you have seen changes in the envelope factory since his predecessor retired. Production rates on all three of Peter's lines are up, wastage rates have dropped, morale in the factory appears to be good, safety procedures are being better observed and housekeeping generally is tidier. However, there are some aspects of Peter's peformance that worry you.

In particular his contribution at management team meetings bothers you. He tends to hog the floor and you have the impression that he is impatient with the other members of the management team, especially the other factory managers. He seems to believe he runs his factory more effectively than the other two – in fact Mark Old, the quality control manager told you that recently in an unguarded moment Peter had described Premier managers as 'just beginning to drag themselves into the twentieth century'. Also, you like to use management team meetings as a forum for the factory managers to discuss problems in their factories and Peter is apparently reluctant to contribute to this. He is happy to offer his advice to the other factory managers (only too readily in your view) but seems secretive about the detailed operation of his own unit.

Something else that bothers you is Peter's apparent willingness to let his staff abuse company resources. For example, the personnel manager mentioned to you the other day in passing that Personnel had had several instances where the mileage clocked by envelope factory staff using pool cars seemed excessive for the journeys involved, although Peter Johnson had signed the expenses claims. The latest example was a claim from Barry Walsh, one of Peter's supervisors for a visit to a raw materials supplier. Apparently Barry had claimed 450 miles for a trip that ought to be about 300 miles return. Another recent incident which rang a warning bell for you was when touring the envelope factory you overheard a conversation between the photocopying machine operator and another of the supervisors, Rob Cooper. It was obvious that he was asking her to do some personal copying for him. When she said people were asking her a bit too often and if Peter Johnson got wind of it she would be for the high jump, Rob merely said that Peter was pretty easy about these things and it was all Ok.

A further area of concern is Peter's seemingly over protective attitude towards his staff. You are aware from the other factory managers that Peter has not been very cooperative on a couple of occasions about temporary transfers of office staff to the other factories when they have been under pressure. Also the personnel manager has mentioned several times that he is having difficulty getting access to Peter's staff to interview them in connection with a job evaluation exercise being done for all three factories.

One other worry for you is Peter's growing liaison with the Director of Marketing. Twice last week when you rang Peter his secretary said he was over with the Marketing Director. You are aware from talking to the Marketing Director that he sees Peter as very helpful and you suspect that Marketing are at least partly behind a paper in your in-tray from Peter which suggests a restructuring of the envelope factory production lines. This restructuring would give greater capacity to the special project line which would allow more flexibility in producing special order, high quality batches – a marketing strategy you are aware that the Marketing Director is keen to develop.

Peter is waiting outside your office for his first annual appraisal interview. . . .

Question

1 What do you think are the appropriate issues for an appraisal interview?

Appendix 1   Appraisal interviewing skills

Premier Manufacturing and Supplies Ltd – Production Department organization chart

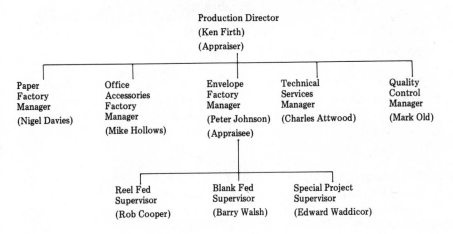

SIX

Maurice Bradley

DAVID BUTCHER AND CATHERINE BAILEY

Maurice Bradley: General brief

Maurice Bradley   Maintenance Section Head

Personal

Aged 35. Married with 2 children (girl 5, boy 3).

Education

Educated at Broomfield Primary School, Totnes Boys Grammar and Southampton University. Graduated with a degree in civil engineering in 1973.

Career

Joined Northshire County Council as a graduate assistant on a three-year training scheme, gaining professional (chartered) status in 1977. Promoted to assistant engineer, highways improvements and then two years later to senior assistant maintenance. In 1981 he moved to Metborough, a semi-rural borough council as head of a small Direct Works Section.

One year ago joined Wessex, succeeding as Head of the Maintenance Section with a staff of two senior assistant engineers, four assistant engineers and one clerical assistant.

See Appendix 1.

Appraiser's brief
(Appraiser: Edward Finch, Assistant Director, Maintenance)

You have been with Wessex for fifteen years and succeeded to your present job eight years ago. You are in your early fifties and now that you are well established in your position you feel able to stand back from the day-to-day running of the department and take a broader view, leaving the 'nitty gritty' to the section heads.

In particular, the majority of your time is spent on department management team matters, policy review and financial control meetings. On top of this you spend a certain amount of time dealing with public complaints. All of this means that you spend less time than perhaps you should with either of your section heads.

It is fortunate, therefore, that on the one hand, as head of the Direct Labour Organization (DLO Section) you have Dennis Marshall, your senior in age, who has come up through the ranks and knows DLOs inside out. He is steady and reliable, if a little staid, knows his men and is undoubtedly good at his job. Your other section head is Maurice Bradley, a young, keen and ambitious engineer. In charge of the Maintenance Section, his responsibility is to identify maintenance required, plan and action programmed maintenance, respond to emergency work required, organize the letting of contracts and if the DLO is involved, brief Dennis on what is required, and to monitor the expenditure of direct works on planned programme works.

Maurice certainly seems to have had a pretty positive effect on departmental performance over the past year. Compared to his predecessor he works within the budget allowed, seems to cope well with changes that call for a reassessment of priorities and rescheduling of work and he also appears to have a better record at responding to calls for emergency repair works.

Recently, however, you have noticed through the monthly financial reports which Maurice prepares, an upward trend in emergency expenditure. You are slightly surprised by this because although Maurice is permitted to authorize small sums (less than £500) on emergency repair works, he is supposed to report back on this to you and you can't think of any such occasion over the last month or two.

You also wonder whether Maurice may be cutting or changing established procedures. Soon after starting the job he applied for an additional member of staff for his section (making a legitimate case, in your view) but the request was refused by Personnel. While you are impressed and pleased that Maurice has apparently increased the effectiveness of his section, coping with an increased workload with a static staff complement, you have a nagging suspicion that it may be at the expense of something you are not yet aware of.

One other area of doubt concerns Maurice's relationship with Dennis. The fact that it is not exactly all smooth and harmonious you see as somewhat inevitable given personality differences between the two of them, and given Maurice's financial monitoring brief of Dennis's departmental performance and the costs of direct works. However, in the past month Dennis has complained to you on two occasions about dissatisfaction among his workmen, caused, according to him, by members of Maurice's section. The first time, a month ago, he just said that his men had been needled, but yesterday he rang specifically to complain that the men were 'up in arms' about Maurice's staff 'breathing down their necks' and telling them how to do their jobs. Dennis said that when he raised the matter with Maurice, Maurice had shrugged his shoulders and told him that his staff were only doing their job. You told Dennis that you would bring the matter up with Maurice today.

You have arranged to see Maurice today to review his performance in accordance with the new staff development procedure just introduced to the department. He is waiting outside your office. . . .

Question

1 What do you think are the appropriate issues for an appraisal interview?

Appendix 1   Appraisal interviewing skills

Wessex County Council
Department of Engineering organization chart

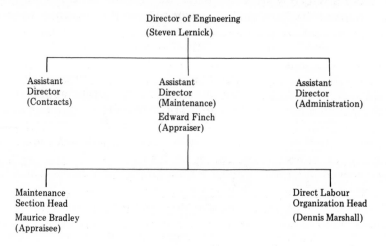

SEVEN

The Industrial Development Authority

ANDREW P. KAKABADSE

In the early 1960s, an Industrial Development Authority was established in order to stimulate business development in the UK. It was considered vital by the then political party in power, that industrial growth and development be conducted on a planned and organized basis. The influential politicians of all the major parties agreed that the organization should be created to promote nationally based industrial growth and thereby generate employment opportunities.

The Authority identified a number of activities to pursue, ranging from technical/managerial courses to offering financial assistance and a back-up consultancy service to small businesses.

Fifteen years on, politicians and influential business people generally agree that the authority has done a good job. However, needs have changed. Many of the courses are considered out of date. The financial assistance and subsidy to small businesses is considered inadequate to meet present needs and the consultancy service is hardly utilized. The results of a recent survey, indicate that proprietors of 'small companies consider the service provided as both inadequate and out of date in terms of meeting their needs.

The Authority's income stems from two sources, central government and a compulsory levy imposed on all businesses. Influential members of the business community have indicated that they resent paying the levy because they could not see how they benefited from such expenditure. The Minister accountable for the affairs of the Department of Industry issued an ultimatum to the Industrial Development Authority – offer a service that the business community finds valuable or else the levy will become voluntary instead of compulsory. In essence, the Minister stated change or be closed down.

The senior directors of the Authority responded rapidly. Working parties and committees were established to try to identify alternative strategies and activities which the authority could pursue.

As a result of these meetings, it became clear that middle management were, and had been, dissatisfied with their bosses and the total organization. Certain outspoken middle managers, in offering their views to the committees and working parties, stated that in order to get on and be promoted in the Authority all that was required was to be 'political'. Competence and hard work came second. Further, many of the problems identified by the Committees had already been recognized by the more capable middle managers. Certain managers even ventured to question how the Authority could be any different in the future, if the same senior managers remained in the post.

It also became clear that certain departments and units in the Authority had become accustomed to 'doing their own thing'. In particular, certain departmental managers had not bothered to inform their bosses of particular projects. Senior management were expected, by influential middle managers, to rubber-stamp their activities.

A report was submitted to Jim Carthy, the Director of the Authority. 'What the hell is happening in this organization?' he demanded at the Directors' meeting. 'The politicians are right. This organization is riddled with splits and disagreements, people running off in all directions and nothing of value being done. The Authority has become unmanageable! This all has to change!' exploded the Director.

The other functional directors shuffled uncomfortably in their seats.

Introducing change

Jim Carthy recognized that something had to be done in the Authority. He saw that to introduce change it had to be done in a planned and organized manner so as to prevent the present anomalies from ever arising in the future. In an attempt to introduce change, Carthy held discussions with each of his functional directors. The one functional director most sympathetic to his boss's views was Henry Mitchell, the Director of Personnel. He recognized that change was necessary and argued that his department should become the agents of change. However, he and Jim Carthy clearly recognized that the personnel managers in his department were not considered particularly pro-active or innovative. If the Personnel Department was to become the catalyst for change within the

Authority, then certain changes needed to be made within the Personnel Department. After substantial discussion, both agreed that they required an outsider to stimulate change within the Personnel Department. After an extensive search they identified a highly recommended consultant, Noel Green, whose specialism was the introduction and management of change.

Noel Green was told that his 'assignment' involved attempting to stimulate the managers with personnel departments to become more pro-active as agents of change. Line managers in the organization needed to develop greater sensitivity and awareness of market conditions and become more assertive in their dealings with their business clients. Essentially, the consultant's task was to change the personnel managers from operating as just administrators to acting as internal change agents/catalysts so that they in turn could help line managers improve their performance. In addition, Noel Green was asked to closely cooperate with Peter Davidson, the management development manager. Davidson had for some time argued that personnel should play a central role in the change and development of the authority. It was considered that Davidson would eventually assume the role of internal consultant.

Green and Davidson began their assignment by talking to a select number of managers in the Personnel Department about their work, ambitions, and the role of the department in the future. It quickly became clear that most of this select sample wanted no change. They were content to remain as administrators. They seemed to be more concerned about their job, role, degree of authority and status differences between themselves, than about the future of the department.

Green and Davidson concluded that most managers in the Personnel Department did not wish for change. How then to go about introducing change?

It was clear to them that before any meaningful discussion could take place as to the future role of the department, it was necessary to attempt to change these managers' attitudes. Their lethargy had to be broken! Their need to identify with the status quo had to be substituted by a wish to explore and become effective at stimulating change in other departments in the organization. In order to change attitudes, however, Green and Davidson needed to identify the values, attitudes to work, thoughts, feelings and potential of each individual manager in the Personnel Department.

Hence their strategy was:

1 Organize a series of workshops in order to gain a perspective on

how the personnel managers viewed their situation and what would be their future direction and objectives for their department.

The managers attending the workshop were asked to identify present problems and also draw up practical solutions to those problems.

The results of the workshops indicated that the lack of drive to do anything new was as much a result of both training and development of the Personnel Department's manager.

Green and Davidson consulted Mitchell as to their next steps. Of course, the problems in the department went far deeper than just a lack of effective interpersonal skills. However, training needs had been identified and the training process could be used as the mechanism for helping the managers change their attitudes, ideas and skills.

2 Organize a series of three-day interpersonal skills training programmes during which managers would have to complete numerous personality tests and leadership/management style type questionnaires.

3 Green and Davidson, with Henry Mitchell's joint agreement, kept a copy of all of the personality and management style test results that were administered on the programme.

4 The two consultants sketched out each individual's personality profile, managerial style, preferred approaches to work, qualifications and task skills. They drew out a comprehensive map of the personalities in the Personnel Department.

5 They began to match people together by personality type, work preference and managerial style.

6 They told Henry Mitchell that the series of three-day courses were a tremendous success. The next step, in order to capitalize on such useful training, would be to initiate a number of small projects whereby people could be given the opportunity to experiment with their newly found skills. They also indicated that they had been able to identify the few managers that really would be unsuitable for the new Personnel Department of the future. They gave him a 'hit-list' of the names and their test scores, recommending that they should be transferred out or sacked.

7 Henry Mitchell agreed, allowing the two consultants to set up a few experimental project teams. At the same time, he transferred or made redundant over 70 per cent of the people on the 'hit-list'.

8 Having removed the most troublesome managers, Green and Davidson organized a few project teams, whose brief was to examine the problems faced by other departments in the organiza-

tion, recommend solutions and if necessary help apply these solutions. Most members of the project teams had all been carefully matched together from their map of the department.

As time passed, the training programme seemed to have made quite an impact on the managers in the Personnel Department. Most of the project teams completed their work and as they had worked on problems faced by the Authority, they displayed their value to the organization by providing practical, workable solutions to the problems they addressed. Certain of the personnel managers were subsequently asked to assist other departments in the Authority in solving both short and longer term problems.

Peter Davidson took over from Noel Green and continued to organize workshops and training programmes to suit the needs of particular managers or groups in the authority. Davidson's brief extended beyond the Personnel Department.

Henry Mitchell was seen by most of senior management as the man who made it happen. In the Authority's newsletter, Jim Carthy publicly congratulated Mitchell for his efforts in developing the Personnel Department.

Henry Mitchell learned a great deal from the intervention of Noel Green. He began to understand his own strengths and weaknesses as well as those of the managers in his department. He appreciated how necessary it was to be skilful at influencing others, especially at a time of rapid organizational change. Most of all, he learned that to be effective, it is necessary to influence others without being identified as a threat. That was a valuable lesson to have learned for the recommendations he was about to put before the Director of the Authority were threatening.

The report

Henry Mitchell submitted a report to Jim Carthy indicating that for the Industrial Development Authority to become anywhere near effective, redundancies were necessary. Further, the Authority lacked individuals who possessed particular skills, hence, in addition to the redundancies, Henry recommended a recruitment campaign.

On reading the report, Jim Carthy became anxious. 'Look Henry, I understand what you are trying to tell me and why, but for God's sake, see it from my point of view; the unions will crucify me,' exclaimed the Director of the Authority.

The discussion did not last for much longer. Jim Carthy said he would have to shelve the proposals.

Henry Mitchell did not give up. He recognized that his boss was highly role and status conscious. Henry began to replan his influence moves concerning the reorganization of the Authority. He approached Jim Carthy once more and suggested that if the above proposals were accepted, the status of the Director within the organization and among the nation's politicians would increase dramatically. He might even be seen as a world leader in the planning of industrial growth and development. As a secondary issue, the organization would also benefit.

After further discussions, and within the next six months, the Director of the Authority accepted most of the Personnel Director's proposals. In particular, the proposals included selected redundancies and redeployments, the continuation of the project teams and the establishment of new projects, and a major eighteen-month management training programme for most senior and middle managers. Henry Mitchell had succeeded in launching one of the largest in-organization change programmes in the UK. Mitchell recognized that he could not solely rely on Peter Davidson and thereby re-hired Noel Green.

The change programme

'The only thing I'm certain about around here is that everything is changing. I don't mind change, but when you get too much of it with little or no support, or training, or anything, I'm tired of it – I just want to stop,' stated a senior manager to the Director of Personnel, when the two met in the corridor on their way to lunch.

The comments worried Henry Mitchell. The senior manager was a supporter of the change programme, but his support was now waning. In fact, the Personnel Department had recently been heavily criticized for not providing sufficient help and support during the various phases of change and reorganization. Henry decided to call Noel Green.

'Ok, let's do that! Let's have a series of short one- or two-day training programmes for our senior and middle managers as we did for the Personnel Managers,' agreed Henry Mitchell on the phone. He had been talking to Noel Green over the phone for the past twenty minutes.

'I agree. Remember when we get together to plan the programmes in detail, we must be very careful about who we invite on each seminar. Getting the right people together who will talk to each other, share their problems and help each other back at work after

34

the programme, is absolutely vital. You and I know that the informal groups are in fact a more powerful force than the formal structure in terms of getting things done or just blocking and making sure nothing gets done. Let's use the existing informal networks for training,' finished Noel.

A few days after their telephone conversation, Henry and Noel met. They identified a series of two-day programmes for the senior and middle managers of the Authority. At the senior manager seminars, the Director of the Industrial Development Authority would give an hour's presentation identifying the needs for change and reorganization and then spend a further hour answering questions and responding to comments from the senior managers. The consultant would then run the programme for the remaining day and a half discussing organization strategy, organization structure and the importance of developing effective teams. The last two hours on the second day would be devoted to action planning whereby the senior managers would be split into pairs, helping each other draw up a six-month action plan that each senior manager could implement on his return to work. It was hoped that by enabling senior managers to generate action plans, that would commit them to doing something positive within the organization. Further, by talking through with colleagues key issues during the process of action planning, the managers would form close relationships and hence help each other implement their action plan.

The seminars for the middle managers would concentrate more on team building, and the generation of action plans. It was considered that the middle managers would benefit more from team development and interpersonal skills training as most of their time was spent within team settings.

The senior managers considered their seminars as tremendously successful, as it was widely felt that their needs were met. It was quickly established that the senior managers had little knowledge of subjects such as strategy and structure. Gaining more knowledge helped the senior managers understand how and what to improve. The participants on the programmes further considered the process of action planning to be invaluable. Most stated that they never realized that others were facing similar problems. Using each other to talk about work problems, and from there identify solutions, helped to form positive working relationships among the senior managers. The Director of Personnel later discovered that many of the senior managers continued to meet and share problems with each other on a fairly regular basis. Six months on, one senior manager commented to the Director of Personnel: 'Your programme helped form one of the best old boys clubs I have ever experienced. You realize that the old man (Jim Carthy) won't be able to cough without asking for our permission.' Henry Mitchell managed to force a polite smile to that last comment. 'You mean, he won't be able to cough without asking for my permission', thought Henry.

The executive merry-go-round

Ray Leonard, Director of Business Development in the Industrial Development Authority recognized the growing influence and stature of the Personnel Department. Ray, the youngest of the five functional directors in the authority, was in charge of the most sought after directorate – business development. Four years on the job, Ray was both feared and respected. His colleagues saw him as clear thinking, intelligent but difficult to talk to and somewhat untrustworthy. Most people considered that at the end of the day, Ray always got what he wanted.

In Ray's eyes, the balance of power within the Authority had shifted. The Personnel Department was now more powerful than Business Development. Personnel were now dictating the pace of change within the Authority. Personnel were calling the shots.

Ray made an appointment to see Jim Carthy. 'One thing is for sure Ray, everyone recognizes the impact you've made on business development. While you've been there, what is it, something like four and a half thousand new businesses have started with your support and help. You also introduced a consultancy service for medium-sized and larger organizations, which is the most profitable part of this whole organization, although strictly speaking we're not into profit making,' said Jim Carthy.

The two men had been talking for over one hour. 'But you think after four years, it's time for a move,' reflected the Director of the Authority.

'As you know, it has been our practice to move directors round every four or five years. It allows for change and vitality in the organization.'

Pause.

'You think you'd like to have a go at personnel – you'd welcome some experience of running a service function.'

Pause.

'Ok! Look Ray, leave that with me. As you know, I'll have to talk to Henry. With all these changes taking place, it may be opportune to switch our directors around as well. Thanks Ray. Speak to you soon.'

The meeting finished. Ray left the Director's office. Jim Carthy remained seated in his chair reflecting on the conversation. That morning, he had held a meeting with senior civil servants from the Department of Industry. He received a clear message from the civil servants – Henry Mitchell, the Director of Personnel in the Industrial Development Authority, sooner or later had to go. Apparently, Henry had made himself unpopular with some of the civil servants, especially Sir Robin Didson. When he disagreed with Sir Robin he said so; what made it worse was that Henry was usually right. Further, Henry and Jim had been contenders for the post of Director of the Industrial Development Authority; Jim won, Henry lost. At the time, certain civil servants had been pressurizing the Minister not to appoint Henry. Those same civil servants, championed by Sir Robin, were now pressurizing Jim to ease Henry out of the organization.

Of all his directors, Jim Carthy respected and trusted Henry the most. Since Jim's appointment Henry had been his loyal supporter. Further, he had done an excellent job as Director of Personnel, especially during this latest and far reaching reorganization. Ray had also done a reasonably good job, he too had his critics, but most were inside the authority.

Jim could see no alternative, Henry had to be moved, otherwise the pressure on him from the civil servants would be too great. He decided on a straight swop between Henry and Ray. He made appointments to see Ray and Henry in that order. Ray accepted the post of Director of Personnel. Then, the appointment with Henry.

'Henry, as you know, it's custom for our directors to move around every four years or so. I've asked you to see me to explore whether you'd be willing to leave personnel for the time being and take on business development. There are particular problems there that need attention, attention that Ray has not been able to provide through no fault of his own,' stated Jim Carthy.

'It's flattering to be considered Jim, but I feel there's a lot more to do in personnel, especially in seeing through this reorganization that we started', replied Henry.

The two men continued talking. An hour and a half passed.

'Henry, my position is clear. Our training centres need sorting out. The training staff are poorly qualified, poorly motivated and incapable of meeting present-day needs. Also training centres are under the wrong directorate. You know this organization as well as I do. If I took training centres and put them under business development, all hell would break loose between Tony Rivers and Ray. Tony does not like losing and even less to Ray. However, losing training centres to business development with you in charge is a different matter. I feel you two have always got on and could work together to improve our training centre's service,' said Jim.

'Jim, I agree with your logic. However, my problem is more personal. You know how unpopular I am with the bureaucrats in the Department of Industry. Taking on business development, especially with the increased responsibility of training centres, is high risk for me. If I am seen to perform poorly, they'll start putting pressure on you to have me out of this organization,' stated Henry.

'Henry! No more talk like this. You are one of the most valuable managers in this organization. Irrespective of what happens or what you decide, I'll always support you,' confirmed Jim Carthy.

The two men continued talking.

'Ok. I'll take it on. You're right. Training centres need to be taken into business development. I'm probably acceptable to Ray and to Tony Rivers and that'll make Ray's and my transition a smooth one. However, I'm suspicious of the Department of Industry. I suspect I'll be asking you for help before too long,' said Henry.

'Henry, let me assure you here and now that if anyone from the Department of Industry puts you under pressure, you'll have my support,' stated Jim Carthy. The meeting finished shortly after.

That evening Jim Carthy attended a dinner at the Department of Industry. He had been in deep conversation with a senior civil servant.

'So it's official then,' remarked Jim, 'Sir Robin Didson will be in charge of Manpower Services. That means our training centres will be under his remit.'

'How come you know so much about his appointment then?' enquired the civil servant.

'Oh, I was one of the people consulted on who should be in charge of Manpower Services. I, like so many others, recommended Sir Robin,' stated Jim.

'Then you've known for some time?' Jim Carthy nodded.

Time I did something about my situation

'He knew. Yes of course he knew!', remarked Henry Mitchell.

It was 11 p.m. and Henry was at home, seated in an easy chair in the lounge, talking to his wife. Henry had spent a particularly harassing day at a meeting with Sir Robin Didson in the chair, a group of civil servants and Jim Carthy. At the meeting, whatever suggestion Henry Mitchell offered was criticized and finally rejected.

Further, Mitchell was heavily criticized for not 'sorting out' the training centres. Mitchell knew that improvements concerning the training centres would take three years. He was only four months in the post.

'Jim did, at times, try to support me today, but he was just too quiet,' reflected Mitchell. 'Yes, he must have known about Didson's appointment when I was offered the business development job,' he continued.

'That does not sound like Jim Carthy. I always thought he was a straightforward sort of man. I also thought you two get on so well,' said Evelyn Mitchell.

Pause.

'Just shows you how wrong anyone can be. What a situation! Jim Carthy working against one of his own top directors,' continued Evelyn Mitchell.

'I'm not sure that Jim Carthy is that political. I think he's just stuck. At the time, Didson was the best. Carthy had to recommend him for the job. The relationship between Ray Leonard and Tony Rivers is worse than ever, but training centres needed reorganization. I was the most likely candidate. Perhaps at the time, Jim Carthy thought he could handle all the pressures and now finds he can't.'

Pause.

'I just don't think Jim Carthy is that political,' finished Henry Mitchell.

Silence.

'Forget Jim Carthy. What about you? What are you going to do?' enquired Evelyn.

'You remember me telling you that I met someone from Rail Transport at a lunch about two weeks ago. Well, he kept telling me that a senior position was about to become vacant, but he did not say what. I wonder if that was a hint,' said Henry.

'Well that would be the ultimate! You going back to managing the railways after, what, twenty years?' laughed his wife.

'Yes, I left the railways to help form this Authority,' said Henry Mitchell.

'Give him a ring. Invite that chap to lunch or dinner here at home. You certainly have got nothing to lose,' stated Evelyn.

'Quite right! Time I did something about my situation.'

Questions

1 If you were Henry Mitchell, what would you do next?

2 How effective do you consider Jim Carthy to be as Director of the Industrial Development Authority?

3 Identify criteria that you would consider suitable for assessing the performance of a senior manager in any organization. To what extent do your criteria seem to be applied in the Industrial Development Authority?

4 From your experience, how important, desired and necessary, is an awareness of the politics played in any organization? Give reasons why.

EIGHT

Guy Roberts

RON LUDLOW

Guy Roberts joined Millard Construction Ltd, on 7th January, 1985. He had worked for eight years as a quantity surveyor with Fry Bros (Builders) Ltd, but in November, 1984, he had lost his job when Fry Bros went bankrupt. The company had never really recovered from the recession of the early 1980s.

Guy was twenty-eight years old and qualified to AIOB level. He had always been considered good at his job, an efficient and accurate assessor of building materials, and his duties at Fry Bros had incorporated control of the Purchasing Department. He had received a basic salary, and an annual bonus.

Married, with a two-month old son, Guy was extremely worried when faced with redundancy. His young wife was unable to work, because of the baby, and the family had moved into a new, detached house some six months prior to his redundancy, incurring a high mortgage.

He was therefore greatly relieved when his wife's brother, Neville, who was the senior quantity surveyor at Millard Construction Ltd, informed him of a vacancy in the company and had recommended him for the job. Millard Construction was a much larger building company than Fry Bros and Guy was offered a higher basic salary. However, he would no longer receive an annual bonus, but instead he was entitled to a petrol allowance. This he welcomed, since getting to work would now entail a forty-mile round trip.

Before getting down to the task of preparing his first Bill of Quantities, he made a brief study of some past assessments and the jobs to which they related. He was puzzled. In each case, he estimated that an excess of sand and cement had been ordered. Making a mental note to query this with Neville, he proceeded to make his first assessment.

Some time later, his Bill of Quantities was returned by Neville, who told him that he had underestimated the quantities of sand and cement. Guy challenged this, and raised the matter of the past assessments. He was told that it was the usual practice to add on a percentage, to be 'on the safe side' and to allow for any accidental loss or damage to materials in transit and on site. Whilst disagreeing with this practice, Guy realized that he was not in any position to argue. He therefore made the necessary amendments, and signed the Bill of Quantities.

The following week, Guy glanced out of his office window, and observed the materials being delivered. Later that day, he was surprised to see the yard foreman loading up a small lorry with sand and cement, taken from this delivery, and driving away. The next morning, Guy observed the Millard Construction lorries being loaded with the rest of the material, for delivery to the building site.

Guy could not settle to his work. He kept remembering the incident of the previous day, and at lunch time, unable to contain his inquisitiveness any longer, he found occasion to see the foreman. He asked him to explain his actions, pointing out that the lorry used by the foreman was not one of Millard's fleet. The foreman refused to give him any answer, stating quite bluntly that it was none of Guy's business. As he walked angrily away down the yard, he called back over his shoulder, 'Take it up with your boss'.

On his return from lunch, Guy went immediately to see Neville and raised the issue with him. To his complete amazement, he was told that the foreman's brother owned a DIY shop nearby, and that for the past two years 'an arrangement' had existed between them. Neville had ensured that sand and cement on all Bills of Quantities was overestimated by a few per cent, and that this 'excess' material was then delivered to the foreman's brother. Payment was always in cash, and was split between the foreman, the senior quantity surveyor and his two assistant surveyors. One of these assistants had recently left Millard's employment, and Guy had taken his place.

Guy listened in stunned silence, as his brother-in-law calmly proposed 'cutting him in on the deal'. He pointed out to Guy that he knew of his financial circumstances, and that he could well do with some extra money. Moreover, if he agreed to go along with them, and say nothing to anyone else at Millard about their little arrangement, his petrol claims would be sanctioned 'without question'. It was apparently common practice for the quantity surveyors to get their local garage to give them blank receipt forms, on the pretext that they had lost some of their original receipts. They would then fill in false receipts and submit them, together with the genuine ones, receiving monthly reimbursement. As the senior quantity surveyor sanctioned all claims, no questions were ever asked.

When Guy recovered from the shock of this revelation, his immediate reaction was one of anger. He absolutely refused to have any part of these dishonest practices. Neville leant back in his chair, smiled slowly, and suggested that he had better think twice before reporting the matter to senior management. After all, his name was already on a falsified Bill of Quantities. In the event of an enquiry, it would not be difficult to contend that Guy had taken a part in the fraudulent practices, and his signature on the Bill would add weight to this statement. Guy realized that he could take the matter no further. He coldly informed Neville that while he had no intention of reporting the matter to senior management, he would, in future, insist on preparing Bills of Quantities for the correct amount of materials.

Almost immediately, Guy noticed the change of atmosphere at work. Neither his brother–in–law nor fellow quantity surveyors would speak to him unless they had to, and he received the same treatment from the yard foreman. This was noticed by others, who started to behave towards him in the same way. The atmosphere became very uncomfortable and Guy's pleasure in his new job quickly disappeared.

At the end of the month, he found that he had not received the correct reimbursement for his petrol claim. When he took this up with Neville, he was told that he had sanctioned all the receipts that Guy had given to him, and that if this did not tally with Guy's estimated figure, then some of the receipts must have got 'lost'. Guy was quite certain that he had given him all the receipts, and that if any loss had occurred, then it had occurred in Neville's office.

Early the next week, Guy was summoned to the yard, where he was told that his car had suffered an accident. Apparently, the foreman had been driving the dumper truck, and had inadvertently reversed it into Guy's car. As a result, Guy was without a car for a week while the damage was repaired, and had to rely on public transport to get him to work. He was also unable to make any visits for his company.

In the following week, Guy was summoned to the manager's office. He was told that the men, working on a job for which he had prepared the Bill of Quantities, had run out of sand and cement. He was accused of underestimating and to prove his point, the manager produced past estimates for similar jobs, all of which exceeded Guy's estimates by up to 10 per cent. Guy was unable to comment.

Later the same month, Guy was once again summoned to the manager's office. This time, some material he had ordered had failed to arrive in time for an urgent job. The manager once more accused him of failing to do his job properly, saying, 'You should be aware of the contingency of late delivery. If you occasionally over-assess on a job, then we will always have a reserve stock to draw on in times of emergency.'

That evening, Guy found his wife in tears. She told him that she had been to visit her sister-in-law, and during the course of their conversation, she had learned that Millard was far from happy with Guy's performance. She reminded him that he was still working through his three-month trial period, and begged him to take care. Her sister-in-law had hinted that he was in danger of losing his job. He decided to tell his wife the truth. When he had told her the whole story, she pleaded with him that, for the sake of family unity, he must say nothing to senior management about Neville's dishonesty. However, she strongly urged him to have another word with him, to see if they could come to a better working arrangement.

The next morning, he approached Neville, saying that he had changed his mind. He would henceforth add 10 per cent to his Bills of Quantities for sand and cement, and while he still wanted no part in the fraud, he would never report the matter. However, he was desperately short of money, and for that reason alone, he was willing to submit false petrol claims. Neville assured him that from that time onward, he would do his best to ensure that Guy's claims were secured against 'loss'.

Guy completed his three-month trial period, without further mishap. The manager informed him that he had been taken on to the permanent staff, and said how pleased they were with his progress. There had been no further incidence of materials running out on jobs for which he had estimated the Bills of Quantities. The atmosphere at work was no longer estranged, and Guy was grateful for the extra money he made on petrol claims.

Questions

1 What are Guy Roberts' values and needs?
2 What are the company's values and norms?
3 If you were Guy Roberts, would you have compromised your values? Why or why not?
4 What measures must the Company take to ensure such practices do not develop in future?

NINE

Grayle Engineering

RON LUDLOW

Grayle Engineering was established in 1936, and was now a public limited company, in which the Grayle family owned the controlling share interest. Throughout its existence, it had relied solely on Ministry of Defence (MoD) contracts for its source of income. Until 1980, these contracts had been placed on a 'cost plus' basis, but with the Conservative Government's policy of reducing public expenditure, the method of placing contracts had been changed to 'fixed price'. Simultaneously, the size of the contracts had been reduced. Instead of the large contract, involving over a hundred employees or more for up to five years, the company was now being asked to handle contracts which frequently involved less than fifteen employees for a duration of under two years. Between 1974 and 1985, personnel levels had fallen from 1500 to 900. Staffing levels in the Electrical Engineering Department had fallen from forty-five to twenty-six over the same period. Between 1981 and 1984, redundancy announcements had resulted in the loss of over 300 employees.

Norman Graham, project manager in electrical engineering, had joined the company in 1977, as a senior electrical engineer, and for the first five years of his employment had worked on one large project. He had not enjoyed this long-term project commitment, and in 1982 had been relieved to find himself transferred to smaller projects. After working on twelve such projects, he was promoted to the position of small projects manager in January, 1985.

During his eight years of employment at Grayle Engineering, he had frequently requested management training, but had only succeeded in getting on to two management courses, one held externally and one in-house, each lasting for one week. Prior to joining Grayle, his industrial experience, extending over twenty years, had started with an engineering apprenticeship, followed by six years with a large computer company and nine years with the

Science Research Council. He was professionally qualified with an ONC mechanical (endorsed by the Institute of Production Engineers) and an HNC in electronics.

Going commercial

Climbing the stairs to his office, one Wednesday morning in January 1986, his thoughts went back to the day he had been appointed small projects manager. He had then put forward his ideas to expand the Electrical Department by 'going commercial', and tendering for contracts outside the MoD, something Grayle had never done before. While this had received the agreement of his Head of Department, Norman was well aware of the problems facing the introduction of small commercial projects, in a company such as Grayle where operations were, and had always been, defined by MoD procedures.

The company had high fixed overheads, exemplified by the quality assurance (QA) system, mandatory for MoD work. The MoD required that all components should be traceable by their batch number, even back to the source of the raw material. Every deviation from the issued drawing had to be recorded and 'concessed' by the Head of Design. Scope for 'judgement' was not permitted by the inspectors – it was either correct to drawing or not correct. Norman realized that one of his first problems was to introduce some scope for 'judgement' if small commercial projects were to be viable.

Grayle had no experience in tendering for commercial projects. MoD contracts required approval documentation with contributions from many department (Systems Analysis, Stress, Reliability). A commercial project did not. It would therefore require considerable effort on Norman's part to prevent these departments 'jumping on the bandwagon', particularly as new work was scarce for all departments, in the current economic situation.

Norman was also concerned about staffing levels. The Electrical Engineering Department's involvement in minor projects could be anything from three months to two years in duration. Yet extra staff could only be recruited if it could be shown that there would still be a shortage in twelve months time. Despite four years of monitoring the situation, the Electrical Engineering Department was always 25 per cent understaffed at any one time because of the difficulties involved in the forward planning of the work load. The recruitment policy remained unchanged. Norman estimated a need for six more engineers. Staff morale was falling. New graduates joined and required training. The 'over 40s' in the department trained the new graduates.

However, there was a dearth of experienced engineers in the twenty-five to forty age group, as a dramatic shortage of engineers generally made it possible for them to exploit good salary enhancements outside Grayle. New graduates saw a twenty-year age gap between themselves and their seniors and felt that promotion was impossible. They left at the earliest possible moment.

The sales operation was also a cause of serious concern for Norman Graham. It was staffed by ex-service officers, who responded to general staff requirements issued by the MoD. They sold only that which the company had already produced and had had approved by the MoD. They did not explore the market, in order to assess its future needs and initiate internal research and development (R & D). The New Business Committee only responded to invitations to tender; such invitations were then passed to the Marketing Department, for assessment. The Marketing Department received information from the company's agents in foreign countries, who fed back 'needs' to Grayle.

A further problem arose in the Manufacturing Department. The continuity of large projects meant that the staff employed at the end of one fiscal year would be employed at the start of the next. The Finance Department therefore had become accustomed to delaying the issue of works order numbers by up to six weeks into the new fiscal year. Minor commercial projects had to be sanctioned anew after the start of the new fiscal year, and this took several weeks after presentation to the New Business Committee. The manufacturing could not proceed without a valid works order number.

The drawing office was required to produce drawings to the strict requirements of Defence Standards. Indeed, it was regularly audited to ensure that it did so. The wider tolerances and the suitable alternative components, permissible in commercial work, produced a laborious drawing burden. The chief draughtsman insisted that draughtsmen worked to the written instructions of the engineer. It was his belief that draughtsmen had no reason to visit the workshops during manufacture. Norman realized that it would be a major task to break down the custom of 'isolationism.'

The Personnel Department moved slowly. Several weeks could elapse between an interview and the issue of an offer of employment. They seemed to be unaware that experienced engineers were at a premium, and that new graduates steadily left after two years, thus exacerbating the age gap. Despite the 'seller's market', salaries of electrical engineers were pegged to other disciplines to avoid 'creating a precedent'. Norman's present staff on small commercial projects numbered four; three were new graduates and one was an engineer with five years' experience.

As Norman reached his office door, he ruefully reflected that so far out of the seven tenders for new small projects, submitted since he became project manager, no contracts had yet been placed. Five of these had been for fixed price MoD contracts and had become 'deferred decisions', a policy decision of the Ministry, but of the two purely 'commercial' tenders, one had gone to a company in Germany (a job for South America) and the other (a job for the Middle East) was still in abeyance. The current commercial work in progress consisted of a contract for Africa.

Norman was determined to get more work into the department and to increase staff levels in order to handle it. He was determined that he would initiate action today in order to achieve this. His first priority was to write a proposal to senior management, via his Head of Department, to increase his authority as project manager on minor projects, so that other divisions would be accountable to him for their performance. He wanted to change the project management structure so that small commercial projects would no longer be organized, as seen in Appendix 1, where the small projects manager could only get input from the various disciplines by making a request upwards via his Head of Department, and once such input had been sanctioned, had no direct control over it on a 'daily basis'. Instead, he wanted to adopt the management structure which already existed for large projects, as seen in Appendix 2, where the projects manager had staff from various disciplines seconded to his project, and had full control over their input, on a daily basis, for the duration of the project. This would specifically give him more control over finance and marketing operations.

He also wanted to stress the need for additional staff, and estimated that his immediate need, regarding commercial projects, was a minimum of two experienced main grade engineers. However, his Head of Department was well known within the company as a man who always put off until tomorrow a decision he should have taken today – his 'in tray' was referred to as the Bermuda Triangle. Therefore, Norman decided to side-step normal company procedures, and to send a copy of his proposal to the chief engineer.

The day begins

The telephone rang. The Progress Department informed him that the paint, required for the transit cases on a current MoD project, was two weeks out of shelf life. As a result, quality assurance had impounded it into the stores to prevent its disposal. Would he please write a memo, accepting it. The alternative would be one month's delivery for a new batch, and a £100 minimum order charge. He had to decide quickly what should be done, and advised them to use the out-of-date paint.

A knock on his office door heralded the arrival of the safety officer. He explained that he could not sign an operational procedure for some test equipment on an existing project, because it did not contain the 'standard paragraph' on the Health and Safety at Work Act. He asked Norman to arrange for its inclusion, or to confirm that there was a disclaimer in operation. Norman promised to check and advise him further that afternoon. He wondered whether or not to delegate this job to one of his new graduates but, after consideration, decided to do it himself, for speed.

The telephone rang again. Purchasing Department advised him that a subcontractor had suffered fire damage, which would delay their delivery of some parts for an MoD small project by twelve weeks. Was this acceptable, or should they go to another firm, which was not MoD approved but could deliver in six weeks, but with a cost penalty. Norman advised them that he would prefer the earliest delivery, but that he would have to see quality assurance for a concession. He promised to call purchasing back in the afternoon with an answer. Glancing out through his office window, he noticed that his staff seemed to be engrossed in their work. 'Oh well,' he thought, 'better not disturb them'. Rising from his chair, he made his way to quality assurance.

It was almost 10.30 a.m. He got up to get a cup of coffee, but as he reached the door, the telephone rang again. This time, it was Finance Department, querying the booking of personnel from Marketing Department on works order numbers issued to Norman Graham. He informed them that, in the case in question, it was quite in order, and hastily replaced the phone to get his coffee.

As he returned from the coffee machine, he heard the phone ringing once more. This time it was publications, advising him that the presentation material for the sales 'push' would have been ready if the slide copier had not broken down. They asked if he could use an overhead instead of a slide projector. The material was all ready, and they wanted to know who would pick it up. He said that he would come over and pick it up straight away.

At publications, he joined in a discussion of their technical difficulties, and received their profuse apologies for their failure to supply him with the material, in the form he requested. He had always enjoyed good relations with them, and consequently allowed them to take up more of his time than he could really spare, given that his morning had been one of constant interruptions.

Arriving back in his office, he dumped the presentation material on the table and noticed that a drawing had been put on his desk, with a memo, requesting him to check it through for errors. Having found one small dimensional error, he reached for his pen and corrected it. He then walked to the drawing office and returned it to the chief draughtsman, informing him of his action, and thinking how much time his modification would save. It took at least a week to get modifications done in the drawing office.

Returning to his office, he looked at his 'in tray'. He noticed a letter from a subcontractor which required his urgent attention. He groaned inwardly, remembering that letters always took at least two days to be processed through the typing pool. Reaching for some headed paper, he wrote the letter himself.

It was now almost 11.30 a.m., and he had not yet chased up the mechanical engineers working on the current commercial project. He knew they were having problems, as one of his subordinate electrical engineers had relayed the information last night. 'Better check it out now,' he muttered, and left immediately for the mechanical section, situated in an office block some 400 yards from his own. 'This is where I could do with more experienced subordinate staff,' he thought, 'but then, would I really want to delegate this sort of thing? A good manager should always keep his finger on the pulse, and there is no better way of doing it than by being seen to be doing it. Besides, I enjoy the contact with other disciplines, it makes for good interpersonal relations.'

On his way back to his office, he was stopped by one of his young subordinate engineers, who told him that he had just become a father for the first time. He congratulated him warmly, and spent a few minutes discussing the joys and burdens of fatherhood. When he finally reached his desk, he dug out the local telephone directory from the pile on his filing cabinet and telephoned Interflora, asking them to send the happy mother a bouquet. He was always interested in the lives of his young subordinates, and believed that a manager should show such concern. Besides it made them feel important, and he hoped it would help promote company loyalty and stem Grayle's staff 'leakage'.

No sooner had he put the phone down than it rang again. This time it was main gate security, informing him that Mr Coleman from CAB Ltd had called. He apologized for not making an appointment, but he had located a supplier of some material which he knew, from his previous meeting with Norman, was being sought. Norman said he would meet him in the foyer. As he descended the two flights of stairs to the foyer, his feelings were ambiguous. He was annoyed at this further interruption but, at the same time, he was very grateful to Coleman for his help. Having taken note of the details supplied by Coleman, Norman glanced at the foyer clock. It was 12 o'clock. 'Well, that's the morning gone,' he thought to himself, and inviting Coleman to join him, he made his way to the visitors' dining room for lunch. Lunch there always took longer, because of the waitress service, but then Coleman had been extremely helpful and he could hardly say goodbye to him at that point in time, without seeming very ungracious.

After lunch

It was just after 1.30 p.m. when Norman returned to his office. He immediately returned to the task of working through his 'in tray'. He had just completed reading the first page of a specification document when the telephone rang. It was the secretary of the New Business Committee, informing him that Wednesday's meeting had been brought forward to Monday because, the Managing Director would be away on Wednesday. He confirmed that he could attend on Monday but that he had not yet received reports from either the Planning, Progress or Finance Departments, and he needed to collate this information before attending the meeting. He telephoned each department, asking if they had their reports ready for him. Planning and Progress Departments confirmed that theirs were ready, but Finance Department informed him that theirs would not be available until Tuesday. He felt a mounting sense of frustration, as he realized that the collation of these reports had been a job he planned to do on Monday, ready for the Wednesday meeting. Now he would have to collect the two reports that were ready, and begin work on them this afternoon, if he was to be ready for the Monday meeting, Moreover, he would have to go to the meeting without the report from the Finance Department. His collated material would be incomplete, and his input into the meeting unavoidably curtailed. He quietly cursed the Managing Director for bringing this situation about.

Putting the specification to one side, he rose to visit the Planning Department. As he reached the door, the telephone rang once more. It was one of his four subordinate engineers, phoning from the inspection area. The assembly of an electronic unit had been undertaken to use available components, but had not been completed because some were long lead items and were still awaited. Unfortunately, the order of assembly did not comply with the planning sheets, even though both the workshop and inspection agreed that it was sensible in the circumstances. Norman's subordinate engineer felt 'out of his depth', with the chief inspector, the workshop foreman and the planner, all arguing. He therefore asked Norman to come quickly, as the situation needed sorting out!

On his way back from the inspection area he called into the Planning Department and then climbed the stairs to the Progress Department to collect their reports. While in the Progress Department, he stopped and discussed two other jobs with them. He regarded good relationships with the Progress Department as an important part of getting things done. He decided to call in on finance, to see if there was any chance of speeding things up but only secured a half-hearted promise that they would try to have it ready by Friday night. 'Oh well,' he thought 'I could read it over the weekend, instead of the Sunday papers!'

Returning to his office he managed to finish reading the specification and made some notes, which he would have to flesh out in the morning. Glancing at the clock, he realized he had not rung back the safety officer. He rang the safety officer to tell him that a disclaimer was in operation. On being told that he had only just caught him, Norman glanced at the clock. It was 5.30 p.m.

At the end of the day

Norman locked his filing cabinet, grabbed his coat and opened his briefcase, to put the remaining paperwork from his 'in-tray' into it, to read later that night. As he did so, he spotted that his briefcase still contained two documents that he had read the previous night. He switched the new for the old, silently promising himself that he would clear all his paperwork in the morning.

At 5.36 p.m. Norman Graham left his office, anxious not to be late home. It was his twenty-fifth wedding anniversary and he had planned a surprise dinner for his wife and family of three at a local restaurant. He got into his car for the drive home, only too aware of his failure to complete that which he had set out to do that morning.

As he drove home through the pouring rain, he had time to review his situation, and question his own competence. 'Am I an effective manager?' he asked himself, aloud. He reflected that he had been instrumental in creating the prototype wiring shop, as an offshoot from the formal shop. He had also introduced the 'roving inspector' and 'process inspection' when end-of-product inspection was inadequate. Had he not also supported the case for radical changes in the electrical 'goods inwards' inspection? Had he not also introduced the 'running errata sheet' for a complete assembly, to overcome the 'one deviation – one concession form' syndrome, which was the custom in inspection? Had he not forced through the drawing office a drawing system which saved 30 per cent of draughting time on printed circuit boards?

With his knowledge of the existing system, and a fair record of sacrificing 'sacred cows', the management considered him the most likely man to succeed in creating a new internal procedure to facilitate commercial projects. Yet, at the same time, he was well aware of senior management's criticism of his methods of dealing with his subordinates. He was thought to be too friendly; senior management believed that managers should adopt a more remote style of management. Norman disagreed; his style had always got things done. His friendliness made people more willing to 'do him a favour', even when this went against company procedures.

That night, returning home with his family from the restaurant, he reflected on his long and happy marriage. However, he was also reminded of the fact that he was now fifty years old. Switching on the ten o'clock news, he sat back to catch up with what was happening in the outside world. He heard, without undue surprise, the announcement that Michael Heseltine had resigned. As he rose to switch off the TV, he smiled wryly, thinking that whoever became the new Minister of Defence would make little difference to his own situation at Grayle. Things would not change as far as MoD contracts were concerned. The amount of work might vary, but the system would remain the same. Pouring himself a double whisky, he reached for his briefcase.

Questions

1 Evaluate Norman Graham's effectiveness as a manager.
2 Describe his style of behaviour and analyse the reasons for it.
3 What can be done, if anything, to improve Norman's effectiveness? Explain why.

Appendix 1 Minor project management

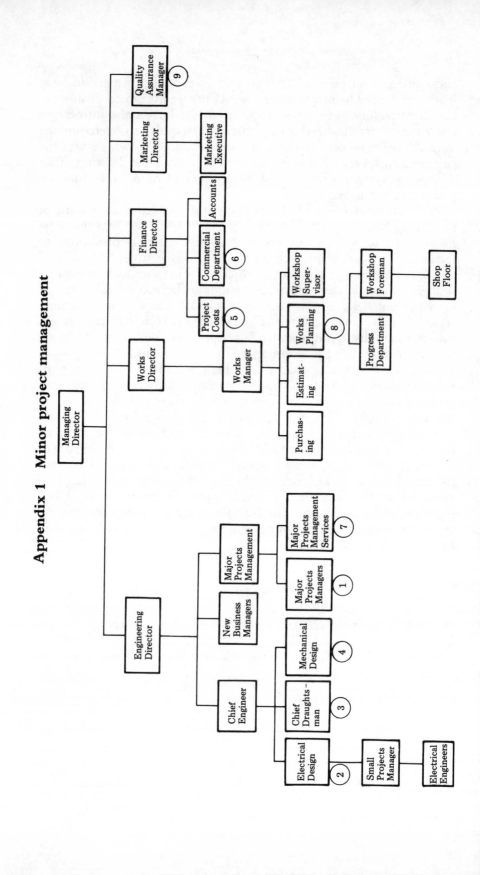

Appendix 2   Major product management

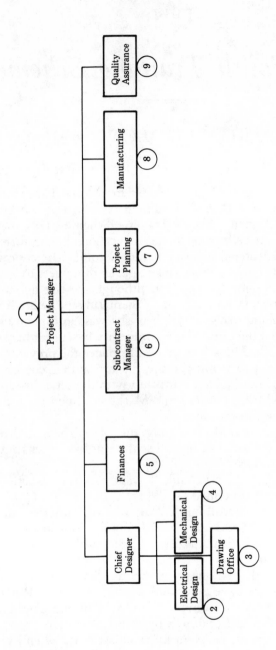

TEN

The Youth Training Scheme

RON LUDLOW

One Thursday morning in August, at 9.05 a.m., Marian Lane received a telephone call from Jane Begley, a training coordinator, working on Rutland County Council's Youth Training Scheme. This they ran jointly with the local college of further education, in the form of a consortium named Rutland Youth Training Group. The coordinator was worried. She had been going to take a group of trainees to London, as part of their off-the-job training, but although she was due to meet them at 8.30 a.m., by 9.00 a.m. not one of them had reported to Rutland railway station. Telling her to stay where she was, in case any of the trainees had mistaken the time, Marian immediately sent for her secretary, Amy Fitt, who had herself been a YTS trainee the previous year.

'Amy, I want you to bring me the file containing copies of all letters sent to trainees. We have a mix-up with the retail group who should have been visiting Harrods and Marks and Spencers today, as part of their off-the-job training.'

Amy promptly appeared, clutching the file. 'They all had the letter, Miss Lane,' she said brightly. 'I sent it out two weeks ago, the day you told me to do it.'

'Give me the copy,' Marian said, 'I want to know exactly what instructions the letter contained.'

'Well, I typed what you told me,' Amy replied, rather resentfully. 'I told them to meet Mrs Begley, the Training Coordinator, at the Station at 8.30 a.m. on 15th August. I signed all the letters on your behalf, as you told me to do.'

'Oh Amy,' sighed Marian, 'you should have typed railway station. You know we have a bus and railway station in Rutland.'

'Well,' retorted Amy, 'it's obvious, isn't it? Anyone would know that the quickest way to London is by train, so station must mean railway station. Anyway, we went by train last year, when I was on the YTS.'

Marian sighed wearily. 'It may seem obvious to you, Amy, but just look at last year's copy letter. You see, it clearly states railway station. You must remember that none of the trainees use the train to get to work. They all live locally and come in by bus each day. To them station would mean bus station.'

As Amy left, Marian lifted the phone and called the training coordinators' office. Finding that only Helen Harcombe was there, the others having already left on their daily rounds of trainee visits, she explained the situation to Helen and asked her to go over to the bus station as quickly as possible. Helen replied that her first call was at 9.30 a.m. and it was already 9.15 a.m. As the call would take her ten minutes by car, any detour would make her late.

'This is an emergency,' snapped Marian. 'At this moment there are fifteen kids somewhere in this town, who are our responsibility and who, by now, should have been well on their way to London, on a visit designed to broaden their education. We must find them, and find them quickly, before either their parents or their employers get to hear about it. It makes us look so incompetent.'

'If I find them, what do I say?' queried Helen.

'Tell them to go straight to work, and explain to their employers that there has been a misunderstanding. An explanatory letter will be sent immediately, both to the parents and the employers.'

'Very well then, I'll go, but goodness knows what time I shall get to my first appointment,' said Helen, grudgingly. 'That car I bought at the auction last week is playing up something rotten. I think I shall take it back. After all, I did get a guarantee with it which said that money would be refunded in twenty-four hours.'

'Are you sure that does not mean within twenty-four hours of purchase?' asked Marian.

'Well, it does not say that,' replied Helen sharply, 'and I made a point of asking the auctioneer what would happen if I was not fully satisfied with the car after I got it home. He definitely said that it was the company's policy to refund money within twenty-four hours if a customer was not completely satisfied with a vehicle bought from them. He did not say anything about a time limit, and neither does the written guarantee.'

After locating the trainees at the coach station, and apologizing for the misunderstanding, Helen set off for the auction yard. However, on arriving there she quickly found out what the guarantee really meant. The auctioneer firmly told her that money would only be refunded if a complaint was registered within twenty-four hours of purchase, and in spite of her protestations about the ambiguity of the guarantee, she realized that further argument was futile. Threatening the auctioneer and his company with a solicitor's letter, she left the yard feeling very angry. Her anger was further fuelled when the car eventually broke down completely, one mile from her first appointment.

At 10.15 a.m., having completed her journey by bus, Helen arrived at the office of a local engineering firm, where she had placed a trainee in the Purchasing Department two months earlier. She had already made two assessment visits, and found the girl to be settling down well. However, she was surprised that on this visit she was greeted by the office manager in a most cold and distant manner. At first she believed that this was because she was so late for her appointment, but after apologizing for this, she discovered that although it was contributory, it was not the principal reason. He told her that the trainee was proving to be quite incompetent, and was clearly unable to carry out even the most simple instruction. He further explained that a week before, he had given the trainee a dictaphone tape to transcribe and she had made several errors, the worst of which concerned an order for biro pens.

'We get through plenty of these in a year,' he explained. 'So when I saw that Pollmans, the office equipment specialists, were offering biros at half the usual retail price, I knew that we could not afford to miss it. I told the trainee to order three gross of these. That would last us well over a year. Imagine my annoyance when the order was delivered this morning, and I found we had been sent only one gross. I can tell you, I have given that stupid trainee a good telling-off this morning and I have told her that you will arrange her removal from our employment.'

'May I speak to her?' asked Helen. 'After all, it is most important that I hear both sides of the story.'

'There is only one side to the story,' retorted the angry Manager, 'I gave her an order, and she failed to carry it out!'

When Tracy Smith, the trainee, was asked to explain the situation, Helen found that this was far from the truth. The girl had saved the tape containing the message in question and she gave it to Helen. What Helen heard soon made the cause of the error plain.

'Send an order to Pollmans, as follows: Three gross (by the way, Tracy, that's 144) blue biro pens. Usual price £14. Special offer £7.'

Helen told Tracy that she had nothing to worry about and that she would sort things out with the manager. She immediately informed him that the tape did not make his meaning clear, in fact it undoubtedly confused the issue, and that Tracy could not be blamed. The manager disagreed.

'Only a fool would make such a mistake,' he said. 'Besides, it is not the only error she has made.'

'You have never complained before,' replied Helen, 'and this is my third visit.'

'Well, when are you taking her away?' demanded the manager.

'I am not,' was Helen's firm reply.

'Then I shall report you to the Manpower Services Commission, for failing to do your job,' replied the manager, his face red with anger.

Back at County Hall, Marian Lane looked at the clock. 'Nearly lunchtime,' she thought, 'and I wanted to be away by 1.30.' Marian was taking six days of her annual leave.

As she started to tidy her desk, she was interrupted by the telephone. The caller was the widowed mother of a trainee, placed in a local factory. The boy had been a poor achiever at school, but was proving to be a hard worker in his placement. His mother had once before talked on the telephone to Marian, because she wanted an explanation of the whole concept of the Youth Training Scheme run by the Rutland Youth Training Group. She was American and although she had lived in England for several years, she was still unfamiliar with many aspects of British life. Her British husband had died six months ago and she was anxious about bringing up her teenage son alone.

'I am sorry to trouble you, Miss Lane, but I am most concerned about this day trip you have arranged for my son's Youth Training group.'

'There is nothing to be worried about,' Marian replied. 'We intend taking the boys on a visit to the Broads, on the last Friday in September.'

'Well, I am sorry, but I really don't think I want my son to be part of this trip,' said the mother, after a slight pause.

'Well, that is a shame,' replied Marian. 'After all, it is our policy to arrange off-the-job training for all our trainees and, as far as possible, we tailor the type of training to the ability and interest of the groups concerned. In your son's case, he is not one of our most academic young people, and his training group at the local college will not be taking any formal exams at the end of their training year. We therefore thought that a visit such as this would be interesting for them, while at the same time, providing them with part of the broad-based education which it is our duty to provide under the Youth Training Scheme.'

'Oh really, Miss Lane,' snapped the mother, 'while I agree that such a visit could be loosely termed educational, I fail to understand why it should be part of the Youth Training Scheme.'

Marian was unable to see exactly what the mother was complaining about. She also noticed that it was gone one o'clock, and she was still far from being ready to leave.

'Look, please don't feel that anyone is forcing your son to go on the trip,' she assured the mother. 'However, I think he would regret it if he does not go. After all, the whole of his group is going, and I am sure he would not want to be the odd one out. All the lads seem excited by the prospect.'

'I don't doubt that at all, Miss Lane, but I hardly feel that this is the sort of activity I want my son participating in, and quite frankly, I am surprised that our County Council would promote such a thing. These boys are all under eighteen years of age you know.'

'What on earth has that got to do with it?' asked Marian, exasperation beginning to show in her voice. 'An educational visit is an educational visit, regardless of age, and I can assure you that Norfolk is a beautiful county. Believe me, with this particular group, such a trip should prove to be both stimulating and enlightening, and introduce them to an area about which they have practically no knowledge.'

'Thank God for that!' retorted the mother. 'Might I advise you, Miss Lane, that as far as I am concerned, I am determined that my son remains unenlightened in this area, at least for another couple of years. He is not going to visit any Broads, and that's that, and it makes no difference to me whether they are in Norfolk or Timbuctoo.'

Marian's patience was at an end. 'Very well,' she said. 'If you don't want your son to take part in this trip, I will inform his training coordinator. There is nothing more to be said.'

'Oh yes,' replied the mother, 'there is certainly more to be said, and I shall shortly be saying it to the Manpower Services Commission. I am sure they would never approve of a scheme which promoted such goings-on, that is, if they ever knew about it in the first place, which I seriously doubt.' The angry mother slammed down the phone, and Marian was left confused, irritated and late in leaving for her holiday. As she left County Hall, she remembered that she had not sent the letter of apology to the parents and employers of the trainees who had failed to make the trip to London that morning.

When Marian returned from holiday, she received a phone call from Rutland Manpower Services Commission. The liaison officer concerned reprimanded Marian for going away on holiday and not informing her, on the grounds of simple courtesy. However, she also delivered a stronger reprimand. She had received, during the week, several complaints about the Rutland Youth Training Group's

Youth Training Scheme and she therefore thought it most advisable to meet with Marian, as soon as possible. She reminded her that the Rutland Scheme was due for validation for the new training year – in exactly one month.

Questions

1 What communication problems can you identify here? Why are they occurring?
2 How would such problems be reduced in the future?

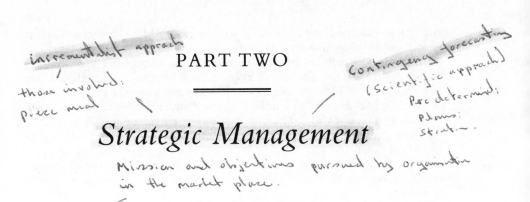

PART TWO

Strategic Management

[handwritten annotations:]
incrementalist approach
those involved; piece meal

Contingency forecasting (Scientific approach) Pre determined; Plans; strat.—.

Mission and objectives pursued by organisation in the market place.

The term strategy has been used in a multiplicity of ways in the management and organization literature. Strategy has been applied at the individual level to indicate the approach(es) a person adopts in order to address particular problems and issues. From an organizational perspective, strategy has been identified with the mission and objectives pursued by the organization in its market place. Equally, the term has been utilized to both describe and epitomize the tensions and pressures at the interface between the organization and its external environment, especially during periods of change.

Even taken from an organizational perspective strategy has been interpreted in two distinct ways. Under the normative school, all embracing models are formed in order to explain the making and effective application of strategic decisions. The emphasis is on a scientific approach to contingency forecasting, in order to draft plans, designs and generate strategies that fit with pre-determined criteria.

In contrast, the incrementalist philosophy projects an intermittent, loosely linked pattern to strategy formulation and implementation, as much influenced by those executives involved in the strategy formulation process, as by organizational, market or external environmental forces.

The cases offered in this section address both philosophies, covering the more haphazard, subjective processes of the incrementalists and the planned, rigorous, objective stance of the normative school.

The case of *The Syntax Corporation* (Part 1) examines the interpersonal processes involved in the development of a newly formed group of senior executives as they progress into becoming a more effective and mature management team. The importance of the behaviour of the team members and other senior executives (non-team members) in the organization, on the organization and its business, emphasizes the importance of understanding what constitutes effective performance at senior organizational levels. The case is sequential and hence parts 2, 3, 4 and 5 can be found in the teaching manual.

The Box Makers: the case of SafePAC plc continues with the theme of performance at senior managerial levels but focuses particularly on how strategy is generated. Depending on the position held by the executive, his vision for the business and its future and his personal values, tensions, conflict and mistrust can arise between the senior managers responsible for strategy formation. The manner in which interpersonal tensions are effectively or ineffectively addressed, is a key aspect of the case.

The role of the consultant in the process of strategy formation, especially when key executives hold different perspectives concerning the future of the business, provides the theme for the case of *The Celtic Woollen Company*. In situations when tensions need to be overcome in order to form business strategies with which senior management can identify, the issue of ethical/ unethical behaviour arises, which provides an additional interesting aspect to this case.

The processes of strategy generation, implementation and the contribution that can be made by a consultant is continued, but from the particular perspective of data feedback as in the case of the *Public Welfare Agency*. The steps to gathering relevant data and its feedback to managers in the organization in order to assist strategic decision making, are crucial learning points in this case.

Having explored the processes of strategy formation/implementation and thereby discussed the range of criteria for assessing executive performance, the case of *Fosbar Electronics* examines the management development requirements of senior management. Particular management development solutions are requested as a part of the case study tasks.

In contrast, the case of the *Olde England Taverns Limited* (Parts 1 and 2), adopts a far broader view by examining the state of the industry before focusing on the case of one company in Part 2. The case can be analysed both from a human resources perspective and from a business policy perspective. The case is not sequential and Parts 1 and 2 need to be issued simultaneously. Part 1 provides the background to the brewing industry and Part 2, the particular problems facing the company.

Similarly, *The Epicurus Leisure Group* case requires that a broader industry perspective be adopted before examining in detail the situation in the company. Having identified the desired strategies for the future, it is important that a human resources strategy be identified and developed which can adequately support the newly shaped corporate plan.

ELEVEN

The Syntax Corporation

ANDREW P. KAKABADSE

Part 1

Syntax is a multinational, advanced computer technology corporation offering a wide range of hardware and software computer products, such as the new micro VDUs on the hardware side and up-to-date packaged management training programmes on the software side. In addition, the corporation has diversified into other areas such as the production of high quality aircraft instruments and vehicle instrumentation and medical and laboratory equipment. Currently, the corporation is split into four divisions, with its head office in Culver City, California.

Medical and Laboratory Division (MLD)

Our attention is focused on the activities of MLD; specifically that part of the division known as 'Rest of the World'. The General Manager responsible for MLD split the division into two – the USA and Rest of the World. Each half of the division is under the control of a President. The President for Rest of the World is an American, Jeremy Bryant, based in London, but servicing the UK and Eire, Europe (including the Eastern bloc), the Gulf States, Africa and the Asian bloc, including mainland China and Japan.

In his current job, Bryant has an impressive track record. He regularly returns a healthy profit. In addition, he holds a reputation in the corporation for picking the right man for the job. His two latest successes are former Lancashire textile worker, Peter Ashcroft, whose selling skills have made him a legend in the corporation, and David Hall, generally recognized as intellectually highly talented. Ashcroft holds the position of Sales Vice President (Rest of the World) and seems to be achieving the impossible – selling advanced medical and laboratory equipment to the Japanese in ever increasing quantities.

Hall has a PhD in physics, a former young university professor, but with an eye for business and product development. Of the two, it is considered by the other influential managers, that Hall will be the one who will take whatever 'big' jobs become available in the USA.

Hall's responsibilities are twofold:

1 To participate as a full member on the Product Strategy Team (PST) which meets periodically in Culver City to decide on the product portfolio of the division. Amongst others, such as the President, MLD/USA (Bryant's counterpart), Bryant himself and representatives from Japan, Europe and other factory sites in the USA, sits Corgill, the General Manager responsible for MLD. On this committee, Hall's task is to represent the British contribution in terms of product design and development, manufacture and the worldwide marketing of all MLD products.
2 To promote product design, development and manufacture of British goods at three sites in South West England, Taunton, Yeovil and Marlborough, and a further site in Carlisle. Hall's position is that of UK Production Vice President.

At present, Hall is the sole UK representative on the prestigious PST.

Both Hall and Ashcroft report directly to Bryant. A third member provides the full complement to Bryant's entourage, Eammon O'Sullivan, the Dublin born, Finance and Administration Vice President for Rest of the World (see Appendix 1). Unlike the commonly accepted stereotype of an Irishman, O'Sullivan is dour, quiet, non-drinker and efficient. He meets deadlines.

MLD, to an outsider, could be seen to operate a somewhat unclear management structure. For the employees, lack of clarity is in reality, confusion, at times leading to disillusionment. The problem is that two structures operate simultaneously, a traditional hierarchical structure and a team structure.

On the hierarchical structure side, appraisals are conducted by the line managers; promotions and pay increases are determined by estabished procedures and guidelines. Most work, however, is conducted by teams. Teams exist for virtually every contingency – long-term strategy teams, medium-term resource allocation teams, segment teams that examine the needs of particular segments of the market, task/production teams that manufacture particular products and leader teams that attempt to identify new markets and their potential. In fact, MLD operates an intricate matrix structure that looks more like a spider's web than the more traditional two dimensional, functional/mission based matrix structure.

Any individual could hold membership to two or more teams whose interests may not be well aligned and yet be supervised by a line manager with whom they may spend less than 15 per cent of their time. Line managers, naturally, turn to team leaders for performance appraisal information in order to accurately assess their subordinates. Such a practice has caused problems, for on numerous occasions, team leaders have provided negative appraisal reports to line managers, which the individual felt was unjustified. The issue is that individuals could hold membership to two or more teams whose interests may conflict. The poor appraisal reports often concern the individual's inability to fit as a team member. From the individual's point of view, the problem is one of a conflict of role expectations.

Although particular problems exist as, a conflict of interests, poor appraisal performance data, switching team membership, being taken off one project on to another before project completion, the moral and motivation among employees (both operatives and management) is high. Starting early, working late, not claiming for extra remuneration and a general preparedness to be responsive to change, has become a norm in MLD.

The birth of a management team

Murray McConnell, Personnel Director, Syntax UK (a subsidiary within MLD) had noticed that a number of co-ordination and communication problems existed in Syntax UK. A few important issues that affected the performance of a number of teams were not being addressed. This was not so much due to negligence, but rather because no one person or team had been briefed to handle these problems. One reason for this, was the now traditional lack of communication and rivalry that existed between the Yeovil and Taunton sites. Yeovil was the bigger of the two as it had the largest production facility of the UK sites, and housed Hall and his team. Taunton, although smaller as a site, housed the marketing, sales and accounts group. Further, for McConnell, Bryant's style of management did not help the situation. Bryant, quite deliberately, had developed an almost perfect delegative style – to the unsophisticated, he sat back and let things happen. McConnell knew that Bryant was aware of the coordination and communication problems but had done little to improve matters. Why should he, he was President for Rest of the World; the fact he was based in London did not mean he had to attend to all of Syntax UK's problems. On that basis, McConnell approached Bryant, indicating that something should be done about the coordination and communication problems in the company.

'Murray, I hear what you're saying. Why not pick a team to handle these problems. I won't interfere. Teams get things done – you know that!' stated Bryant.

McConnell did just that and invited six influential managers (Tony Capella – manufacturing; Robert McSweeney – product development; Jerry Jones – sales; Andy Taylor – accounts; Damien Carter – marketing; Russell Peters – sales) to sit with him on a newly formed team. All but McConnell reported to Ashcroft, Hall or O'Sullivan. McConnell invited these managers for four reasons – they were well known, influential and respected in Syntax; they represented each of the major functions; also they were well known to each other and shared McConnell's concern for the problems facing the organization.

'Hell, we are not just an operational group, we are a management board,' thought McConnell.

So was formed Syntax (UK) Management Board, on which neither Bryant, Ashcroft, Hall nor O'Sullivan sat.

Questions

1 What would you consider the nature of some of the co-ordination and communication problems mentioned?
2 What particular problems and issues are McConnell's team likely to face?
3 What criteria would you consider appropriate for assessing effective team performance?

Appendix 1: Syntax (UK) Organization structure

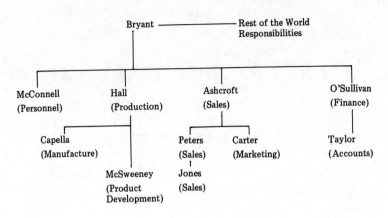

TWELVE

The box makers: the case of SafePAC plc

ANDREW P. KAKABADSE

The period of growth and expansion in the box-making industry in the UK was in the late 1960s and early 1970s. Goods were placed in boxes to transport to another locality for sale or further distribution. The introduction of containerization of goods on shipping, roads and rail systems induced further demand for strong, robust boxes as packaging materials. Large amounts of well-packaged goods could be stacked into large containers relatively cheaply and efficiently transported to other foreign or national localities. Customers could receive the purchases relatively quickly, but most important, undamaged and in good working order. The box-making business responded positively to the packaging needs of British industry.

The oil crisis of 1974 disrupted this happy state of affairs for the box-making industry as for so many other industries. Fuel costs rose and products became more expensive.

At the time, key decision makers in the box-making industry showed little concern. Yet their products, similar to most others, had dramatically become more expensive. Like everyone else, the box makers passed their increasing costs to the customers. For the large corporations in the industry, the dominant view was that the companies were simply too healthy (financially), powerful and big to be seriously affected by what was (or so it was thought) Arab retaliation in reaction to Israeli military achievements. It was thought that the crisis would pass without seriously affecting profit margins.

Market-place performance for 1974 to early 1976 seemed to justify this view. Most box-making companies were holding to their previous profit margins despite rising costs and inflation.

There were, however, certain individuals who did not accept the predominant view that market stability and prosperity would return.

Peter Girling, the chief executive of one subsidiary company (SafePAC plc) of a USA corporation entitled PAC Corp., argued that the bottom had fallen out of the market. He was convinced that the market had matured. The prospects for the future were only that of a declining market. Such decline would not be entirely due to rising oil costs, but more to technological advances that had gone unnoticed. For certain industries, packaging goods in a box was now a redundant concept. It would be more efficient, and in the long run cheaper, to utilize new stocking and distribution methods that require no boxes.

The box makers knew of such developments, but did not consider them a threat. Prior to 1974, it was still cheaper to pack goods in boxes. The chief executive, prophesying market decline, stated that rising fuel costs would make boxes more expensive. Valued customers would switch to alternative forms of more economically viable stacking. In the longer term, certain valued customers would probably have switched to alternative forms of packaging. Rising oil costs had merely accelerated that process.

Most influencial decision makers in the box-making industry took little notice of this one lone chief executive. Most sincerely believed it was simply a matter of surviving the storm and waiting for the return of a profitable, stable market.

Within SafePAC itself, most of the executives took a similar view to the other chief executives in the industry – there simply was no need to restructure the shape of their business. The situation came to the fore when the Director of Business Services, Denville Harper, at one of his meetings stated that he was concerned that the company was holding too much stock for sale.

'Look, John, I know we can't take it further at this meeting, but we really need to sit down, some time after work, and just see why we have consistently held so much stock. Despite our efforts, for the last three years we have been returning a small loss, as far as corporate are concerned . . . I know, why the hell should we care about corporate, but Girling is going to be breathing down our necks. He's been on about high level of stock for quite some time, so why not three or four of us meet some time this week, preferably one evening?' asked Denville Harper. Denville Harper had been talking to John Frenkel, the newly appointed American Manufacturing Director.

After numerous discussions between the Business Services Director and Sales, Marketing and Manufacturing Directors, it was decided that a consultant should be hired to examine the situation. A suitable consultant was identified, interviewed and hired. The consultant's first recommendation was that he hold individual discussions with each of the directors, sales managers and, if necessary, salespeople.

After a number of interviews a fairly clear picture emerged. The Sales Director had, over the years, developed a strong network of customers and clients. In the early to mid-1970s the most attractive customers to pursue were large companies and local and central government departments. Those large bulk customers tended to reorder the same sorts of large quantities annually. Selling to large customers required little effort; they merely had to be wined and dined. As a result the numerous smaller customers were ignored. A centralized sales organization had evolved with the Sales Director at the centre of a web of contacts of bulk customers.

However, the recession disrupted this comfortable network of customers. Government budgets were slashed. Large companies closed down parts of their own organizations in order to remain solvent. The last thing in the mind of government officials and the purchasing managers of larger companies, was boxes. Orders for boxes fell dramatically.

This information was fed back to the Director of Business Services: 'We should have been chasing the small time customers!' exclaimed Denville Harper. He thought for a while. 'Hell, the sales organization is far too centralized for that to happen,' he replied angrily. 'Yet I cannot blame the Sales Director. We all fell into the same trap.'

The Chesterfield plant

SafePAC faced other problems, especially the poor record of the Chesterfield plant.

The Chesterfield plant had been unprofitable for some time. Productivity was low, quality of produce was poor and plant operational costs were high. Further, the Chesterfield plant had a particularly active group of shop stewards who, in the past, not only reacted adversely to any attempts to improve productivity but threatened action if any attempts were made by management to alter circumstances in their own and other plants. Understandably, the directorate had made no real effort to confront the situation at the Chesterfield plant, fearing industrial action that could well spread to other plants. Finally, the directors, some reluctantly, decided to close down the plant. In anticipation of such a move a number of middle managers, a large number of supervisors, shop stewards and operatives jointly signed a petition demanding that their jobs be safeguarded by keeping the plant operational.

The directors of the company responded by attempting to negotiate with the various groups of employees in the plant. The employees would not compromise their objectives that the plant should remain operational. Fearing disruption in other plants, the directors agreed to review the situation at their next board meeting.

That particular meeting was tense, not so much for what was said but more because of the different positions adopted by the members of the board. However, in order to understand the comments and views of the board members, it is important to appreciate the structure of the company. The structure of SafePAC was geographically split into five regions – Highlands and Ireland, North England, Midlands and Wales, South West and London and Anglia – with a general manager (GM) responsible for each region. The five GMs reported to the Director of Business Services. The GMs attended board meetings in an ex-officio capacity, as much for them to be fully informed of events in the company as to identify closely with the directors in order to stimulate closer working relationships. However, the GMs had no voting rights on the board. The full board members were the five directors – Business Services, Sales, Marketing, Personnel and Manufacturing – the latter holding a dotted line responsibility over the manufacturing managers at plant level. Peter Girling chaired the meetings of the board of SafePAC.

Each area was serviced by a large plant manufacturing cardboard boxes. Midlands and Wales area had long been considered a problem. It had two plants, with the Chesterfield plant being considered the spare capacity plant, manufacturing boxes according to the demands of all the areas when they could not be fully serviced by their own plant. Despite the labour relations and poor product quality problems, the other areas had frequently called upon the Chesterfield plant to service their excess needs. As far as the GMs were concerned, they were pleased to read that one of the agenda items for the forthcoming board meeting was a review of the situation at Chesterfield.

The board meeting

At first, the directors and general managers simply asked for clarification. The reason given by Peter Girling was that SafePAC needed to become more profitable. Its overheads were too high. Corporate needed to see improved financial returns as they required capital for new investment programmes. Economies needed to be made and Chesterfield would make an attractive proposition to any prospective buyer.

'Well, I don't think that's very attractive,' remarked John Rumpole, the South West general manager, considered one of the elder statesmen of the group. John had only twenty-three months to go to retirement and was never careful about what he said at meetings.

'Undoubtedly, profitability is on all our minds. Apart from anything else, being unprofitable leaves you in a difficult position at corporate, which makes us all vulnerable when Slater (Group Chairman) wants something from you,' continued Rumpole, addressing himself to Peter Girling. Before Girling could respond, Rumpole continued 'Instead of closing Chesterfield plant, what about simply reducing this ridiculous head count overhead costing system on the areas . . . hm . . . hm?'

'Look, we've been through all this before. Overhead costs have just got to come down!' responded Girling.

'That's not good enough!'

'To close Chesterfield would virtually mean closing down the Chesterfield district. To reduce Chesterfield would mean redundancies which we could not handle, as much from the redundancy payments point of view, as from the potential union problems that could spread to other areas. Then there's the knock-on effect if we really mean to aim for greater profitability,' stated Stanley McPherson, London and Anglia general manager.

'What do you mean?' asked Rumpole.

'When we had that last discussion about Chesterfield, one or two of us said that this plant was not the problem; the real problem is increasing profitability. You know, there's only one way to make more money and that is to get better quality boxes to the customer, on time. That means more cooperation between manufacturing and sales and more effort on the sales side to build up our network of small time customers. And that means district sales managers and plant managers working closer so that sales don't accept jobs that plant cannot fulfil on time. You Henry (Henry Tyne – Sales Director) have got to get more together with the general managers and reorganize and revitalize the sales force. What I'm really saying is that we all need Chesterfield if we mean to really go for greater profitability!' responded McPherson.

Silence.

'Also there's the obvious point,' continued Rumpole, 'that as we are organized on an area basis to keep in close touch with our customers, Jim Price (the Chesterfield district sales manager) would face a real problem. He gets on well with the boys at the Chesterfield plant and, I know, they give him priority when he puts orders

74

through. To close Chesterfield could mean giving the district lock, stock and barrel to a competitor, or reorganizing each other area so that salespeople would have their patches changed just so that we could maintain some sort of parity in the system!'

'Just because Chesterfield is a problem does not mean that that is the problem on which we should concentrate! What about this area head count tax?' questioned Denville Harper.

Pause.

'As far as head count costing is concerned, you know we need that to keep our own head office going, plus each of the subsidiaries is subscribing to corporate venture capital for the Information Technology project,' stated Girling.

'Well, without that tax, even Chesterfield would break even', stated Stanley McPherson.

The discussion continued for some time.

'We need Chesterfield to cope with the additional capacity, re-affirmed Rumpole at one point.

The arguments continued late into the night. The meeting finished with the directors and general managers agreeing to arrange another extraordinary meeting four days away. Most of the members of the group resigned themselves to the closure and sale of Chesterfield. What they found particularly unpalatable was the way Girling decided to behave over the next four days. One by one, Peter Girling visited each of the directors and general managers at their office to discuss with them the Chesterfield proposal and review their area's performance. Girling obtained from each of them, unknown to the others, a commitment to support him in the Chesterfield closure proposal. To the surprise of each board member, the Chesterfield proposal was agreed to fairly quickly at the extraordinary meeting of the directorate. It was months later that the group members discovered that each of them had been visited by Girling. From thereon, it was more or less understood that each of the group members was to do their own thing, irrespective of what was formally agreed at meetings.

Peter Girling's view

Peter Girling had long recognized the problems facing SafePAC; the lack of team identity and even unwillingness to implement proposals agreed at directorate; the lack of profitability of the areas; the poor industrial relations record of the company, a problem which incidentally plagued the whole group, even in the USA, and the difficulties he faced with Aubrey Slater, the Group Chairman.

Aubrey was set on exploring new business areas. The group had predominantly concentrated on the wood, pulp and paper, and toiletries industries. Certain new ventures had succeeded, such as Sunflight, their profitable holiday package firm. However, other ventures had failed miserably, such as the plastic coating escapade and the failure of their hospital equipment business. Currently, Aubrey Slater had persuaded the main board to authorize the necessary capital to establish an information technology company. On top of his other problems, the greatest proportion of the venture capital was to be subsidized by SafePAC.

'What the hell is he trying to do with SafePAC, or even me?' thought Girling.

Girling also wondered about Denville Harper. All the general managers reported to Harper. They liked and respected him. They probably preferred Harper to him. Yet Harper had never really opposed him. On the other hand, Harper had never really brought the general managers together as a team. What's more, Harper had never really addressed the areas' profitability issue.

One more consultant

It was Girling who identified people problems as one of the key concerns of the company. He invited a human resource consultant to conduct a shop floor audit of the organization, on the premise that the fundamental human relations problems existed at the supervisory/operative level, i.e. at the bottom of the organization.

After initial discussions with Girling and certain other directors, the consultant concluded that severe relationship problems existed at the top of the organization. The consultant confronted Girling with this view, stating that attention should focus on the directors and general managers of the organization. The consultant recommended that he should interview each of the directors and general managers to gather their views concerning the organization, the way it was being managed, their jobs and the future. In addition, the consultant recommended that a one-day workshop be held whereby the board members could freely discuss and identify their problems and solutions to those problems. In order to allow for open debate, the chief executive should not attend the workshop. The chief executive agreed to all of the consultant's proposals.

The result of the interviews and the workshop were not quite what the chief executive expected. Virtually all the directors stated they strongly resented the chief executive. He was seen as a forceful, controlling personality, who tended to impose upon the other directors, the direction and strategies for the future. Although acknowledged to be an exceptionally talented individual, flaws in the strategy he imposed were identified. The closure of Chesterfield was one example given by most of the board members. Further, trust between the board themselves was low. Girling's behaviour during the Chesterfield discussion, of picking off the board members one by one in order to get them to back his policy of closure, left the other board members with a feeling of mistrust in each other. Girling was also criticized for having the annoying habit of changing his fellow directors' diary commitments. If Girling wanted any of the directors or general managers to meet an important client, he merely changed their commitments in their diaries held by their secretaries. After a while the board members ceased to confront Girling about such activities and give each other sufficient warning if Girling was to make such moves. In addition, the board meetings were considered to be poorly conducted. Even when decisions were overtly agreed to, covertly some of the board members had no intention of implementing the agreed strategies.

On reading the consultant's report, Peter Girling showed little surprise. He commented that generally speaking his views, visions and data analysis forecasts were accurate. For some time, however, he had been concerned that he was unable to motivate his colleagues to work as a team.

'You are considered as trying to simply railroad your views on others and all you are seen to be is someone who wants others to accept your solutions and not discuss the problem,' commented the consultant.

Girling listened and then said, 'I am the chief executive of a subsidiary, not my own company. I sit on the main board of this multinational, but so do a lot of other uncompromising people!'

Girling then recounted the problems and pressures he was facing.

The main board had, over the last four years, made a number of decisions that had adversely affected his subsidiary. No matter how strongly he had resisted the other main board members, decisions were agreed and he, along with other directors, had to implement them. Furthermore, he felt his position in the company to be insecure. He considered himself as unpopular largely due to his strong disagreements with the other directors of the main board, especially Aubrey Slater, the Group Chairman. He knew that the recent decision of the main board to reorganize would make life more difficult for him.

Slater wanted greater profitability. SafePAC came under considerable criticism largely because of its poor profitability record and high overhead costs. The closure of the Chesterfield plant was the one point in Girling's favour.

'All this and then my own board that cannot work with me!'

Pause

'OK! What do I do?' questioned Girling.

Questions

1 Identify, list and discuss the problems faced by SafePAC plc.
2 How effective is the management style of the chief executive, Peter Girling?
3 If you were the human resource consultant, what strategy would you adopt to help the board of SafePAC?

THIRTEEN

The Celtic Woollen Company

ANDREW P. KAKABADSE

'As you can see, we were a very traditional company with still some changes to come', finished Jim Peters, Personnel Director of the Celtic Woollen Co.* Jim sat back in his comfortable black leather chair, awaiting a response.

Jim had been talking to Neville Sims, a senior consultant of Management Associates, a large consulting firm offering a number of different services ranging from marketing surveys, feasibility studies, organization design and structure, personnel consultancy, recruitment and selection and management training. Neville Sims specialized in organization structure and design, the management of change in organizations and management training. The Celtic Woollen Co. had frequently used the services of Management Associates for marketing surveys, feasibility studies and recruitment and selection. This was the first time Neville Sims had been approached by the company.

Sims reflected on Jim Peter's account of developments in the Celtic Woollen Co. He examined the organization chart of the board of the company that Peters had drawn for him (see Appendix 1).

The Celtic Woollen Co. had been transformed from a small family business based in Dumfries to an organization of considerable size and repute by Hamish McArdle, grandfather of Rory McArdle. The McArdles had been wool manufacturers for five generations but serviced only local needs. Despite the 1930s recession, Hamish recognized the potential of the American market and negotiated short-term contracts with the more reputable Chicago and New York department stores. The American retailers considered the

---

* This is a true case but not based in the woollen industry. Hence the name, Celtic Woollen Co. is fictitious, and thereby no commercial relationship exists between the Celtic Woollen Co. and any other organization mentioned in this case.

products of the company to be of high quality, manufactured at the right price but in short supply. More through the persuasive powers of the American retailer, rather than Hamish's desire for considerable expansion, did the company take a calculated risk and purchase two further factories in Inverness and Motherwell. In fact, the risk was small. The American retailers recognized the market potential of traditional manufactured woollen clothing goods imported from regions such as Ireland or Scotland. The 'Made in Scotland' label was suitably large and placed on each item of clothing.

Hamish's second son, Robert, showed the flair, capacity and potential to take over the company. In 1950, he was duly elected Managing Director of the Celtic Woollen Co. in succession to Hamish. Robert considered the company's dependence on only certain American retailers to be a risky policy. For a start, Hamish's counterparts in the USA had either retired or died. Robert had neither the time nor inclination to negotiate the same trusting, informal relationships with the new generation of professional manager retailers as Hamish had done with the owners, or family representatives, of the American retail outlets.

Further, Robert had questioned why just the American market? What about the English or even European markets? The House of Fraser, a well established Scottish family business, had purchased a considerable number of retail outlets in England, with the star of their portfolio being Harrods.

During the 1950s and 1960s, Robert negotiated numerous long-term contracts with several retail outlets in England, notably the House of Fraser, the Burton group and the Austin Reed chain of men's retailers. In order to service this increased demand, Robert opened a fourth factory in Glasgow. In addition, he invested considerably in modernizing the other three factories. Unfortunately, Robert had to retire prematurely due to a heart condition and his eldest son, Rory, was elected Managing Director in 1974.

Rory McArdle and his father had, to say the least, a somewhat strained relationship. At the age of thirty-six, portraying the image of the young, energetic, competitive, 'about to change everything' executive, Rory took over the company with the expressed intention of introducing changes to the company's product portfolio. Although over two generations the company had grown, increased its manufacturing capacity and negotiated lucrative retail outlets, the product range had hardly altered. The company manufactured chunky woollen knit sweaters, scarves, woollen hats and pure wool kilts. Apart from minor design changes, or changes of colour pattern, the product line remained the same. It was Rory's intention to introduce new designs, enter the women's fashion market, and the up-market cashmere sweaters, cardigans, scarves and coats. Further Rory considered the current manufacturing technology to be outdated, labour too expensive, and a management too traditional and set in its ways to introduce the drastic changes he desired.

From 1974 to 1981, Rory worked on two fronts:

1 Introducing new and updated manufacturing technology and information systems.
2 The opening of two new plants in Nicosia, Cyprus and Galway, the Republic of Ireland, manufacturing cashmere sweaters and scarves.

The traditional clothing-making skills, the abundance of cheaper female labour and the attractive subsidies offered by the home governments had made Eire and Cyprus two particularly favourable areas for the location of additional manufacturing plants. The cashmere product ranges were selling well in up-market stores such as Harrods and Debenhams in London, top stores in Brussels and the Marshal Fields group of stores in Chicago and New York. Rory considered the manufacture of cashmere coats to be the next addition to the cashmere product range, to be manufactured in Galway and Nicosia.

Although he introduced substantial changes to the production side of the business, Rory made little impact on the management structure of the company. He had met with considerable opposition from his own board to the Galway and Nicosia projects. Unable to act without the support of his board, Rory made considerable concessions to the three long-standing directors in the organization: David Price – Production Director; Alex Campbell – Marketing Director; and Alistair McIntyre – Sales Director.

All three in their late fifties or early sixties; all three started as apprentices in the company; all three the appointments of Hamish or Robert McArdle. The only changes Rory had introduced on to the board was the appointment of Jim Peters as Personnel Director, ex-personnel manager from Philips, the rapid promotion of Jonathan McArdle (Rory's cousin) to Finance Director and the introduction of an entirely new functional directorate – product design, under the directorship of Aelish Patterson, another of Rory's cousins, previously married to an American, now divorced. Aelish's skills and experience were particularly relevant as she had been product designer with one of the more experienced American fashion houses but returned to Scotland shortly after her divorce.

It was common knowledge in the organization that on most issues

Rory would face most opposition from the production, marketing and sales groups.

'You say Rory wants his managers to be more capable of managing change. Also your managers have not really undergone any form of management training and you would at least like to consider what sort of training would be useful and how much it would cost,' reflected Sims.

'Don't forget, Rory would like to look at the needs of the production and sales department first and then marketing and finance. Personnel Department has been charged with master minding the whole programme, but where do we start?' enquired Jim Peters.

'Look, I can't see the point of training your managers to appreciate all the various aspects of business. Why not train them to handle what you, I and they consider to be the problem issues? Why not hold a series of workshops with say six to eight managers at each workshop for them to identify their needs. We can then create whatever programmes are necessary from the ideas and issues these guys generate?' questioned Neville Sims.

'Sounds a good idea. Look why not come to Dumfries and meet Rory and any other members of the board that may be there,' responded Jim Peters.

'Good! Why don't I give you a few dates and then you can see which of them is most suitable to the others in Scotland. Finding dates is such a problem. Well here's mine. I'm free on. . . .'

'Mr Sims. Do come in. Nice to meet you. I hope you had a pleasant flight from London. Yes, do sit down.'

Pause.

'I've arranged for a number of my colleagues to meet you at lunch. Any further discussions that are necessary, perhaps you could conduct on a more individual basis after lunch,' said Rory McArdle.

Rory then re-told Neville Sims the history of the Celtic Woollen Co., its current state of affairs and needs for change.

The luncheon meeting was a lively, friendly and informative affair for Neville Sims, attended by David Price, Alex Campbell, Rory and Jonathan McArdle and Jim Peters. The group discussed the company's present state of affairs, its need for change and the need for improved managerial skills in the organization. Jonathan McArdle indicated that the company had not sufficiently explored different market sectors. Whatever developments had taken place, the company was still in the high quality woollen knit garments business. Alternative markets that should and have not been considered, are men's wear (i.e. jackets, trousers and suits) and the more giddy world of women's fashion such as dresses, blouses, skirts, tops, etc. Rory stated the company was not ready for such expansion. During the conversation, Jim Peters quietly spoke to Sims stating that a meeting between David Price, Alex Campbell, Peters and Sims had been arranged for after lunch. Sims thanked Peters for organizing the meetings as David Price had hardly contributed to the luncheon conversation but most of the initial workshop activity would involve a substantial number of managers from production. The lunch meeting finished with Rory pledging his support for the workshops and any ensuing activities.

Neville Sims and Jim Peters made their way to David Price's office.

'Gentlemen, enter,' said Price, 'perhaps if I can outline the purpose of the meeting. Well what I want is to know what you intend to do in line with Rory's statement on making our managers more sensitive and capable of managing change.'

'I think it's important that before anything is done, you, the directors know what we are trying to do. Towards the end, it's crucial that the problems, constraints and opportunities faced by the various levels of management are identified and understood. Although Jim and I have not specifically mentioned this, I would have thought the top managers of the organization should be included in this initial process of investigation,' stated Neville Sims turning to Jim Peters.

'Yes, I see. Uhmmm . . . to what extent have you been briefed on the developments in this company?' asked Price.

'I'd say fairly fully with no punches pulled,' responded Sims.

'So you appreciate some of the basic issues facing this company, and especially this board!'

'Yes, I have been told what's happening,' stated Sims.

'Then why start mainly in production and partly in marketing departments?' asked Price.

'I can answer that,' responded Jim Peters. 'You see, the parts of the organization that are likely to be most crucially affected by change are principally production and to a certain extent marketing and sales. I think whatever we as a board decide, the greatest impact will be on your people.'

'Yes, that I appreciate. How do you intend to proceed, Mr Sims?' questioned Price.

'Initially, identify key and influential managers in production and marketing who would be sympathetic and interested in talking about and identifying present and future problems. Then invite them in small groups to two or three, one and a half day workshops. The findings of these workshops would be presented to you and other interested directors. From there on, the directors can debate what should be done,' finished Sims.

'That's interesting; get the managers to identify their own problems and their own solutions, by the sound of it. Mmmm. Ok. What do you need from Alex Campbell and myself?' asked Price.

Campbell had not commented throughout the meeting.

'What we need are the names of people whom you would consider suitable for the workshops. For instance, they could be people who are sympathetic to change, those opposed to change, those who are influential in the organization; you know, a complete cross section'.

Pause.

'Thinking about it, we would also need just a few representatives from sales, finance and personnel. In that way we will have a complete cross section,' commented Sims.

'That's fine by me,' said David Price.

'You may find Alistair objecting to some of his sales boys taking part. As for the idea itself, that's Ok with me,' stated Alex Campbell.

'I'll speak to Alistair and Jonathan,' interjected Jim Peters. 'Although I can't promise anything. As far as my people are concerned, I think it's a good idea that some should attend the workshops.'

Four, one and a half day workshops were organized, and held at monthly intervals. The venue was a comfortable hotel in the highlands of Scotland equipped with full conference facilities. Neville Sims, as workshop leader, stated the objectives of the workshops and then split the plenary into a number of subgroups.

Each group was asked to identify the problems facing the company. From these findings each group was then given the specific responsibility of identifying particular courses of action, which the company could specifically adopt.

The workshop participants used flipcharts to make their presentations. At the end of each workshop, Sims collected all the flipcharts and wrote a short report, concentrating on the key issues/problems identified and the proposed courses of action to overcome those problems. Each workshop participant received a copy of the report, as did the members of the main board.

After the fourth workshop, Sims drafted a summary paper for the members of the main board. The paper contained the following comments.

Key issues facing the Celtic Woollen Co.

Relations between management and staff

- Industrial relations between management and labour force is poor.
- Managers consider that the trade unions have weak full-time officials who lack control over shop floor workers.
- Managers feel that the workforce is at times better informed than management.
- There exists a general indifference to authority on the shop floor.
- It is considered that there is a reluctance on the part of the trade unions to identify with the longer term future of the organization.
- The company is seen as very much concerned with the development of its managers.

Diversification and new developments

- The company has experienced a number of changes over the past few years which has caused anxiety among its employees.
- Further changes, in terms of utilization of new technology, is likely.
- Demand for certain of the company's products is likely to stabilize or decrease. In particular, the chunky knit products are likely to decrease but cashmeres are likely to increase.
- There is a need to explore new market areas, such as fashionable male/female clothing, but using other fabrics – silks, linen, rayon, etc.
- An expected increased variety of goods means an increased work load for management and workforce, thereby creating remuneration problems.
- Costs of machinery, raw materials and products is likely to increase.

Work opportunities and career development

- There is no master plan for career development within the organization.
- Managers tend to be moved to different jobs with little initial training in their new post.

- Currently, the lack of formal career development is not viewed as problematic. It is considered that the better managers occupy the more responsible jobs.
- The company is still of a size that the better managers are personally known to various members of the board.
- If the organization plans to grow further, career development is a key issue which requires immediate attention as current practice will be unsatisfactory.
- There is a need to recruit further personnel into the organization due to the potentially ageing work force.
- Succession planning needs to be considered as an issue in career development.

Relations between departments and production units

- Communication problems are identified between departments and production units leading to lack of cooperation and antagonism between important sections of the organization.
- The main board is identified as being divided and split on certain key issues. If the main board members are unable to cooperate why should others?

One point in particular concerned Sims. Namely the lack of impact on the organization by the Personnel Department. True, the company faced a number of strategic problems which needed confrontation and some training and development work was needed with the main board. However, the workshops highlighted a number of key human resource issues that should have, in Sims' opinion, been addressed some time back. Sims wondered whether he should highlight the lack of penetration by the Personnel Department into the organization. Up to now, Jim Peters had been Sims' client. Sims recognized that the relationship between the two would be severely shaken if the Personnel Department was seen to be criticized by the consultant they hired in the first place.

Sims delayed submitting the report to give himself time to consider how to report the Personnel Department's involvement in the organization. He had, for some time, been dissatisfied with Jim Peters. In fact, most of the criticism levelled against the Personnel Department was criticism of Jim Peters. Peters seemed unable to grasp quickly the key issues in particular problem situations, and certainly did not present himself well at the workshops. On the other hand, he had recognized the problems faced by the organization and forcefully argued for and supported Sims' intervention. In this split, diversive and somewhat bitchy organization, Jim Peters had taken a considerable risk in inviting Sims.

Sims decided to have an informal talk with Rory and not emphasize personnel's deficiencies. Sims submitted the report to Jim Peters to circulate to the other board members. The main board meeting to discuss the report was set.

'Having now talked it through, the issues facing us are not just what business areas do we or don't we enter, but also what sort of managers, their skills level and I suppose what sort of organization we want,' commented Rory.

The main board meeting discussing the Sims' report, had now entered its second hour.

'I think the issues are more linked than that. For example, the sort of business you want to be will dictate what sort of managers you require. Let's face it, you are a functionally structured organization that really is fairly centralized in terms of decision making. You talk about profit centres and giving greater responsibility down the line. That's not just a training problem. You may have to restructure your organization. In reality, you as a main board, may not wish to become that decentralized,' responded Neville Sims.

'I think what's interesting with this report and our discussion is that a number of problems have been highlighted. Our image as a board is not that great. Our managers all too readily have spotted our internal squabbles. Production in itself is not seen as a particular problem but new technology and new areas of business could severely influence the way the whole of production is managed. What's more, personnel have not come out as the shining heroes. I've been saying this for years, and yet production has been blamed for most of the problems in the organization', snapped David Price.

The heated debate continued. Throughout the discussion, Sims noticed the tension between Rory and Jonathan McArdle. Rory seemed to be emphasizing staying with the present product lines and increasing the marketing activity in those areas. Jonathan was strongly arguing in favour of entering new market sectors, especially the world of women's fashion, ranging from formal, casual and even trendy sports attire for women. Throughout, Jim Peters was being criticized for his lack of planning and development of managers and the labour force in the organization. Two hours later, the meeting finished. The board members decided that the following two action points should be pursued:

- Jim Peters, together with Neville Sims, would together work out a manpower plan for the organization with particular emphasis on training and career development.

- Jonathan McArdle, together with Aelish Patterson, were asked to explore new market sectors. Jonathan indicated he would commission particular consultants to conduct feasibility studies in particular markets.

Rory asked for a short meeting with Neville Sims after the meeting.

'Neville, be honest. You heard what was said at the meeting. What's your opinion of Jim Peters? You've worked with him,' said Rory.

'Probably most of what was said of the Personnel Department, and Jim in particular, is true and accurate,' replied Neville.

'I was afraid you'd say that. Jim's been with this company a long time. He's loyal and always supported me. However, I'm not too sure he really appreciates what his job is all about.'

Pause.

'It'll probably come as no surprise to you that I've been thinking of moving Jim out of that job. Problem is, to move him into anything else would be to downgrade him. I reckon it has to be early retirement. I know you've worked closely with Jim and I would like you to continue doing so on this management development blueprint thing. However, I also need a new Personnel Director. Would you be willing to informally and very confidentially start an informal search process for the right man?' asked Rory.

'Yes. Yes I would. I'm not sure you have any other choice,' replied Neville Sims.

'You don't need to say anything to Jim; I'll talk to him. Ok?'

'Fine,' responded Neville Sims.

Jim Peters and Neville Sims embarked on the project of drafting a management development blueprint. Each job in the organization was analysed in terms of task content, in terms of objectives to be achieved, skills required and the training needs of the incumbents. Numerous meetings and discussions were held with the managers of various departments and units.

One day Jim Peters commented to Neville Sims: 'I had a meeting with Rory yesterday evening. We talked about the changes required for the future and why we need a younger management, especially on the board. He suggested I might consider early retirement after I finish this project and another one he's got in mind for me.'

'I see,' came the reply.

'I must tell you, I'm not too happy with the situation. Financially, no problem. This company is still old fashioned enough to look after its employees, even when it sacks them. What aggrieves me is that it would have been impossible to do anything substantial until now. Can you imagine David Price allowing personnel to take a look at his part of the organization? Who would have bothered turning up to workshops? Who was capable of running workshops? It took all my time to get Rory's support for you to come into the organization,' said Jim.

'Mmm. Yes, I can see that,' mumbled Neville.

'I also understand from Rory that he's asked you to search for my replacement.'

'Yes, that's true.'

'Are you doing this because you agree with him?' asked Jim.

'Yes. I'm afraid that's true. I do agree with him on this issue,' responded Neville.

'I see,' said Jim quietly.

Jim Peters turned away and left the room.

The management development blueprint was completed and the report presented before the board. The board accepted the key recommendations of the report. Shortly after, Jim Peters was appointed Project Director to manage the start up of a new factory in Portugal, which was to manufacture cashmere sweaters. This project, championed by Rory, had been commissioned and agreed to before Neville Sims had been approached by the company. Within a year, Jim Peters had retired. Tony Waters, the training manager, was placed temporarily in charge of the Personnel Department. Within two months, the new Personnel Director was in post.

Neville Sims was commissioned to implement certain of the proposals accepted in the management development blueprint. Sims initiated an assessment centre available for all levels of management, training programmes for managers and shop floor supervisors and completely reorganized the entire performance appraisal documentation, and instituted appraisal training in an effort to ensure more effective appraisals were conducted down the line.

During this period, Jonathan McArdle submitted his fashion wear feasibility study, which was strongly supported by Aelish Patterson, David Price and Alex Campbell. Jonathan highlighted three particular issues:

- Fashionable sports and leisure wear.
- Fashionable clothes for the executive woman.
- Evening wear for men and women.

Rory, together with Alistair McIntyre and the new Personnel Director, refuted certain of the recommendations made by Jonathan. After substantial debate and two extraordinary board meetings, it was agreed by majority vote that the company should enter the sports and leisure wear and fashionable clothes for the working women, markets. By now, the majority of the cashmere products were being manufactured in Portugal.

The Galway plant was being run down. The bulk of the sports wear items were sited for manufacture at the Galway plant. The fashionable female executives' clothes were to be manufactured at a new factory to be opened in Connemara, Eire. State financial support in the Republic of Ireland for new business was generous. The Celtic Woollen Co. made use of all facilities offered in the Republic.

After the start up of the Connemara plant, Rory called in Neville Sims and indicated that David Price would be taking early retirement. Neville was commissioned to search for his replacement. At the next board meeting, Jonathan McArdle questioned why David Price was opting for early retirement and why Neville Sims, in particular, had been asked to find his replacement. Jonathan was heard to have muttered that there were better hatchet men around.

Within six months, David Price's replacement was identified, appointed and in post. Neville Sims is substantially involved with the Celtic Woollen Co. as he regularly runs training programmes for them and is the only person qualified to administer the psychological tests used in the assessment centre. Jonathan McArdle has submitted another paper to the board, basically arguing that the company should enter the fashionable evening wear market. So far, only Aelish Patterson has publicly supported the proposal.

Questions

1 If you were the consultant, how would you have handled the intervention?
2 How would you define ethics in business?
3 How important do you consider the ethics of consultancy practise?

Appendix 1: Celtic Woollen Co. organization chart

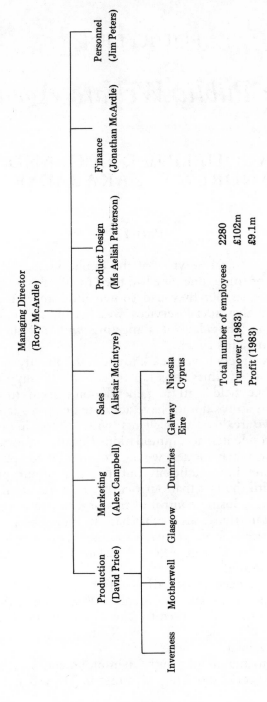

Managing Director
(Rory McArdle)

Production
(David Price)

Marketing
(Alex Campbell)

Sales
(Alistair McIntyre)

Product Design
(Ms Aelish Patterson)

Finance
(Jonathan McArdle)

Personnel
(Jim Peters)

Inverness   Motherwell   Glasgow   Dumfries   Galway   Nicosia
                                                  Eire   Cyprus

Total number of employees	2280
Turnover (1983)	£102m
Profit (1983)	£9.1m

FOURTEEN

The Public Welfare Agency

JACQUELINE DRAKE AND
ANDREW P. KAKABADSE

Part 1

The Director of Social Services of the Public Welfare Agency had
been worried for some time. She had tried to talk about her concerns
with her colleagues but they had shown little interest. It was the
director's view that social services was becoming inefficient and
ineffective. One Thursday, at a meeting with her directors, she
voiced her complaints again.

'Our social workers have been known to go directly against what
we stipulate and, at times, this has been with the support of their
supervisors. The field staff in general don't seem to fill in the
necessary forms so we do not have accurate or up-to-date information on what we are doing with clients, with children in care, or with
old people in residential accommodation. Equally important, we do
not know how much money we are committed to spending. We
have to become more efficient but that's a minor problem in
comparison with the fact that our field staff do not seem to respect
us. We are simply losing control of this organization!'

'Come on Joan, things aren't that bad. It's never been an easy job
and with the recession its got even tougher. Our people are doing
their best', soothed George Allen, Assistant Director, Administration and Accounting.

'Trinworth has been particularly badly hit, what with the closure
of Bailey Components and the Stenley Works not taking on any
more apprentices . . . they used to take a lot of young lads between
them, got nothing now,' Trevor Keating, Area Director for
Trinworth explained.

'Don't talk to me about youth unemployment, idle little tykes!
Don't want to work, more like it', burst in Tony Blair, red in the

92

face. 'Prefer their mothers to go out and work all the hours God sends while they get up to all kinds of monkey tricks. Our paper work will never be up-to-date with the likes of them. If anyone needs discipline, its them – not us. We've been taking too soft a line for a long time. I've said it before, I'll say it again, some proper authority, like we used to have, that's what we need out there . . . and in here', he added, half under his breath.

Despite being made Area Director for Ipstone, Tony Blair had never fully accepted the reorganization Joan had pushed through shortly after her appointment.

'Let's not all get excited now,' came back George Allen 'there probably is room for improvement, so why don't we all look into our own departments and see what we can do?'

There was general agreement and a sense of relief that someone had provided an escape route from what seemed to be something of an hysterical outburst by the director. 'Typical of a bloody woman', thought more than one of the managers around the table.

Joan felt thwarted. She knew they were brushing their problems under the carpet. They wouldn't do anything even though performance was not what it should be. A problem existed, she was convinced of that. An irritating sound brought her back to the meeting. It was Lionel Edgely, clearing his throat.

'While I am perfectly prepared to look into efficiencies in my department, I should like to make it quite clear that as Assistant Director for Residential Services, I know (a) what is going on in my area and (b) what financial commitments we have made. I would be disturbed to think it might be otherwise.'

Two weeks later the Simpson case broke. Fourteen month old Jennifer Simpson was beaten to death by her father. The social services had long been involved with the Simpson family. The social worker and his supervisor had made an error of judgement in releasing the child from care to her parents. The Director of the Social Services department showed just how angry she could become at the next management team meeting.

'Everyone here knows that the Simpson case need never have happened.'. . . Pause . . . 'And why did it? Because the field staff are a law unto themselves. I've been stating that fact for too long. Up to now you've persuaded me otherwise. Well, I tell you, I've made up my mind what I am going to do. First, I've asked Harry Francis to take responsibility for a special project on problem families. He will have a roving brief and report directly to *me* and second, I'm going to call somebody in to look at our organization, just to tell us where the problems lie!'

The others looked at her. The Assistant Director, Residential Services, spoke first.

'I don't like people poking their nose into our affairs. The press have just done that; one more snooper will destroy all our good work. Anyhow, who are you calling in, someone from Whitehall or is it some slick management consultant?'

'Neither, it's a university researcher whose specialism is public welfare administration,' she responded.

Shortly after the meeting finished, Lionel Edgely turned to one of the other Assistant Directors in the corridor and stated.

'Just how is that stupid woman going to solve any problems by bringing in some know-it-all academic? Apart from which, I just don't trust her.'

Everyone heard his comments but no one responded. The Assistant Director, Residential Services, was even more unpopular than the Director of Social Services.

Joan Armstrong prowled around her office feeling that she had a problem. She considered that most of her Assistant Directors (members of the top management team) and Area Directors (the middle management) neither liked nor trusted her. Not that she really blamed them. On being appointed director, she had introduced some dramatic changes. She removed two levels of advisory management, reducing what was, in effect, a seven-level organization to a five-level organization. She also introduced a policy of decentralization, creating six geographical 'areas' from what had previously been five. The combined effect of these two major changes was planned to increase the number of people working in the field. It also dismantled what Joan considered to be a 'bureaucratic nightmare of an organization' so that it could better fulfil its primary mission, that of providing a helping service to members of the community. Nobody lost their jobs in the reorganization but Joan Armstrong felt the resentment. People saw themselves as demoted. Many felt they had lost their status. Others did not wish to go back to fieldwork activities; they were quite content to administer the system.

What made matters worse was that she, at an earlier stage of her career, had been employed as a social worker in that very same Social Services Department. Some of the managers in the organization remembered her as a rebel, a person who complained that the bureaucracy in the organization was 'getting in the way' of good social work. Joan then left and practised social work in the USA for a number of years. On her return to England, she was appointed director of the same department. Certain managers found it difficult to accept such a role reversal with her. Two Area Directors in particular found it difficult to accept that a woman, who had been their subordinate, was now their boss.

Joan bore her colleagues no resentment; in fact, she quite liked them. She wanted her policy of decentralization to work and also for personal relationships to improve. Two of her supporters had urged her to fire at least two of her opponents. Joan flatly refused to follow such a line. She saw her colleagues as basically honest and sincere people who had not yet 'seen the light'. However, opposition to Joan was increasing and her policy of decentralization was not being implemented to her satisfaction. What should she do?

In order to maintain her policy of introducing major change while sticking with her existing group of managers, Joan recognized that she lacked information as to what was 'going on' in the organization.

'What do people feel about me, my managerial style and how committed are they to the reorganization?'

She decided to call in Saul Becker, a bright young professor from Cornell University (USA) on sabbatical at Oxford University. Joan first met Saul when she had been working in the USA.

'Saul's the only one I know who would know how to handle these guys and get them to answer these questions', thought Joan.

'Hello Saul, nice to see you again', said Joan, shaking hands with Saul Becker as he was ushered into her office by her secretary.

'Something very English, would you like some tea?' asked Joan.

The two of them talked about old times.

'Y'know Joan, the issue is not just getting some relevant information together, it's deciding from whom to get it. I could be more of a hindrance than help asking them to complete question-naires. People will become more suspicious than they already appear to be, according to the way you have described the situation. We need to discuss who you think I should interview and why, and how I should approach them.'

By now the conversation had become serious. Joan asked her secretary for a copy of the organization chart (Appendices 1 and 2). She explained to Saul why she reorganized, the logic behind the new role structure and her opinion as to the strengths and weaknesses of key people in the structure.

'As far as I can see Joan, there seem to be three groups that we must get on our side; the Assistant Directors, the Area Directors and the supervisors. The Assistant Directors are vital because if any one of those people does not agree to let me into his department, the project is virtually dead,' stated Saul.

The two continued to talk about each of the personalities in turn.

'Look Joan, I know you want to get this thing going, but I urge you just to be a little cautious. Try this out for size. You organize a buffet lunch for the Assistant Directors so that they can meet me under fairly informal surroundings. With a bit of luck, I will be able to arrange to see each one in his office some time after the lunch. I don't think we need to be that sensitive to the Area Directors and supervisors. Why don't you identify those Area Directors and supervisors that are forceful characters, those that are likely to support the project and those that may be a bit 'anti'. We can then organize a couple of one-day workshops and invite a handpicked number of Area Directors and supervisors to attend. We can get these people to talk about the problems they see in the organization and their jobs, introduce the project to them and even get them to think about how to carry it out,' said Saul.

'Good thinking! That's probably the way to do it,' responded Joan.

The lunch and workshop seminars were organized. All went well. Saul, however, faced problems with both the Assistant Directors and the Area Directors.

First, and as expected, Lionel Edgely raised his objections at the lunch.

'This isn't New York, Mr Becker. Far from it. I don't know how you think you can tell us what to do. Your knowledge may be all very well over there but things are very different in this country.'

'Sir, I recognize things are very different over here. I have no intention of "telling you how to do your job", nor is that what I was brought in for. My technical expertise helps me to understand what's happening and what alternatives may be open and I will share these with you as and when appropriate but my *primary* role here is to help you to identify and work through your own problems. Now, to do that we need to work together and I look forward to that.'

The idea of a survey was mooted by Saul who soon had the support of most of the Assistant Directors. However, he did not have everything his own way. Edgely persisted in his objections to the extent that Saul suggested that a steering committee be formed to review the results of the survey and indicate what further steps, if any, should be taken. Lionel Edgely was invited to act as chairperson to the steering committee. Saul made it clear that each individual's responses would be kept confidential. Only Saul would have access to each person's data. The committee's responsibility would be to help interpret the overall data in terms of trends, provide administrative and other assistance, if and when required, and generally to explore the implications of the findings in terms of the structure and management of the social services organization.

Second, the Area Directors proved to be more difficult than Saul or Joan anticipated. Their problems emerged at the workshop. They suffered a lack of role clarity and role identity. Since the reorganizations, the Area Directors did not understand what was expected of them and what, in essence, decentralization meant to them. They also suspected Saul's presence in the organization and the workshops as a manipulative attempt by Joan to introduce further change. Saul concentrated on helping the Area Directors identify the supports, constraints and key activities in their roles. By the end of the workshop, the Area Directors seemed comfortable with the process.

'Saul, I think this is a valuable exercise. I will arrange for you to see all my supervisors and social workers,' enthused Tony Blair.

'Will you be putting them through a workshop, or seeing them one-to-one, or what?' enquired Trevor Keating.

'Oh. It will be one-to-one. I need to gather the data fairly quickly now,' responded Saul.

'I suppose it will be much the same as we have had; questions on people's work, their working relationships, job satisfaction, their views of their team and of the organization in general. Is that right?' asked Brian Eversley, Area Director for Brympton, the smart part of town.

'Yes, very similar indeed,' replied Saul.

'Then I'm in favour. I think we should all give Saul Becker every possible assistance,' chimed in Trevor Keating.

Questions

1 What has happened so far:
   (a) Is there a problem?
   (b) Is it important?
   (c) Whose problem is it?
2 How effective do you consider Joan Armstrong to be as the Director of the Public Welfare Agency?
3 What strategy should Saul adopt in order to address the problems facing the Public Welfare Agency? In your answer identify the factors Saul should be taking into account.

Appendix 1: The Public Welfare Agency organizational structure: pre-Armstrong reorganization

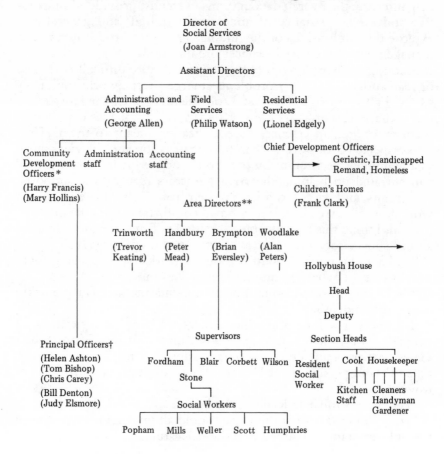

Director of
Social Services
(Joan Armstrong)

Assistant Directors

Administration and   Field   Residential
Accounting   Services   Services
(George Allen)   (Philip Watson)   (Lionel Edgely)

Community   Administration Accounting   Chief Development Officers
Development   staff   staff   Geriatric, Handicapped
Officers *   Remand, Homeless
(Harry Francis)
(Mary Hollins)   Children's Homes
                                    Area Directors**   (Frank Clark)

        Trinworth   Handbury Brympton Woodlake
        (Trevor   (Peter   (Brian   (Alan
        Keating)   Mead)   Eversley) Peters)
                                                    Hollybush House

                                                    Head

                                                    Deputy

                            Supervisors   Section Heads
Principal Officers†
(Helen Ashton)   Fordham   Blair Corbett Wilson   Resident   Cook Housekeeper
(Tom Bishop)   Social
(Chris Carey)   Stone   Worker   Kitchen Cleaners
(Bill Denton)   Staff   Handyman
(Judy Elsmore)   Social Workers   Gardener

                Popham   Mills Weller Scott Humphries

* Professional specialists; advisors to Assistant Directors.

† Specialists in drug abuse/alcoholism, child welfare, marriage guidance, psychiatry, home teaching for the blind. Advisors to Area Directors, supervisors and social workers.

** Each controls a sector of town, being line manager to five supervisors. Each supervisor is line manager to five social workers.

Appendix 2: The Public Welfare Agency organizational structure: post-Armstrong reorganization

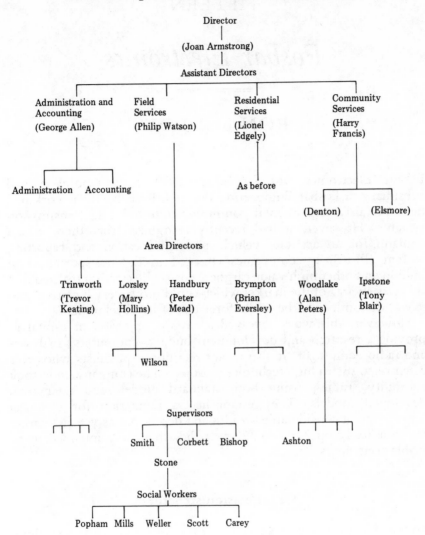

FIFTEEN

Fosbar Electronics

RON LUDLOW

Fosbar Electronics was formed in 1979, as a wholly owned subsidiary of Fosbar Engineering Limited. Initially, their work had been in fairly fundamental communication and data transmission systems. However, it had recently recognized that there was a demand for an accurate vehicle position location and reporting system (PLRS) by companies engaged in the transportation of bullion and other high value cargoes. Fosbar Electronics realized that this was an area of the market which could prove very lucrative, and it was determined to be at the forefront of its development.

However, this work involved a massive injection of capital to provide a research and development budget, computers, analysers and radio equipment. It also meant recruiting specialists who were essential to such a high technology project. The company undertook feasibility studies, using both standard models and their own developed models. They established a reputation for technical knowledge of considerable breadth and depth, but as yet the market had not really opened up. When it did, they fully intended to be viable contenders.

Organization structure

Fosbar Electronics was an engineering company organized along functional lines. Its departments were staffed by engineers, technicians, scientists and mathematicians, with each technical discipline located in its own department.

All engineering aspects were headed by the Engineering Director, Ralph Doe, to whom the Department Heads reported. The line management continued to group leader, section leader, and then to the main grade engineers and technicians.

The lines of communication were clear and formal. The family tree of the department was pinned to the wall in the office of the Department Head's secretary, and could be seen easily through the glass panels facing the main office area.

All group leaders, but few section leaders, had side offices. However, their status was recognized by eating in a separate canteen from the rest of the factory, including the main grade professional engineers.

In 1985, Fosbar Electronics set out to bid for a contract which represented a major part of the vehicle location and reporting market. Without doubt, this was the biggest opportunity which had come to the company. A long-term project, it would restore a healthy cash flow and give financial stability for several years.

The electronics content was the largest the company had ever had to face and the Department Head, Reg Fryer, was instructed to fill the position of project leader with an engineer of high calibre. The position was offered to Jack Savage, who saw the opportunity as his 'big break'. Assuming that the company's bid was successful, he believed that as the market grew so too would the electronics section. At this point, the matrix system was incorporated with all participants of the new project being located in one building and reporting on a daily basis to a project manager. Jack had previously handled all the estimating and feasibility studies in his group (Group C). There were two other groups in the department, but they did not interact with C group.

Jack Savage's departure from the group left a vacancy for a group leader, which had to be filled. The new project would last at least another five years (even the proposal stage would last eighteen months). Before Jack Savage left, he was asked whom he considered the best candidate to fill the vacancy. He declined to answer, pointing out that the Department Head would need to work with, or delegate to, his new group leader. In the circumstances, therefore, Jack felt that the Department Head should choose.

The choice was between two men only. The group was run as three sections. Len Bartholomew headed the data handling section, which covered a variety of small projects, including in-house test gear and training equipment, and was the section which had been most involved with the workshops and marketing division.

The second section was headed by Gareth Stevens and handled the software requirements of the group, electromagnetic compatibility (EMC) studies, and the effects of radio frequency radiation on electrical and electronics systems.

The third was undermanned, having no designated section leader, but handled the detailed analogue design work.

The problem was that the background and characters of the two section leaders were totally different. Gareth Stevens was forty-two years old with a BSc in electronics, and had been at the company for ten years, six of which had been in the electronics department. The first few years had been spent in a theoretical studies group, before a lateral transfer. He had a thorough knowledge of the effects of high frequency radiation microwave theory and he was a sound mathematician and theoretician. His software knowledge was broad, but not deep, and he thoroughly enjoyed 'putting it on the computer', which was always done with careful analysis but lacked clarity of presentation. He had a background of analysis in the aerospace industry and experience in formal reporting of experimental data. One of his shortcomings, however, was that he was almost totally humourless and, to some, too dogmatic on every issue.

Len Bartholomew was totally different. At forty-eight, he had twelve years with the company behind him, all in the electronics section. Academically, he had obtained three O-levels at school and had proceeded to the Civil Service, followed by National Service (a period in history unknown to everyone else in his department except the Department Head). At night school, he had acquired a HNC in electronics and an ONC in production engineering, while 'rising through the ranks' from workshops to design office, via the drawing office and experimental laboratory of a small electrical company on the South Coast. His background was in hardware, with a flair for ergonomics. It was varied, but not specialized, and he could see the broad picture. Yet, he was not good at detailed work, much of which he dismissed as 'nit picking' and 'exercises for word-smiths.'

Unfortunately, he had not done any computer programming; indeed his software knowledge was virtually zero. Despite a notoriety for 'not suffering fools gladly', he also had a reputation for possessing negotiation skills and patience. He was often described as being able to 'think on his feet and talk his way out'. During a period of rapid staff turnover, he had become the section leader and unofficial training officer for the new graduates (a position which Gareth had steadfastly refused) but his irreverent sense of humour perturbed Reg Fryer. Yet, at the same time, he admitted that Len always had his feet on the ground.

Reg Fryer went to Ralph Doe who accepted his choice of Gareth. Ralph had some unspoken doubts, but conceded that it was Reg who would normally deal with Gareth. He also acknowledged that Gareth did have the more formal education behind him.

The following day, a new issue of the family tree appeared on Reg's secretary's wall. Len's attention was brought to it by one of the technicians in the laboratory. Len was not happy and objected to being 'leap-frogged'. He pointed out that in the previous year, when there had been staff turnover turmoil, he had carried the group. Gareth had refused to have even the software people reporting to him, until he was virtually ordered to. Len's annual report recorded how he had responded to the situation. Reg accepted that Len had a wider variety of skills, but he wanted more depth in his department. He accepted that the group needed 'a Len Bartholomew', but not as their leader. Gareth had, after all, taken on the work involved in applications for capital equipment, which Reg felt was very important. His decision stood. He expected Len to report to Gareth in the same way that he had done to Jack Savage.

Len continued his work, reporting to Gareth as he had done to Jack which was, 'I'll shout when I need help.' This had always suited Jack, who trusted Len not to get out of his depth but also not to 'get in his hair'. He wanted Len only to shout when he really meant it, and he, in turn, would provide help. Len's progress reports were short and succinct. Gareth, however, wished to know the details of the task, which Len regarded as intrusive and insulting. Gareth regarded this response as uncooperative.

To combat his lack of computer experience, Len proposed to Reg that he should have a budget to convert his estimating system and format for proposals into a departmental standard. This would put his methods clearly on paper for others to follow, as well as giving Len some 'hands on' experience of minicomputers. Reg was sympathetic and enthusiastic, but the new project was currently soaking up all the available funds. He did have some money, but the requirement did not fall into the correct category.

Len then asked if the categories included another of his pet ideas – to produce a set of modules for use on data transmission systems. The need for these had appeared in four 'spin-off' proposals the previous year, and the design and development costs could not be written off over the four proposals. They had to be carried by one, and the development costs were making the estimates too high. This too was refused on the grounds that the R & D budget did not include it. Len interpreted these refusals as deliberate blocks: first, in an area where it was acknowledged that he was not proficient and second, in an area where he was considered to be constructive. He attacked his Department Head for being obstructive and negative.

Four months later, the annual review of staff took place. The form had a space for 'work undertaken in the previous twelve months' which the individual concerned filled in. Beneath this was the assessment format. The centre column was marked 'normal for the grade and position', and had two squares above and two squares below it. These were normally filled in by the immediate supervisor; in Len's case, Gareth.

Len proposed that he should fill in his own assessment, as a self-appraisal. That would only have left the difference between the appraisal by Gareth and the self-appraisal, to be discussed at the annual review with Reg. Gareth agreed.

On the form, there was one slot for 'other abilities'. Len inserted, 'presentation skills' and assessed himself 'above average'. Five years of night school lecturing, plus active parts in the local drama group had, he believed, given him the ability to present information. Reg regarded such claims as 'unnecessary and extravagant'. Len claimed that engineers 'talking into their shirt buttons' created a bad impression. His remarks regarding the company's lack of training for presenters led to more heated words on general lack of training and retraining available from the company, and the annual review ended less than amicably.

In the ensuing months, Len found the development work on which he was engaged being curtailed in favour of the large project. Works order numbers became scarce. Demands for a 'waiting time' number rose. Accounting for 36.5 hours per week became embarrassing.

Len required hardware to pass through the department in order to exercise his skills, but there was no hardware. This was regularly pointed out to Reg and Gareth, but the development of the total system was still incomplete. Without hardware, there would be no expansion and no promotion. Len considered his position. He was forty-eight years old; there was no hardware design planned for the immediately foreseeable future. Did he have a future at Fosbar Electronics? Reg considered the position. 'There is only one Len Bartholomew in the department,' he told Len. 'There is no one else who can do what you do; but I don't need two!'

Reg pondered. Financial strictures had prevented Len from training himself in the areas he knew to be a personal weakness, and the current climate had hidden Gareth's weakness. He could not promote Len to an equal position with Gareth, without expansion in the department; but if Len was not returned to the position in which the younger staff had regarded him, he would lose face and the new members would lose faith. If he didn't do something, he felt that Len's departure would be imminent.

Meanwhile, Len flicked through a borrowed book, *The Psychology of Management*. The book fell open at Chapter 13, 'The Male Menopause – A Crisis of Confidence'.

Questions

1 What are the implications for management development at Fosbar Electronics?
2 What steps would you take to improve the situation for:
   (a) Fosbar Electronics?
   (b) Gareth Stevens?
   (c) Len Bartholomew?

Appendix 1: Fosbar Electronics organization chart

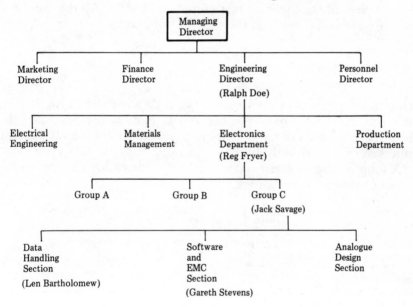

SIXTEEN

Olde England Taverns

TIM NORMAN AND
JACQUELINE DRAKE

Part 1   The brewing industry in the UK

This review of the industry was compiled in 1983. All the indicated trends were still evident at the time of publication.

Introduction

The brewing industry comprises over eighty brewery firms which between them own over 140 breweries. Nine firms dominate the industry, six of them have their own public houses estates and the others are involved only with production.

A long period of concentration in the industry has resulted in the present number of breweries:

Table 1   *Number of breweries*

	1950	1955	1960	1965	1970	1975	1982
Breweries	567	460	358	274	177	147	142

Source: Brewers Society.

The largest nine firms are responsible for about 75 per cent of total beer production, some 36.5m bulk barrels (see glossary) in 1982. This represents a 3 per cent decrease on 1981 total beer production, and was the lowest figure for ten years. The long-term decline in the demand for beer has forced the brewery firms to concentrate their competition more through the amenities in their public houses

(PHs), and through price competition on off-sales through super-markets and off-licence chains.

The industry employs 57,700 people directly in manufacturing with nearly another 300,000 employed in PHs. In total the industry is estimated to employ approximately 750,000 people covering trans-portation, manufacturing of beer, liquor and soft drinks, etc.

Since 1976 those directly employed in the manufacture of beer has declined from 68,000, a fall of 15 per cent, although those employed in PHs has increased by 21 per cent. This increase is due to the growth in the number of on-licensed premises (see glossary). In 1976 these numbered 122,036 and increased to over 130,000 by 1981, the largest area of growth being in the restricted on-licence sector (see glossary).

The on-licensed sector includes restaurants, night clubs and discotheques, and has expanded from 17,000 to over 22,000 outlets in the five years to 1981. The brewery firms' share of all types of licences fell from 35.5 per cent to 31.0 per cent in the same period, victims of the growth in independently owned outlets, known as the free trade.

The industry contributes nearly 7 per cent of all state taxes in the form of VAT and excise duty, and in the year 1982–3 the total revenue was £4,130m, of which £2,450m came from beer. Con-sumer spending on alcohol and government revenue raised on beer sales since 1976 is shown in Table 2.

As an indication of the effects on the industry of taxation, for each bottle of Scotch sold for £6.50 there is a tax of over £5.00 and for each bottle of wine of £2.25 there is a tax of over £1.00. Also, since 1979 the total tax on a pint of beer has increased from 10p to about 22p, which is double the rise in the RPI.

The 1950s and 1960s was the period of greatest concentration for the brewers, partly because of the fall in beer demand in the post-war decade and partly because of the intervention of both non-brewery firms and their attempts to buy the assets of the brewers cheaply, and the more aggressive brewing firms, willing to compete with those established in local oligopolies. The mergers and takeovers were therefore mainly defensive in nature.

As a result of these amalgamations, national beer brands (initially for bottled beer) began to establish themselves. With the introduc-tion of keg beer and the consequent demise of cask-conditioned beer (see glossary), the smaller brewers were faced with the alternatives of combining or of going under.

During the 1970s there was a move away from keg beer to lager, and this brought about an increase in the demand for beer for the first

Table 2 *Consumer spending on alcohol at 1981 prices (£m)*

	1976	1977	1978	1979	1980	1981	%1981 Total
Beer	3282	3788	4182	4838	5656	6395	56.1
Spirits	1559	1648	1981	2425	2708	2900	25.1
Wines	995	1103	1308	1610	1836	2100	18.5
Total	5836	6539	7471	8873	10200	11395	100.0

Source Central Statistical Office.

Table 3 *Government revenue from beer sales (£m)*

	1976	1977	1978	1979	1980	1981	1982
Customs and Excise	652	809	893	893	917	1130	1440
VAT	209	259	297	317	611	755	850
Total	861	1068	1190	1210	1528	1885	2290

Source Customs and Excise.

time in two decades. However the increase was short lived and the last three years to 1983 had seen a fall of 7.8 per cent in beer demand.

The resulting increase in competition between the brewers had forced them into price wars and expensive advertising campaigns, mainly for their lager products. It had also caused them to compete more heavily in the free-trade, offering loans to independent publicans in return for them selling the brewers' products. In recent years the brewers have realized that their tied estates, and in particular their managed houses, have become increasingly reliant on income from gaming machines.

During 1983, the EEC recommendations regarding the tied house system in the UK had caused great concern to the industry. These recommendations meant that PHs could only be tied to beer products and not spirits and wines, etc. The brewery firms made high margins on the non-beer products sold to their tied houses. In fact, it was often the case that they were more expensive than if the publican had purchased them from a supermarket or off-licence.

A final area of importance for the brewers is the growing realization that the food sector can be very profitable, not just with the introduction of simple operations in their PHs but also with the development of chains of specialist catering outlets, mostly combining pub and restaurant together.

Grand Metropolitan is probably the best placed in this segment of the market with around 150 Berni Inns and 130 Schooner Inns. Allied with Cavalier Steak Bars, Bass with Toby Inns, Whitbread with Beefeater Steak Bars and Courage with Chaucer Inns and Falstaff Taverns are in direct competition with the Grand Metropolitan chains.

Other non-pub experiments include Whitbread's Pizza Hut and Grand Metropolitan's Huckleberry operations. All of these developments underline the brewers' move away from their reliance on their tied estates and the concentration on volumes, and their move towards more competition on price, service, 'value for money', and in the utilization of their property through new concepts and experiments.

This current scenario in which the brewers find themselves is the result of years of change, which began with the declining beer demand after 1945 and the changes in the structure of the industry that occurred at that time.

Structure of the industry

Since 1950 the number of breweries had declined and there has been a concentration of both production facilities and in the ownership of public houses. In recent years however, the number of public houses owned or tied (see glossary) to the main brewers has declined as a proportion of the total PHs. While there were some eighty brewing firms in 1982, the market was dominated by nine firms: three of them are purely manufacturing firms (Guinness, Carlsberg, Harp) while the remaining six also control their own PHs. These firms are Bass, Allied Breweries, Watneys, Whitbread, Courage and Scottish & Newcastle (S & N).

Changes since 1950

In the early 1950s the national brewers accounted for 18 per cent of beer production. National brands were nearly all bottled beers as these could be easily transported and also had a longer life than cask-conditioned beer.

Some firms, Worthington for instance, relied on independent bottling firms for their production but others, like Whitbread, employed local brewers who were under its 'umbrella', to bottle its beer. (The 'umbrella' arrangement involved Whitbread buying 20–30 per cent of an independent brewers' shares to give them a chain of outlets through which to distribute their beer.) Bass also had similar arrangements with some small brewers.

By 1960 Whitbread had access to 15,000 PHs through its 'umbrella' which were able to offer its beer to their customers. Eventually the 'umbrella' became the vehicle for the amalgamation of the small brewers into the Whitbread group. (Appendix 1 shows the major firms which made up the group.)

The expansion of Whitbread products through such a large outlet chain created a national identity in the public's mind for those products. Other brewers began to follow.

Behind this push toward national brands there lay three factors common to the large brewers: the determination to penetrate competitors' outlets; the desire to sell main brands through small brewers' PHs and finally, to increase their share of the free trade.

The same could be said of the regional brewers who, by the 1950s, constituted a significant force in the industry. At that time there were between 30–40 regional brewers with over 300 PHs, and which formed local oligopolies against which the larger national brewers had to compete. Many of the regional brewers had been the result of a series of amalgamations and mergers. Against a background of declining demand, a company operating in a relatively concentrated market could only grow either by merging with one of its major competitors or by acquiring smaller breweries with trading interests close to themselves.

Factors behind the mergers

One of the most important reasons for the mergers within the industry during the 1950s and 1960s was the declining demand for beer during the decade after 1945. Table 4 shows this decline which

Table 4 *Trends in drink consumption, 1945–75*

Year	Beer (barrels) m	Spirits (gallons) m	Wine (gallons) m
1945	31.0	8.3	4.4
1950	25.8	9.8	11.6
1955	23.6	11.5	16.9
1960	26.6	14.2	27.0
1965	29.9	19.1	36.4
1968	31.5	19.0	45.6
1970	33.5	18.0	48.4
1975	38.5	20.7	77.5

Source EIU.

was not overcome until 1968, although demand for other products increased quite significantly during the period

As a consequence of this demand trend, defensive mergers took place to protect the local oligopolies that had been established.

Another impetus given to the merger boom was the expansion of the bottled beer market. This placed the smaller brewers at a disadvantage since the bottling plant was expensive, and only an economic investment if the brewer had sufficient outlets through which to sell relatively large volumes of bottled beer.

Also the dispersion of population away from the major urban areas gave the large metropolitan brewer a strong incentive to spread his tied trade more widely. The small city brewer did not have the resources to be able to distribute beyond a limited geographical area.

Both the cost of plant and distribution were put even more out of the reach of the smaller brewer in the 1960s with the expansion of keg beer. The keg beer made it possible for the first time for draught beer to be distributed outside the immediate area of the brewery. The high cost of the plant made the need for many outlets even greater, and this could now be achieved through the transportation of keg beer.

Between 1957 and 1969, it has been estimated that 59 per cent of the 166 firms which made up the industry were absorbed by mergers. An indication of the concentration during the whole period is given below. The largest five brewers increased their share of production from 18 per cent in 1954 to 64 per cent by 1968. However, even by 1968 the industry concentration ratio was slightly below the average for manufacturing industry as a whole.

The most active period of concentration was between 1959 and 1961, during which time there were thirty-five combinations out of the ninety-eight that took place in the industry. (A summary of the major mergers etc. is given in Appendix 2.)

Table 5 *Concentration ratios in the brewing industry.* Five largest firms' share of total

	1954 %	1958 %	1963 %	1968 %
Net output	18	23	42	64
Employment	19	22	49	61
Purchases	23	23	43	52
Capital spending	21	32	33	63

Source Censuses of Production.

The acceleration of mergers at this time was also due to factors outside the normal trading of the brewers. These were the intervention of financial insitutions looking for 'asset situations', i.e. buying a firm with undervalued assets and then selling them off at their true market price.

Most of the brewing companies' assets were both undervalued and underutilized, and this was (and is) especially true of their licensed property. The most famous instance of an attempted takeover by an outsider was in 1959 with Charles Clore's company, Sears Holdings' bid for Watney Mann. The bid was unsuccessful (more through good fortune than Watney's defence) but Watney's had learned its lesson and undertook a series of defensive mergers with smaller brewers (see Table 6).

Table 6

Year	Company	Area
1959	Wilsons	Manchester
1960	Ushers	West Country
1960	Phipps	Midlands
1961	Morgans	East Anglia
1963	Steward & Patteson	East Anglia
1963	Bullards	East Anglia
1965	Drybrough	Scotland

Another intervention from an outsider concerned the development of United Breweries (UB). This was the vehicle through which a Canadian entrepreneur, E. P. Taylor, amalgamated a series of small breweries in order to gain outlets for his main product, Carling lager, which he had built up in North America.

He acquired the Hope & Anchor Brewery in the early 1950s and by 1961 had built up a chain of 2800 tied houses. However, he was never able to break into 'the big league' in terms of the number of outlets that he had tied through UB. The reason for this was that the 'family' of small brewery firms did not welcome the attentions of an outsider. They preferred to merge with other small brewers with whom they had close connections in the local area. He was therefore 'shut out' of the club.

But Taylor had influenced the industry by his direct approach and also the trend toward the national branding of beer products, with Carling lager. By 1968, after a decade of horizontal mergers 73 per cent of beer production was in the hands of the seven major firms.

Since 1968 the major firms have increased their share further, partly by the acquisition of smaller firms, but also by greater penetration in the free trade. The most significant events to occur during the maturation of the industry were the acquisitions of Watney Mann by Grand Metropolitan in 1971, of Courage by the Imperial Group and of Truman's, also by Grand Metropolitan, in 1972.

Despite this further concentration, the national brewers have reduced their holding of licensed premises in recent years. This can be illustrated in the changing pattern in the types of licences available.

Licences

In the UK alcohol can be sold through several different types of outlets, each of which requires a particular type of licence. These are explained in the glossary.

In 1981 the percentage shares for each of the different types of licences were as follows:

1	Full on-licence	public houses	44 per cent
2	Restricted on-licence	restaurants night clubs	13 per cent
3	Club licence	private members clubs	19 per cent
4	Off-licence	supermarkets off-licences	24 per cent

Between 1945 and 1975 the total number of on-licences in the UK grew considerably, although the full on-licence category decreased. This is illustrated in Table 7:

The number of PHs in the UK declined by 9.5 per cent during the

Table 7 *Number of on-licences (in thousands) in the UK, 1945–75*

	1945	1955	1965	1975
Full	81.4	79.7	75.4	73.7
Restricted	—	—	6.3	15.8
Club	16.4	22.3	25.3	30.5
Total	97.8	102.0	107.0	120.0

Source Home Office.

thirty-year period, although the number of restricted on-licences grew to nearly 16,000 after their introduction in 1962. The club sector grew from 17 per cent to over 25 per cent in the same period.

Since 1975, however, the number of PHs has begun to expand again but not at the same rate of growth as the restricted and club sectors, both of which continue to expand rapidly. Since 1975 the total number of on-licensed premises has increased by 7.3 per cent, but the major brewers' share of them has actually decreased by 5 per cent (see below).

The same pattern is repeated for off-licences, where the growth since 1975 has been 14 per cent, yet the brewers' share has decreased by 2.3 per cent. Overall, their share of all licensed premises has declined by 4.5 per cent.

The fall in brewery-tied PHs has meant that in recent years there has been a considerable return to the free-house system, over which the brewers have actively competed. It has also brought about the re-emergence and popularity in regional brands of traditional draught beers.

Table 8 *Number of Licensed Premises in the UK (000s)*

	1976	*1977*	*1978*	*1979*	*1980*
On-licences					
Full	74.3	74.5	75.2	75.7	75.8
Restricted	16.7	17.8	19.1	20.5	22.0
Clubs	31.0	31.8	32.4	32.7	33.1
Total	122.0	124.1	126.7	128.9	130.9
Off-licences	37.1	38.4	39.8	41.1	42.3
Total	159.1	162.5	166.5	170.0	173.2

Source Home Office.

Table 9 *Brewers' Share of Licensed Premises (per cent)*

	1976	*1977*	*1978*	*1979*	*1980*
Full on-licences	69.0	68.1	66.6	65.3	64.0
Off-licences	13.6	12.5	11.4	11.3	11.3
Others	0.5	0.4	0.4	0.5	0.5
All premises	35.5	34.3	32.9	32.0	31.0

Source Brewers Society.

Olde England Taverns

Although most of the major off-licence chains are now firmly in the hands of the brewers, much of the expansion in this sector has been due to supermarkets' willingness to compete with the established chains of off-licences, offering very competitive prices. Even the brewers have been tempted by the large volumes turned over by the supermarkets, and have given them the opportunity to buy brewers' wines and spirits at lower prices than are offered by the brewers to their own tied houses. This is true even when comparing the wholesale prices paid by the tied houses and the retail prices offered by the supermarkets.

Table 10 *Break-down of full on-licences (000s)*

	1976	1977	1978	1979	Percentage change 1976–79
Managed houses	14.8	14.4	14.1	14.0	−5.3
Tenanted houses	36.4	36.3	36.0	35.4	−2.7
Free houses	23.1	23.8	25.1	26.3	+13.9
Total houses	74.3	74.5	75.2	75.7	+1.9

Source Brewers Society.

The rationalization programmes undertaken by the brewers can be clearly illustrated in Table 10. The fall in the number of managed houses and tied houses, and the rapid rise in the number of free houses is one of the reasons why the brewers compete, through price and offers of loans etc., between themselves in the free trade sector.

Table 11 *Brewers' ownership of public houses/off-licences, 1981*

Brewer	Number of on-licences Outlets	% Total	Number of off-licences Outlets	% Total
Bass	8150	10.7	975	2.3
Grand-Metropolitan	8050	10.5	550	1.3
Allied-Lyons	7600	9.9	930	2.2
Whitbread	7100	9.3	650	1.5
Courage	5300	6.9	400	0.9
Scottish & Newcastle	1500	2.0	225	0.5
Total	37700	49.3	3730	8.7

The rationalization programmes have attempted to first, dispose of unprofitable PHs and then second, to improve the amenities and appearance of the remaining PHs through large investment schedules. This trend has continued since 1979 and, in terms of the brewers' commitment to improving their PHs, has accelerated.

Summary

After the concentration period between 1950 and 1972 the industry has stabilized whereby the major brewers own nearly half of all PHs in the UK in 1981 (see Table 11) and about 9 per cent of off-licences. For all of them, apart from S & N, their managed houses represent about 25 per cent to 33 per cent of their total estates. For S & N managed houses constitute about 60 per cent of their estate.

Given the rationalization programmes and the competition from the free-trade, the trend for the major brewers' PHs would seem to be one of a gradual decrease both in the absolute numbers, and also in their share of the total number of PHs.

The demand for beer had remained reasonably stable between 1976 and 1981, at which time there was a fall of 5.5 per cent and then, in 1982, there was a further fall of 3.1 per cent on the 1981 figure. This has resulted in plant closures by the major brewers (e.g. Ansells in Birmingham, Courage in Southwark) and any continued fall in beer demand will certainly bring about further reductions in brewing capacity.

The Market

A marked feature of the UK alcohol market between 1960 and the mid–1980s was the fact that it remained buoyant during periods of recession. In terms of output the peak was reached in 1979 with beer consumption reaching 41.7m bulk barrels, which is equivalent to 12,000m pints. Since then the annual per capita consumption has fallen for both beer and wines, the latter having had many years of rapid growth. Both these trends and the per capita figures for spirits are given in Table 12.

Although per capita spending on beer has risen from £58.73 p.a. to £101.10 p.a. the underlying market trend has been downward, with beer consumption falling from 4.4 per cent to 4.1 per cent of total consumer expenditure from 1976 to 1980.

The declining consumption is counter to the trends of other beer

Table 12 *Beer consumption (m bulk barrels) and per capita consumption for beer, wine and spirits 1976–1981*

	1976	1977	1978	1979	1980	1981
Total beer consumption	40.7	40.3	40.4	41.7	40.0	37.8
Per capita consumption						
Beer (pints)	209	208	214	214	206	200
Wine (pints)	10	11	13	14	15	15
Spirits (pints)	3	3	3	3	3	3

drinking countries, and although the UK is third in terms of production (behind the US and West Germany), it was only tenth in terms of consumption in 1982.

The fall in the beer market has been offset to some extent by the increasing demand for wines and spirits. Since 1970 the proportion of consumer spending on wines out of the total spending on alcohol has risen from 14 per cent to 19 per cent in 1981. For spirits it has risen from 23 per cent to 25 per cent, while beer has fallen from 63 per cent to 56 per cent.

One of the reasons for this change in consumption patterns could be because the increase in beer prices has been greater than for those of wines or spirits, and other goods. The price for beer has risen by 74 per cent since 1976, while the price of other goods has risen by 64 per cent (see Appendix 3). The main causes of this rise are:

(a)   Excise Duty.
(b)   Labour, raw materials.
(c)   Transportation.

Because of the increase in the number of clubs, and the price cutting in the free-trade and supermarket sectors, it seems likely that the actual price increase of beer in tied PHs has been greater than this 74 per cent. However, it would appear that it was not until 1979 that the price increases began to provoke consumer resistance, deterring beer-drinkers in large numbers.

The most dynamic segment of the beer market has been lager, which has expanded by nearly 40 per cent in the years 1976 to 1981 (see Appendix 4). This is equivalent to 9 per cent of the beer market. All other types of beer have fallen, and for the largest segment of the market, bitter, this has meant a fall of 4 per cent.

Despite the dominance of the big six and the rise in popularity of first keg beer in the 1960s and then lager in the 1970s, local tastes have remained an important factor in any regional market and particularly influence lager penetration levels.

The regional preferences can be seen below, and by comparing the SE with 27 per cent of the total beer market but 31 per cent of the lager market, while the NE has 18 per cent and 14 per cent of these markets respectively.

Table 13 *Beer consumption in 1979 by region and type (percentages)*

Region	% total beer market	% non-lager	% lager	Lager as % beer sales
SE	27	26	31	33
NE	18	20	14	22
Midlands	16	17	15	27
NW	16	18	12	22
Scotland	9	7	14	45
SW	8	6	7	31

Source The Financial Times (March 1981).

Some of the reasons for the growth of the lager market are:

(a) Increased consumer preference for bland, light and carbonated beer.
(b) Lager's quality as a refreshing drink.
(c) Increase in the take-home trade and the importance of canned products.
(d) Massive advertising campaigns launched by the brewers.
(e) Increase in women's beer market.
(f) Increase in the concept of a 'young person's drink'.

The rapid growth of lager has resulted in the proliferation of lager brands as the brewers seek to gain as much market share as possible, using price, advertising and different distribution channels (supermarkets) as competitive tools.

Indeed the changing pattern of consumption has been matched by a change in the distribution of alcohol. In volume terms 86 per cent of beer, 35–40 per cent of spirits and 30 per cent of wines are sold through the on-trade, although the off-licence trade is increasing. This is illustrated in Table 14.

By increasing the competition in the free-trade and off-licence trade, the brewers have effectively made their tied houses less

Table 14 *Retail distribution (percentage of volume sales)*

| | 1977 | | 1981 | |
	On-trade	Off-trade	On-trade	Off-trade
Beer	91	9	86	14
Whisky	45	55	40	60
Vodka	59	41	53	47
Gin	49	51	45	55
Wine	31	69	30	70
Vermouth	37	63	24	76

Source Trade estimates.

attractive to the consumer in terms of beer price, because the profit margin on the beer sold through these channels is in fact less than that which could be got from the tied houses. The same is also true for spirits, where brewers' brands are substantially cheaper in supermarkets than in their own PHs.

Even the increasing interest in 'real ale' throughout the 1970s, epitomised by the expansion of CAMRA (Campaign for Real Ale) did not significantly alter the growth of lager or the trend toward off-licence sales.

Summary

The increase in the lager market had resulted in a high level of competition between the brewers in price advertising and promotional activity. Watneys, for instance, introduced Foster's lager three years ago even though its main brand, Carlsberg, was the market leader. After extensive promotion Foster's has replaced Carlsberg as the number one brand.

The brewers still regard wine as a necessary evil although their expansion of wine bars and catering operations has resulted in an increased market for wine.

Both the expansion of the lager and wine markets has contributed to the growth of the off-licence trade, because both products are conveniently packaged in cans, bottles and bags. The pricing policies of the brewers has also contributed to this expansion.

The major brewers dominate not just the beer market but also those for wines and spirits through their subsidiaries. These holdings are included in the following section.

The brewery firms

The six main brewers have, since the late 1970s, undertaken a rationalization of their estates, combined with large improvement programmes on their remaining managed houses.

In the three years to 1985 it was estimated that £850m would be spent by Britain's eighty brewers on the 49000 PHs which they own. Overall support for retailing activities would be £1180m which represented 75 per cent of the brewers' total capital investment planned over the three years. There would be a shift away from expanding production and distribution facilities, in line with the forecast fall in beer demand.

Free houses, independent of the brewers, and clubs would get their share of support, mainly by way of loans from the brewers whose spending would total £175m over the three years. At the end of the financial year 1982, loans to the free-trade were over £200m, so brewers expected to expand their support to an even greater level (see Appendix 5). S & N, for example, had loans to the free-trade which amount to £49m and which is equivalent to 11 per cent of its total assets.

The turnover and profit figures for each of the firms is given in Appendix 6, together with those same figures for the groups of which they are part. In the cases of Whitbread, Bass and S & N, the brewing and retailing figures are the same, or virtually the same as those of the group.

Although it is not possible to attribute those assets dedicated to the brewing and retailing divisions within the groups, the consistency of the profits to sales ratio seem to suggest a commonality in margins etc.

Despite the recession in recent years, the results of the brewers appear to have remained stable even though the demand for beer is declining. As Dun & Bradstreet conclude in a recent report (April 1983):

'The brewing industry often complains that it has felt the effects of recession over the past few years, but this analysis indicates that it has held up remarkably well. This may be a reflection that the brewers' profits are now derived less from the production of beer and more from the sale of food and other beverages.'

This would appear to be consistent with the planned expenditure on PH refurbishment.

A profile of each of the six main brewery firms is given on the following pages.

Note A summary of capital expenditure and disposals in years 1980 to 1982 is included in Appendix 5. Both turnover figures and profits for each of the brewers are given in Appendix 6.

Bass

Controls thirteen breweries and is generally considered the largest UK brewer with over 20 per cent of all beer sales. Bass is also Britain's largest publican, with some 8150 tied outlets and control over 1000 off-licences including the Hedges & Butler, Galleon and Sado & King chains.

Its principal products include Tennants lager, Charrington and Bass beers. (A summary of the main brewers' non-beer products is included in Appendix 7.)

As well as its brewing activities, Bass acquired Coral Leisure Group in 1981 which includes Pontin's holiday firm as one of its subsidiaries.

In 1981 Bass employed 69,000 people which was a fall of 5000 over the previous year. In 1983 it plans to spend a further £47m, as part of its continued strategy to improve its PHs.

Allied–Lyons

Is one of the world's top ten food and beverage groups. Brewing activities go back to the 1960s with the merger of Ind Coope, Ansells and Tetley. Seven breweries are operated and the firm runs nearly 7500 PHs and owns the Victoria Wine and Grants of St James's off-licence chains. Allied-Lyons accounts for 14–16 per cent of all UK beer sales with over fifty draught and packaged brands.

Among its brands are Double Diamond, Arctic Lite, Skol, Long Life lager, Babycham, Britvic and Burton beers. Its regional breweries include Benskins, Taylor Walker and Tetleys.

In 1978 it expanded outside the brewery business when it acquired J. Lyons Ltd the catering and beverage group.

Whitbread

Is third in the market with 13–14 per cent of beer sales. Outlets include 7850 on-licensed premises and a further 700 off-licences including the Threshers and Stowells of Chelsea chains.

Its main products are Trophy bitter, Mackeson, Heineken, Stella Artois and Fremlins' and Whitbread beers.

It, too, expanded its interests by buying a wines and spirits company from Nabisco in 1982 for £57m. The company, Julius Wile Sons & Co. will give Whitbread the opportunity to expand its sales into the USA. It also purchased Goodhews Ltd in 1982, a small PH company providing it with another independent brewer to integrate into its estate.

It has also entered into a very successful joint venture with the Pepsico Corp of USA in developing its Pizza Hut operation in the UK, selling pizzas through its chain of fast food restaurants.

The emphasis on retailing is underlined by its continuing expansion of its Beefeater chain of steak houses, which numbered over 100 in 1983.

Grand Metropolitan

Has Watney Mann and Truman Brewers as its main brewing subsidiaries among the ten regional breweries which it operates. (A summary of the regional divisions is in Appendix 8.)

Tied outlets total more than 6500, while off-licences, including Peter Dominic and Westminster Wines, provide over 1000 further retail outlets. The Watneys group is estimated to account for 12–13 per cent of the beer market.

Its main products are Stag and London bitters, Wilsons and Ushers beers, Foster's Lager, Carlsberg, J & B Scotch and Gordons Gin.

Watneys have diversified into the fast food business, building on its earlier successes with the Schooner Inns.

Scottish & Newcastle (S & N)

Based in Edinburgh is the fifth of the big six accounting for about 11 per cent of the market. S & N is considerably weaker in terms of distribution outlets with only 1500 PHs, although its position in the off-trade has improved with the acquisition of the Gough Brothers chain to complement its ownership of Cannongate Wines.

Main products are McEwans and Wm Younger beers. It does have a small exporting operation which turned over £13m in 1982. However, a fall of 37 per cent in the managed house profits has accelerated S & N's rationalization programme, returning many of them to tenancy. It intends to continue pub improvements, financed mainly by disposals.

It also intends to continue to expand its promotion of the free-trade with its loans to customers which amounted to £5.5m in 1982. This leaves a total exposure of £49m in the balance sheet, with total assets of £440m.

Imperial group

Owns the Courage brewery firm. On-licensed premises number just under 4000 outlets, while the Saccone & Speed and Arthur

Cooper off-licence chains form the major part of the Courage estate of 500 outlets. Market share is approximately 8 per cent of sales.

Main brands include John Smith's and Courage beers. Its diversification programme has resulted in its ownership of the Happy Eater chain of family restaurants, the Chaucer and Falstaff steak houses and Anchor Hotels.

Much of its capital expenditure has been on modernizing its productive facilities.

Regional brewers

As well as the major brewers, there are several others which operate on a regional basis, and whose presence can often be quite important to the local market. Among the more famous of these regional brewers are:

Youngs   West London
Boddingtons   Manchester
Greenhall Whitley   Warrington
Vaux   Sunderland
Wolverhampton & Dudley   Midlands

These local brewers are often more profitable than the major brewers. A report by stockbrokers Hitchens Harrison in 1981 found that during the 1970s the profits achieved by the smaller brewers were proportionally almost twice the levels achieved by the major companies.

Profits of the big six and Guinness in 1979, as a return on capital on a weighted average, were 7.9 per cent on estimated values. Of the smaller brewers, Ruddles had a return of more than 30 per cent, while in 1980, W & D had a return of 21.4 per cent and Mansfield a return of 17.4 per cent. By contrast Bass, the leading brewer, could manage only 11.6 per cent.

One of the reasons for this difference is that the smaller brewers have a lower number of PHs and a more limited geographical area in which to have to distribute their beer. Another reason lies in the increasing interest in 'real ale' and a reaction against the national brands such as Double Diamond. The image of quality and tradition of real draught beer has proven to be attractive to the free-trade. On the other side, the major brewers have been associated with bland, carbonated, pasteurised, fizzy beers. Such is the selling power of 'real ale' to the consumer that Watneys have introduced Ruddles County beer into many of its tied houses.

The smaller brewers have therefore been able to maintain their volumes even though the rest of the industry has been suffering a decline in demand. They have also been able to keep price rises lower than those of their bigger rivals, who decided to maintain their margins at the expense of volume.

To counteract their relatively declining market position, the big six have moved towards adopting some of the methods and tactics of their smaller competitors. They have begun using regional names for beers and also of pricing on a more localized basis in an attempt to compete more effectively. Allied has revived some of its constituent companies, discarded particular beers and expanded its portfolio to over fifty beers. Watneys has undergone a massive reorganization in order to decentralize its brewery subsidiaries in order to establish local brands, e.g. Wilsons bitter, which it can then 'export' to London. It has also reverted to the original names of its breweries, e.g. Trumans has returned to be known as Truman Hanbury Burton.

As if to underline this process even more, Watneys has recently opened its first in-pub brewery and plans to expand this concept into a chain of such PHs.

Summary

Since the peak of 1979 beer consumption has fallen by 8 per cent. Part of this fall is due to the major brewers' decision to maintain their profit margins in their tied houses and, at the same time, to keep their volumes up by aggressively competing in the free and off-licence trades.

This has coincided with the rapid growth in conveniently packaged products, e.g. wine and lager, which are easily sold through supermarkets and specialist chains of off-licences which have expanded in recent years.

The brewers have rationalized their estates and invested heavily in decor and amenities in order to milk their tied houses through high prices.

After many years of being conservatively and defensively managed, the brewers have realized the vulnerability of their reliance on beer volume. They have expanded their interests into catering and leisure businesses, while disposing of brewing plant and PHs.

The likely change in the EEC laws governing ties between retail outlets and manufacturing firms will change the industry by making it more competitive, as the brewers seek to gain market share through price and promotion. A foretaste of this has already arrived with the competition in the free-trade. In future, therefore, greater emphasis will be placed on the management of the major brewing groups to adopt the attitudes and techniques of fast moving consumer goods firms such as Mars, Lever Bros and Proctor & Gamble.

Appendix 1   The Whitbread 'umbrella': major acquisitions

Company	Region	No. of PHs	Year
Tennant	Yorkshire	NA	1961
West Country	Wales and West	1250	1962
Flower	Midlands	1125	1962
Dutton's	Lancashire	820	1963
Rhymney	Wales	680	1966
Threlfalls	North West	800	1967
Fremlin	Kent	920	1968
Strong	South	750	1969

Source Brewing Trade Review.

Appendix 2   Main brewery mergers and acquisitions, 1955–72

1955 onwards	Start of Whitbread 'umbrella'.
1956	Courage merged with Barclay Perkins.
1958	Watney, Coombe, Reid merged with Mann, Crossman and Paulin.
1959	Ind Coope acquired Taylor Walker.
	United Breweries formed.
1960	Courage merged with Simonds.
	Tetley merged with Walker Cain.
	Scottish Breweries merged with Newcastle Breweries to form S & N.
1961	Ind Coope, Tetley Walker and Ansell merge to form what was to become Allied Breweries.
	Bass merge with Mitchells and Butlers.
	Courage acquired Bristol Breweries.
1962	Charrington merged with United.
1967	Bass merge with Charrington.
1970	Courage acquired John Smith's Tadcaster Brewery.
1971	Grand Metropolitan acquired Trumans.
1972	Grand Metropolitan acquired Watney Mann.
	Imperial acquired Courage.

Appendix 3   Percentage price increases of beer, alcohol and all goods

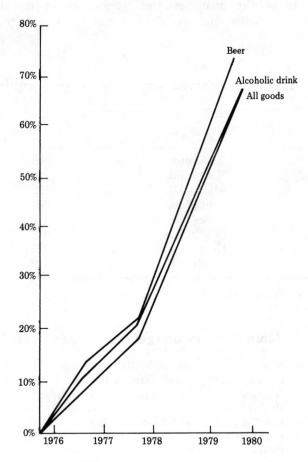

Source Central Statistical Office.

Appendix 4   Trends in sales of different beer types, 1976–81

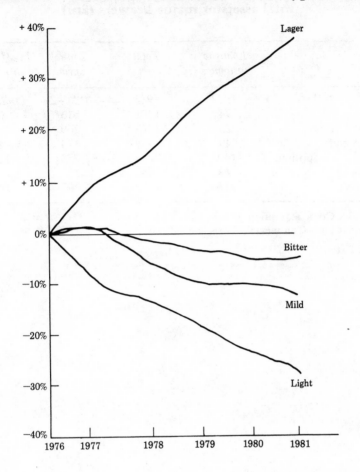

Appendix 5 Capital expenditure and disposals, loans and total assets of major brewers (£m)

	Loans to customers	Total assets	Capital spend	Fixed assets disposals
	1982	1982	1980–2	1980–2
Bass	74	1351	513*	61
Allied-Lyons	23	1348	269	124
Whitbread	49	958	174	44
Grand Metropolitan	NA	2218	773†	125
S & N	49	440	137	10
Imperial	NA	1072	495	146

* Includes Coral acquisition.
† Includes Inter-Continental Hotels and Liggett.

Source Extel.

Appendix 6   Sales, profits and fixed assets of major brewers

(£m)	sales	Group total profits	assets	Brewing only sales	profits
Bass					
1980	1263	133	931	1184	122
1981	1713	153	1145	1332	129
1982	1861	162	1185	1380	136
Allied-Lyons					
1980	2200	113	988	1456	106
1981	2268	112	991	1579	106
1982	2398	141	1021	1674	119
Whitbread					
1980	738	60	492	738	60
1981	782	66	798	782	66
1982	842	72	814	842	72
Grand Metropolitan					
1980	2583	213	1659	671	66
1981	3221	277	1892	744	73
1982	3849	355	1910	1357★	167
S & N					
1980	498	46	283	496	46
1981	588	48	320	585	47
1982	621	48	368	617	46
Imperial					
1980	3929	141	805	540	42
1981	4526	147	903	734	50
1982	4614	191	865†	815	59

★ Includes Liggett acquired in 1982.
† Disposal of food interests.

Source Extel.

Appendix 7 Brewers' ownership of spirit brands

Brewer	Distilling firm	Brand
Allied-Lyons	Wm Teacher & Sons Grants of St James's (30% share) Philips	Teacher's Scotch Romanoff Vodka Mainbrace Rum Plymouth Gin
Bass	Grants (30% share) Hedges & Butler	Standfast Scotch Bacardi Rum Zamoyski Vodka
Courage Greenall Whitley	Saccone & Speed G & J Greenall	Dry Cane Rum Vladivar Vodka Greenall's Gin
Grand Metropolitan	International Distillers & Vintners Gilbey Vintners	J & B Scotch Smirnoff Vodka Gilbeys Gin
Scottish & Newcastle	Charles Mackinley	Mackinleys Scotch
Whitbread	Grants (30% share) Philips	Scotch Plymouth Gin

Appendix 8 Grand Metropolitan regional breweries

Brewery name	Region	Products
Watney Combe Reid	London	Stag bitter
		London bitter
Phoenix	Sussex	Tamplins bitter
Ushers	West Country	Triple Crown bitter
Manns	Midlands	Bitter/mild
Wilsons	Manchester	Bitter/mild
Drybrough & Co.	Scotland	Pentland ale
		Heavy bitter
Samual Webster	Halifax	Yorkshire bitter
		Green label
Norwich Brewery	East Anglia	Bitter
Truman Ltd	London	Bitter

Other products distributed by Grand Metropolitan

Foster's Lager
Carlsberg Lager
Holsten Export
Holsten Diet

Glossary

Managed house	A public house owned by a brewery company and managed by an employee of the company.
Tenanted house	A PH owned by a brewery company and let to a tenant, who runs it as his/her own business.
Tied estate	The managed and tenanted PHs and off-licences owned by a brewer.
Free trade	Licensed premises not owned by a brewer, although they may be linked to one or more firms by short-term contracts to purchase their products.
Licensed club	Usually a proprietary club which requires a justices' licence.
Registered club	Issued by a magistrate's court, and available where sales are non-profit making or where it is for the benefit of the members.
On-licences	(*Unrestricted*) a PH or some hotels which may be tied or free.
	(*Restricted*) restaurants, wine bars and residential hotels are typical of these.
Off-licences	To sell alcohol for consumption off the premises only.
Keg beer	Pasteurized, carbonated beer filtered to remove the yeast and stored in metal casks.
Cask conditioned beer	Traditional beer, stored in casks (often wood), with the yeast still working allowing secondary fermentation.
CAMRA	Campaign for Real Ale, effectively a consumer pressure group.
Bulk barrel	36 gallons (288 pints).

Part 2 Olde England Taverns

Introduction

On 20th October 1982, Tom Oliver, the Managing Director of Olde England Taverns (OET) heard that the company had not only achieved its profit plan of £20m, but had bettered it by £2m to £22m for the year ending September 1982.

There had been rumours that Oliver was under pressure for his job, and so the news could not have come at a better moment. There had been substantial changes in other parts of the Retailing and Brewing Division of International Leisure plc, of which OET was a subsidiary. With this result, however, there appeared to be little reason for changes to be made to OET.

Background to International Leisure

At the financial year end 1982, International Leisure was one of the largest companies in the UK with interests in brewing, hotels, public houses (PHs), liquor distribution, gambling and bio-technology. Its turnover for the year was £3,848m with profits of £355m.

International Leisure was founded in the late 1940s by Frederick Goldstein, trading initially in property before entering the hotel business in 1948. During the 1950s and 1960s International Leisure grew rapidly concentrating mainly on hotels in central London and capitalizing on the rising property prices.

Between 1969 and 1972, Goldstein completed a series of remarkable acquisitions, including International Casinos, Wine 'n' Dine Steak Houses, and Fortress Brewery. This last takeover was the first large scale incursion of an outsider into the brewery business. The pinnacle of his coups in the early 1970s was that of East Ham Brewers, which was among the largest takeovers in stockmarket history in the UK. This was a bitterly fought battle, and resulted in the complete removal of senior East Ham management once Goldstein had won.

Almost at the end of his career, there were still two more spectacular takeovers to come. The first, in 1980, was of the Virginia Group (tobacco and whisky distribution) in the USA, which was also a strongly contested affair involving court action before success was achieved. The second was that of Riviera Hotels for £267m in 1981.

In July 1982, Goldstein resigned as Chairman, although he remained a director. A few months later in September 1983 Frederick Goldstein died.

International Leisure's style

International Leisure is managed on a decentralized divisional basis with emphasis placed on cash-flow and 'bottom line profits'. There is little corporate planning and the International Leisure Head Office consists predominantly of accountants and finance specialists, and acts more as a merchant bank than anything else. There is no interference in the operations of the divisions, as long as they achieve their required profits.

One of these divisions is Fortress and East Ham Brewers (FEHB), which was formed during the years after their takeover by International Leisure. During the 1970s, International Leisure was severely short of cash, and had an over-abundance of debt. In 1974, its total debt was £528m with shareholders' funds amounting to only £134m. Consequently, there was little cash for the modernization of plant and PHs that was needed.

One of the most attractive parts of FEHB was the managed house estate, and its attraction lay in the fact that it was a cash business with virtually no external debtors. FEHB's managed houses became Olde England Taverns Limited.

Olde England Taverns background

Olde England Taverns (OET) was set up in 1976 as a separate subsidiary of FEHB in order to operate the managed houses of most of the division. The reasons for setting up a separate company included:

1 The specialized nature of the managed houses which required a specialized management team, able to market and promote the houses as individual businesses.
2 Both line managers and pub managers could be trained and developed to establish a separate identity for OET as the foremost licensed trade retailer in the UK;
3 The retailing part of FEHB could be separated from the brewing part. It could also escape from East Ham's 'Swinging London' image, which was believed to have damaged FEHB. The 'Swinging London' promotion, launched in the late 1960s, was adopted by FEHB in an attempt to unify all the FEHB pubs in the public's mind.

In October 1976 OET consisted of 1313 houses, which were run by thirteen operating companies. Nearly half of the houses were in and around London, and so the Head Office (HO) of OET was situated there, with a small HO team. Each of the operating companies established its own regional HO.

By establishing thirteen new offices the administration costs of the new company were, it was known, going to be higher than those costs associated with the managed houses in the past. However this was deemed to be necessary if the management of the houses was to be efficient, and if the objectives for setting up OET were to be met.

Every OET operating company had a similar complement and structure. Each company had a director and general manager, a management accountant and an assistant, four district managers, a surveyor and about eight to twelve district assistants-cum-stocktakers. There were also a few secretaries and a pub promotion girl. Each company operated approximately 100 houses, subdivided into four districts each of which was managed by a district manager, who in turn had two district assistants reporting to him.

The director and general manager (D & GM) reported to an assistant managing director (AMD), of whom there were two, and these in turn reported to Tom Oliver. The board of directors therefore consisted of two AMDs, Finance Director, Personnel Director, Company Secretary, Managing Director and the Chairman.

The D & GM had almost total autonomy in terms of his staff and the house managers, their remuneration and perquisites. The board believed in decentralization and this policy was adhered to, such that there were few centrally generated rules. Salaries between managers in the same position, but in different companies, varied greatly, especially as a large part of the remuneration package was in the form of perquisites. These included company car (with extras), monthly personal expenses, accounts at company restaurants or pubs, free petrol, liquor, cigarettes, etc.

It could also include a free holiday as an incentive prize, such as a weekend in Paris or a luxury holiday in the Greek Islands or Jamaica. There were also a series of incentives for days at Ascot or Wimbledon or concerts for Frank Sinatra, Tony Bennett, etc.

Incentives were looked upon as a means to:

- Reward good management performances.
- Motivate other managers and staff.
- Bind line managers and pub managers together, through holidays etc. and thereby lowering conflict between them.
- Create a company identity, especially amongst the pub

managers, who generally had little company loyalty, moving on at short notice and at frequent intervals.

The company placed great emphasis on man-management and as a consequence many of the line-managers (i.e. D & GMs and DMs) were ex-services personnel. This also extended to the board, and the established culture set by it within OET was both militaristic and one which encouraged a 'macho' style of management. OET employed very few women in line management, and in 1983 there was only one woman DM.

One of the main reasons for this emphasis on man-management was the incidence of fraud by the pub managers. It is quite difficult, even with modern point of sale tills to establish exactly what a PH takes in sales. It is common practice for managers to 'buy-in', i.e. to purchase their own beer, spirits and food and sell it to the customers, keeping the money for themselves.

The DMs task is therefore, to establish what a PH should be taking in sales and then to persuade, cajole or threaten the manager to give that amount to the company. This negotiation process requires strong personalities on the company side, if it is to achieve some success in recouping its money. It is impossible to estimate exactly how much 'shortages' are worth, but a conservative estimate would be about 5 per cent of bar sales, which in 1981–2 would have been worth £10m.

The fraud is institutionalized and maintained:

1 Because the company does not usually prosecute when managers are found to be defrauding the company.
2 Because there is usually little difficulty in discredited managers finding another job. Due to the shortage of experienced managers, it is not unusual for one OET company to hire a manager recently sacked by another OET company.
3 Because managers' salaries are kept low. Salaries in London are £9–12,000 p.a. on average, (this amount includes the managers' wives' salaries).

Both line and pub-managers tend to move within the company fairly regularly, a process that the company encourages in order to keep motivation and interest in the job high. In fact, OET had undergone a series of changes, both because of internal reorganizations and because of incorporation of the remaining Fortress and Albany estates.

The reorganizations were undertaken in 1978, 1980 and then in January 1983. One of the reasons for these was to promote some managers without appearing to penalize others.

The reorganizations

Having only been set up in 1976, the OET board decided to reorganize the company in 1978. The objectives, stated in the Corporate Plan 1979–81, were to achieve:

1 Shorter lines of communication.
2 More effective operational decision-making.
3 Increased responsibility for pub and district management and, therefore, improved quality of personnel.

The assistant district manager-cum-stocktaker role was split up in an attempt to motivate the more able ADMs without seeming to discriminate against the rest, who were made stocktakers but kept on the same grade. One OET London company was disbanded, and another in Brighton set-up and the PHs involved were transferred to and from other OET companies. Hundreds of PHs were interchanged, increasing some companies and decreasing others. In this way, the opportunity was created to promote some D & GMs and DMs without appearing to demote others.

Some of the board members were retitled, although their duties remained the same.

The main administrative problem caused by the reorganization was that it took place at the start of the OET financial year, and consequently the annual plans for the PHs involved were later disowned by the D & GMs. They argued that they had not set the plans themselves and so should not be expected to take responsibility for them.

Also, the length of time needed by the line management to get to know the PHs and their managers meant that it took some months before they were able to make effective decisions about their new PHs.

In 1980 OET undertook another major PH reshuffle, this time also incorporating the remaining Fortress managed estate of nearly 300 houses, and then, a few months later, the fifty Albany managed houses.

Two new AMDs were internally recruited and OET was divided into four regions, each with an AMD who was responsible for four operating companies. Two new divisional HOs were established and a small number of staff hired. The four AMDs also took responsibility for newly set-up OET HO functional committees, which were to coordinate marketing, training, etc. to meet the needs of the 'grass roots' of the company.

At the time of both reorganizations new D & GMs and DMs were recruited (most internally) and some older ones were retired. However, it was not OET practice to fire mediocre line managers even though some operating companies and districts consistently underperformed.

As well as the problems caused by the house transfers to the budgeting and reporting system, there were also difficulties caused by the fifteen limited companies which now made up OET, each of which had a separate legal identity and administration centre.

Although each of them were wholly owned subsidiaries, the transfer of assets etc. created much additional work for the companies' accountants. Much of their time was taken up with the administrative details of the transfers. This encouraged the accountants to 'politicize' their work by, for example, loading expenses on to those PHs to be transferred or by adjusting the annual plans to their advantage.

This created many disagreements but the accountants were encouraged to be proficient at such tactics, and were rewarded by their D & GMs for any success they had with them.

In the latter part of 1982 plans for another reorganization were being assembled, and expected to be implemented in early 1983.

The financial costs of the reorganizations are illustrated, to some extent, by the growth in the administrative costs, which grew from £4.4m in 1977 to £14.3m in 1982. What are not quantifiable, however, are the 'disruption costs' caused by the reorganizations in terms of reduced profits due to such matters as learning time needed by line management to get to know their new PHs.

Finance

The balance sheets and operating statements (OPST) for years 1977 to 1982 are given in Appendices 9 and 10. The Fortress and Albany estates are included in the results for 1980 and 1981 respectively, and thereafter. In 1980 there was a revaluation of the assets, which added about £90m to the balance sheet.

The notable item in the OPST is the very rapid rise of machine income (MI) from £3.8m to £16.0m in the six years to 1982. This source of profit represented 73 per cent of PBI in 1982. Much of the growth in MI has been due to the 'video boom' of the early 1980s, a market which has now begun to decline.

The largest proportion of MI is generated by AWPs (amusement with prizes machines) i.e. fruit machines. One of the advantages that licensed clubs have over PHs, is that PHs can only offer maximum prizes of £3.00 per machine, whereas the clubs are not restricted.

To counter this reliance on machine income OET attempted to

redevelop their PHs in such a way that they attracted customers other than by video machines and AWPs. It entered several agreements with regional brewers to sell their beer in OET PHs, with the brewers often agreeing to contribute loans to OET for the redevelopment of the PHs concerned.

The main intentions behind OETs investment policy in PHs were:

1 To bring the estate up to certain minimum standards, for example toilet facilities;
2 To redevelop PHs in order to alter their character and attract a different clientele, with greater emphasis on catering operations;
3 To acquire or build new PHs. Some of the acquisitions were leasehold properties owned by regional brewers, with OET agreeing to manage the PH, often after improving it with OET's own cash. The original beer portfolios were maintained in these cases, and even when the PHs were freehold or built by OET, there was generally some 'foreign' beer available in the PHs. (Foreign beer being non-East Ham products.)

Total capital investment since 1978 is given below together with the spends on repairs:

Table 15

	1978	1979	1980	1981	1982
Capital spent (£m)	7.0	10.4	13.9	17.6	19.8
Repairs (£m)	3.3	3.8	6.0	6.5	7.1

Of all the projects undertaken by OET during this time the most adventurous and ambitious were two catering concepts.

OET new catering concepts

In 1978 OET launched two new food operations, the first was called Merlin's, which was to sell hamburgers, fish and chicken meals. The fast food expertise was obtained through a franchise agreement with Tasty Burgers Corp of the US, although the image was developed for the UK by OET.

In charge of the Merlin's experiment was an ex-Army officer who had been D & GM of an OET company managing the banqueting suites and catering operations at the Lord's and Oval cricket grounds. Both he and other OET personnel involved in the new company undertook several weeks training in the US.

By 1982, Merlin's had acquired an additional five sites with the purchase of Nelson hamburger sites in Central London bringing the total number up to ten. Total losses to 1982 were £1m and capital investment was £6m.

The second concept was called Pickwicks, which was intended to be a chain of carveries. It was an attempt to repeat the success of the Wine 'n' Dine steak-bars in the 1970s, by aiming for the same family market with an emphasis on 'value for money'. The company ceased trading in 1982, and the three sites which constituted the chain at that time were returned to other OET companies to be incorporated back into the PH estate. Total losses were £0.6m and total investment had been £1.4m.

During 1982 both concepts were revamped. Merlin's acquired a totally new management team, which had experience in fast food and which put forward an aggressive, expansive corporate plan. Pickwicks was relaunched, but not as a separate company. Together with the original three sites, another ten pub-restaurants within the OET companies took on the Pickwick name, image, etc. and changed their menus in line with the carvery operation.

OET investment planning

Despite the often optimistic and ambitious plans of OET investment projects, many proved to be less successful than predicted by the line management. This was especially true for the larger projects i.e. over £250,000. Perhaps a main reason for this was the inexperience and lack of training for the line management in the planning and execution of building projects. The company employed architects and quantity surveyors, but these were usually brought in after the capital budgeting process had finished. Consequently the average overspend for the larger projects was 13 per cent against budget, and this made the eventual returns lower than planned. Also, much of the capital budgeting was done 'bottom-up', i.e. the profit was established on the basis of what was necessary to achieve a 20 per cent return on capital. This rate proved to be too optimistic in most cases.

Of the £97m spent by OET in the five years to 1982 about £65m was on acquisitions and/or developments. The increase in profits was from £14.4m to £22.0m, but during this period OET did take on both the additional Fortress and the Albany estates, and therefore the effect of this investment would appear to have been minimal.

Summary

During the period 1977 to 1982 OET was managed in a very decentralized manner, allowing maximum freedom to line management. In order to give opportunities to the more able, OET underwent two major reorganizations altering its management structure and the composition of the PHs within the operating companies.

At the same time, International Leisure allowed OET to reinvest most of its profits in developing its PHs and expanding its interests into other areas such as the fast food industry. However OET's profits did not increase as planned, because many of the investment projects proved to be less successful than predicted.

January 1983

After three months of speculation and rumour, a major reorganization within International Leisure removed Oliver from the Managing Directorship of OET. Initially he was given a new division of International Leisure with a turnover of £30m, but within three months he had resigned in order to take up a senior position with one of the other 'big six' British brewers.

Questions

1 What are the key issues associated with the management of decentralized profit centres in International Leisure?
2 What are the skills required to function effectively in decentralized profit centres in International Leisure?

Appendix 9 Olde England Taverns balance sheets 1977–82 (£m)

	1977	1978	1979	1980	1981	1982
Sources of finance						
Share capital and reserves	70.4	72.2	76.2	174.3	193.9	197.8
Deferred tax	5.2	6.9	9.5	12.1	0.4	(0.3)
Tax	2.3	4.7	4.4	10.4	4.1	6.9
Loans	—	—	—	0.1	0.1	0.1
	77.9	83.8	90.1	196.9	198.5	204.5
Invested in						
Fixed assets	90.0	95.7	102.1	208.3	264.1	286.2
Long-term loans	—	—	—	—	—	—
Goodwill	0.4	0.4	0.4	—	—	—
	90.4	96.1	102.5	208.3	264.1	286.2
Current assets						
Stocks	6.6	7.5	8.2	7.3	9.3	11.4
Debtors	1.1	1.5	2.0	2.5	3.4	4.0
Inter-group	—	—	1.7	9.1	11.8	14.9
Cash	9.8	6.0	5.2	3.5	3.5	—
	17.5	15.0	17.1	22.4	28.0	30.3
Less current liabilities						
Creditors	9.3	13.3	20.3	22.0	27.4	18.7
Inter-group	12.9	4.3	—	5.8	52.5	66.7
Current tax	5.1	5.2	5.8	2.5	9.8	8.2
Proposed dividend	2.7	4.5	3.4	3.5	3.9	8.4
Overdraft	—	—	—	—	—	10.0
	30.0	27.3	29.5	33.8	93.6	112.0
	77.9	83.8	90.1	196.9	198.5	204.5

Note: Fortress included from 1980 and thereafter. Albany included from 1981 and thereafter. Revaluation in 1980 of approximately £90m.

Appendix 10 Olde England Taverns operating tables 1977–82 (£m)

	1977	1978	1979	1980	1981	1982
Sales						
Bar	100.6	114.3	127.2	169.4	182.9	202.6
Food	11.6	14.1	16.4	21.1	26.1	28.5
Other	1.0	1.1	1.3	1.5	1.5	1.5
Total	113.2	129.5	144.9	192.0	210.5	232.6
Gross profit	46.2	53.8	62.6	88.0	96.9	106.7
Wages	13.1	15.2	18.7	27.1	29.1	31.2
Expenses						
Controllable	8.3	9.5	11.0	15.8	17.9	19.7
Fixed	10.7	11.6	13.7	20.3	25.4	28.4
Other	5.1	6.4	7.8	11.6	13.8	15.2
Total	24.1	27.5	32.5	47.7	57.1	63.3
Income						
Machine	3.8	5.7	7.8	11.8	14.9	16.0
Other	4.0	4.6	5.2	6.1	6.8	8.1
Total	7.8	10.3	13.0	17.9	21.7	24.1
HO costs	5.5	7.0	8.3	10.7	13.8	14.3
PBI	11.3	14.4	16.1	20.4	18.6	22.0
Number of public houses	1285	1297	1280	1571	1569	1580

Note: Fortress and Albany estates included from 1980 and 1981 respectively.

SEVENTEEN

The Epicurus Leisure Group

SHAUN TYSON

The case is set in 1982 when the Epicurus Leisure Group, a large British-owned group, seemed to be at the peak of its success. The group employed 9000 people throughout the leisure and entertainment industries, including catering, leisure, and sports centres, bingo halls and a company which rented television receivers to over one million subscribers. As a group, its main period of growth had been from the mid-1960s to the late 1970s. The growth had slowed down between 1977 and 1982, when there had been no significant acquisitions. During this time, the group had come to rely on the television rental company for 60 per cent of its turnover.

Epicurus Rentals Limited

The main concern of the case is the television rental company, Epicurus Rentals Limited. The business in 1981 was simple, it started with the rental of TV sets when TV was a new phenomenon, and grew on the backs of successive technical and broadcasting innovations (ITV, BBC 2, colour TV, etc.). The original marketing idea proved durable up to 1981. By first selling the idea of cheap viewing and overcoming fears of unreliability by ensuring quick, competent service, with replacement sets wherever the need arose, customers were encouraged to rent. There were a number of reasons why people rented sets rather than purchased them:

1 The periodic advent of new developments encouraged customers to rent so they could have the latest set.
2 High cost of TV sets when first produced helped form the renting habit, especially among low wage earners.
3 Given the low value of second-hand TV sets, customers were not interested in purchasing new receivers.

4 The 'drug' effect of TV – customers wanted assurance that they would never be without a TV receiver, even if there was a breakdown.
5 The product was seen as being technically 'sophisticated' – customers felt the need for advice, support over problems of reception/TV aerials, etc. which they received from the continuing relationship with a rental company.
6 Government regulations on hire purchase made rental as attractive as purchase.

The rental business was highly competitive. In addition to the 'giants' many small retailers were also able to carve out a local corner of the market, but the advantage had stayed with the big battalions until recently.

In addition to rental, the major development was the home video recorder. The company forecast a large growth in demand for the rental of these and for video tapes, and made plans to exploit this. Among the marketing ideas being discussed at the time were the rental and servicing of home computers, and the rental of video films.

This company was represented throughout the UK with a network of 480 showrooms (mostly small, but on prime sites), 200 servicing depots and a total staff of 5000 people. The turnover in 1981 was £113 million p.a.

Company organization and people

1 The organization chart was as given in Appendix 1. The company was reorganized into this form two years ago. The Chairman of Epicurus Rentals was the Chairman of the Epicurus Group, and the Managing Director of the rental company was a member of the group's board.
2 Staff numbers and the labour turnover were as shown in Table 1:

The technicians' jobs included the servicing of TV receivers, calling on customers to deal with technical complaints, helping in the installation of video equipment etc. Apart from about 150 apprentices all were trained to repair colour TV equipment. A small number had already been retrained to service home computers; and another group to service/repair video recorders.

Receptionists were based in the showrooms. Their work was to collect payment from customers, to sell the service to potential customers and to prepare the rental agreements.

Table 1 *Epicurus Rentals, staff numbers and turnover*

	Staff numbers	*Labour % turnover p.a.*
Technicians (almost all male)	1935	10
Receptionists (almost all female)	506	20
Representatives	840	30
Showroom managers	450	18
District/regional management staff and senior technical staff	200	5
Cleaners (mainly part–time, female)	440	8
Drivers	100	10
Stores assistants/warehouse staff	130	10
HO staff	400	13
	5001	

Showroom managers were shop managers although they only had one receptionist working for them in some cases.

Representatives called on customers and potential customers in their homes, in order to sign agreements; they also installed and repossessed equipment, and collected bad debts.

Industrial relations

85 per cent of the technicians were members of the EPTU and 49 per cent of the remaining staff were members of other unions.

The relationships with management were very good. There were formal procedures for disputes, grievances and discipline to which both management and unions were committed.

There was one strike over pay about ten years ago, but since then the technicians in particular were satisfied with their pay and conditions. There was an annual pay award, negotiated to take effect on 1st July each year.

There were common conditions of service across the Epicurus Group for pensions, life assurance and senior management conditions.

The corporate plan, as at August 1981 for Epicurus Rentals Limited

The corporate plan proposed that the Company would remain and develop within the home entertainment field – TV, video, video games, cassettes rental; and would simultaneously develop the renting and servicing of home computers.

The company forecast that changes in the marketing environment such as greater reliability and easier servicing of the later models would gradually make inroads into the subscriber list, as more and more people decided to purchase television receivers, rather than to rent them.

The proposed net profit figure in the five year plan were as follows:

Table 2 *Net profit forecast*

1981–2	1982–3	1983–4	1984–5	1986–7
£25m	£20m	£18m	£24m	£47m

These forecasts were founded on the assumption that the rental of TVs would fall steadily until 1983–4, even with the marketing initiatives (e.g. capturing more of the contract rental market in hotels, encouraging rental of second TVs etc.), but that there would be a steady increase in the rental of video equipment to take up the shortfall. The figures also represented a modest growth in the field of home computers but assumed that they would remain a minor contributor for the next five years.

The 'new reality' of 1982

Due to a number of factors, the outcome was rather different from the plan. At the normal profit forecast at the end of first quarter of 1982 a number of disturbing factors were noted:

1 The trend towards owning rather than renting had accelerated.
2 The recession had forced more terminations of rental agreements in areas of high unemployment.
3 The video 'boom' in rental was projected at a time when supplies were difficult, and demand was growing. Demand had not increased as projected, and a number of Japanese manufacturers had started dumping cheaper videos on the market, thus encouraging purchase.
4 Costs had been rising sharply, for example the rates on premises, staff costs and distribution costs.

As a result, the projection for 1982–3 was now zero net profit.

Question

1 Take the role of Epicurus Rentals Limited's board of directors and consider what alternatives there are (e.g. new products, new initiatives) and the implications for the human resources of the company in each case. In particular you should undertake to examine these questions:

    (a) Look at the possible impact of the human resource strengths/weaknesses on the alternatives considered above.

    (b) What personnel policy outcomes should derive from these changes in corporate plan?

Appendix 1   Epicurus Rentals Limited organization chart

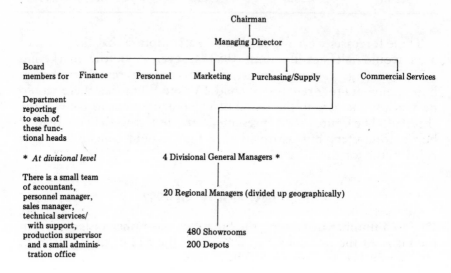

PART THREE

Personnel Planning and Systems

The case studies contained in this section are concerned with how to turn corporate plans and management strategies into actions. They are about policies and systems which will make strategic changes of direction actually happen, and as such they describe situations where the original plan ran into difficulties, they show that often there are a number of policy options available, and they indicate with varying degrees of detail what those options actually are. In the following cases it is possible to see how the interventions of personnel specialists or consultants can influence the options available. The cases cover all the main personnel management areas: manpower planning, reward structures, training and management development, recruitment and selection, as well as the personnel role.

The Pallas Electronics case focuses on manpower planning in a situation where the original plan has not been achieved. Appropriately, as the first case in the section, this case study underlines the need to see the interrelationships between the different personnel policy areas.

Archon Engineering looks at the problems of establishing a personnel role in an organization at a time of rapid change. While allowing the reader to address the organization structure issues of establishing a new role, the case also highlights the ambiguity so often associated with personnel specialists, who often experience a disjunction between power and authority.

Lysander Products puts the reader in the position of a new personnel manager, being asked to help create a new reward structure in a company where most personnel systems have fallen into disuse.

For the old established firm of *Thomas Nestor* there is a more favourable climate for the personnel specialist's intervention. However, this is a crucial time for decisions to be made about the company's future management development policies.

The *Recruitment Case* illustrates the significance of recruitment policy and provides an opportunity to explore a range of questions which must be addressed when undertaking personnel selection.

EIGHTEEN

Pallas Electronics

JOHN BERESFORD AND SHAUN TYSON

Pallas Electronics was a manufacturer of electronic equipment for the telecommunications industry. Components were manufactured and assembled at five large factories in the UK. The company was organized in a traditional way, with a large production function, research and development, marketing, and finance departments (see Appendix 1).

Attention is focused on the Bristol factory of Pallas. Each factory was run by a small team, which included the personnel manager, production control, transport manager and accountant. The organization chart is given in Appendix 2.

The factory had been established for three years, and in addition to the supervisory staff, employed 200 female operatives.

The national marketing manager was able to negotiate a substantial order, which could only be met by a large increase in production. All the factory managers were called in to discuss how this could be achieved, and it was agreed that the Bristol factory would play an important part in the achievement of increased production, since there was room for expansion on the site and a good supply of labour was available.

The decision was made to build up the labour force to 300 operatives. Production was to be maximized as soon as possible, so the recruitment plan was an intake of 100 new operatives over the next six months. The plan, and its expected results are shown in Table 1.

The labour turnover was around 20 per cent per annum, and was expected to increase during the build up of labour. The utilization of labour at 40 per cent was rather low at the outset, compared with the four other factories, where some of the older established plants achieved 75 per cent utilization. During the first six months layout improvements were prepared, together with altered production

Table 1 *Six month recruitment plan and expected results*

Month	Planned recruits	Expected numbers	Expected utilization
0		200	40
1	25	221	43
2	25	240	46
3	25	259	50
4	25	277	54
5	15	290	57
6	12	300	60

methods, and a new pay and productivity incentive scheme was introduced. These changes were expected to improve utilization to 60 per cent at the end of six months, and to over 70 per cent by the end of twelve months. The term 'utilization' is used here as a rough measure of productivity – the number of units actually produced compared with the expert view of production management of the capacity of the factory for any given number of workers.

At the end of the six month period, the position was as shown in Table 2.

Table 2

Month	Recruits	Actual numbers	Utilization %	Units of output expected	achieved
1	25	216	40.3	950	870
2	25	231	42.0	1100	970
3	25	245	45.3	1300	1110
4	25	258	48.9	1500	1260
5	15	261	51.0	1680	1330
6	12	263	52.3	1800	1380

The recruits had been engaged as planned, and the quality of the applicants was good. They seemed to be attracted to the pay and the working conditions were good for the area. However, both the build up of numbers, and the utilization of the factory fell seriously below target. Converted into output units, the running rate at the sixth month was seriously below target and there was considerable management concern at a senior level. A running rate of 2100 units of output per month had been expected by the end of a year, and the order intake to the company and thus to the Bristol factory depended on a good delivery performance. Production could not easily be switched to the other factories without disrupting their operations. Cumulative output was already so much in arrears that a month of output needed to be recovered as soon as possible, therefore making the problem worse over the next six months.

There was some concern about the ability of the training department to cope with a larger intake of people. The personnel department was under strong criticism in general, and various, excessively high, turnover rates were being quoted, some of the estimates being in excess of 40 per cent. The board gave a directive to the Bristol factory management team to produce a report on what had happened, and an action plan which should show how and when the optimum labour force of 300 would be reached.

Questions

1 You are in the position of the factory management team. Now that the first six months has passed, comment on the original plan in the light of the results, explaining in your answer the likely reasons for the variation between the planned and the actual results.
2 Produce a plan and a monitoring procedure for the next six months.

Appendix 1 Pallas Electronics organization chart

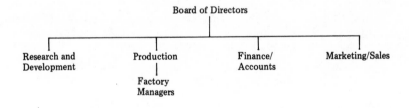

Appendix 2   Bristol factory organization chart

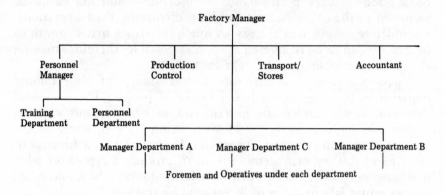

NINETEEN

Archon Engineering

SHAUN TYSON

Background

Archon Engineering was founded in the mid-1930s as an engineering company which manufactured a range of small components used in the automotive and aircraft industries. The Second World War saw a diversification of the company's activities, and after the war the company expanded to take over a number of smaller businesses in the fields of chemical and consumer products, valve manufacture and pipe manufacture.

The general style of management had been paternalistic. The original entrepreneur who had formed the company, Arthur Cohen (hence the 'Archon' name) had been succeeded by one of his sons, and his other son was also on the board. For many years the Archon Group had been based in a suburb west of London. The Head Office was in the converted old house of the founder, and the close proximity of the rest of the companies in the group strengthened the paternalistic style. However, growth and diversification brought formality into relationships. The need to expand their capital base had resulted in the group becoming a public company in the early 1950s.

As the 1960s drew to a close, Archon was changing its style and organization structure dramatically. This case history concerns the events and the people who were involved in this period of growth and change. There was a growing requirement for more capital in 1969, which resulted in the group floating a rights issue. In order to impress the City of London, Sir Horace Scott was appointed Chairman of the Archon board. Sir Horace had many friends in the city and was already a non-executive director of several well known companies. He had been seen as an ideal figurehead, aged in his late fifties, it was thought his presence would add 'weight' to the board, without upsetting the balance of power. In practice, he was much more vigorous than expected. By a series of deft political man-oeuvres over a period of a year he was able to bring in several of his friends as directors. As a consequence of one year's bad results he was able to exploit differences among the members of the board, so that the Managing Director, John Cohen, 'retired' with a handsome settlement.

The Archon Group in 1971

By 1971, when this case is set, the group employed around 4000 people, had a turnover of £500m created from about twenty small companies in the UK and abroad. Sir Horace and his board decided that a more formal, professional and consciously organized approach was necessary. The decision was made to 'divisionalize' the group into four divisions, and to give greater autonomy to the Divisional General Managers, who were directors of the Group, and who would be accountable to the Board as a whole for the profitability of their divisions. The new organization structure is given in Appendix 1.

The divisional structure

Each division of the group employed a management team which acted as the functional specialists for the operating companies. There were divisional marketing, finance and personnel managers, whose role was to provide expert advice to the operating company Managing Directors, and to produce a divisional strategy for acceptance at group level. Apart from the directors, at Head Office, there were only administrative departments covering for example the group pension scheme, and a secretariat which dealt with legal and insurance matters for the group. When the divisional strategy was formulated, therefore, it was the directors who evaluated the plans put forward.

The consumer products division

The consumer products division consisted of three companies: each operating company had its own products, style and traditions. The products were paints and chemicals, domestic products (window furnishings, blinds etc.) and radiators. The divisional general manager of the consumer products division was Alexander

Robertson, one of the new directors brought in by Sir Horace. The divisional personnel manager was Neil Jones who was regarded as the most professional personnel manager in the group, where he had been the personnel manager in the engineering company. Personnel departments were well established in the radiator company, which was fully unionized with a closed shop, and in the paint company, an old established company dating back to the eighteenth century which the group bought in 1958. The other two companies merely kept personnel records and left all personnel decisions to line managers, and ultimately to their Managing Directors.

The organization structure of the consumer products division is given in Appendix 2.

The division employed 1200 people in small factories and offices throughout the UK. The total divisional turnover was £30m.

When the new structure was announced, it was made clear that personnel managers reported to their operating company Managing Directors, but had a 'dotted line' functional relationship with the divisional personnel manager. The divisional offices were located on the largest site in the division where the paint company's manufacturing facilities were.

The divisional personnel manager's position

The divisional personnel manager arranged to meet Robertson when taking up his appointment. Jones was keen to discover how he should perform this new role.

The interview with Robertson

Robertson had a strong view of the personnel role. Putting his views simply, Robertson viewed the personnel function as an arm of his own policy. In particular, he wanted to rid the division of a number of managers whom he disliked; he regarded them as 'useless', unable to cope with new conditions and not sufficiently in tune with his divisional philosophy.

Among the specific proposals discussed was Robertson's opinion that all the companies in the division should offer the same conditions of service. These, he felt, should be based on those pertaining in the paint company. Jones said he would investigate but managed to avoid committing himself. Robertson was prepared to appoint further executives to the divisional personnel function, but there was a strong feeling in the meeting that Robertson did not want to build a personnel function on a separate power base from his own.

He wished to take all the major decisions on personnel, and to see the personnel department as a source of data for him about people in the division.

Neil Jones reflected on his meeting. He decided to discover what the Managing Directors of the operating companies thought before setting out his own position on the role of personnel specialists within the division.

Interview with the paint company's Managing Director

Geoff Wayne was the Managing Director of the paint and chemical company. Employing 600 people, a substantial number of whom were hourly rated, the paint company faced more problems than Wayne was prepared to admit at first. The paint company was desperately in need of new products and of a marketing image which would distinguish the brands of colour paints from other manufacturers. The factory was as old as the company, and there were many breakdowns due to the old machinery. Wayne regarded his managers as loyal and hardworking, but untrained. The Personnel Department consisted of an ageing ex-naval officer who spent most of his time on recruitment, and attending to the personnel records, and a welfare officer who also had responsibility for the canteen. Industrial relations was handled by line management who negotiated with the Transport and General Workers Union, and the General and Municipal Union who represented most of the hourly rated personnel. There was a strong rumour that ASTMS were recruiting among the supervisors, and managers, many of whom expressed their dissatisfaction with their pay and conditions. There were no fixed pay scales for management, and salary administration was rudimentary.

By contrast, the separate chemical plant which manufactured degreasers and chemical cleaning fluids only employed around thirty people, most of whom were in sales. This was a highly profitable plant with modern automated equipment and was often held up by Wayne as an example of how the paint company should operate.

Interview with the consumer products company's Managing Director

This company employed around 400 people and was regarded by its Danish Managing Director, Per Nielson, as a part of the 'home fashion' industry. He could see no logic in associating it with the other companies in the division. Indeed he was openly hostile to Jones, whom he saw as Robertson's stooge.

Although the company only had a small financial turnover it was highly profitable, with a record of steady growth and reliability in performance. The managers who worked there were loyal to the consumer company, rather than to Archon. There was no trade union membership, and no Personnel Department. Personnel records were kept by the chief accountant who made whatever personnel decisions were necessary in conjunction with Per Nielson. The majority of the employees were female, and worked in small factories spread all over the UK on subassembly work. Most employees were only trained to a semiskilled level, and there was a growing trend towards the employment of part-time staff and subcontract when orders justified this, instead of extra permanent employees.

Interview with the radiator company's Managing Director

This company employed around 200 people, mostly male. Manufacturing was in a West Country factory which was highly mechanized. All employees were trade union members, except the senior management group, and a post entry closed shop was operated by the AUEW. The Managing Director, Arthur Wilson, was a gloomy individual – he was aware his company was making losses, but considered this to be the fault of an incorrect pricing policy imposed by Archon. He was complacent about his own organization, and pointed to the small numbers employed already when questioned about the efficiency of his operation.

There was a small Personnel Department. The personnel officer was largely concerned with the maintenance of existing agreements with the unions, and leant heavily upon the Engineering Employers Federation for advice. Conditions of service and pay were well above the minimum, however, and there were some especially generous sick pay and holiday benefits. Jones, impressions when he left were of a cosy atmosphere, where the greatest sin was to suggest change.

Jones had promised he would go back and talk with Robertson about the role personnel should play.

Questions

1 From the perspective of Jones, how do you believe the role of the personnel function should be structured at divisional level?
2 What priorities would you suggest to Robertson?

Appendix 1 Archon Group organization chart

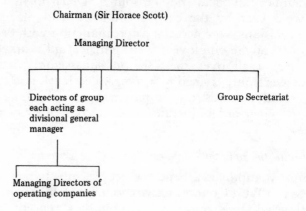

Appendix 2 Consumer products division organization chart

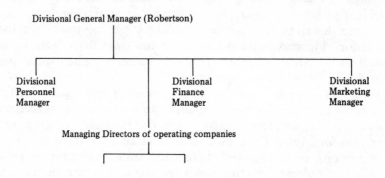

TWENTY

Lysander Products

SHAUN TYSON

Background

This case is set in 1982. It concentrates on the problems of job evaluation and salary administration in a company where the personnel systems had fallen into disuse. Lysander Products was the UK subsidiary of Lysander Incorporated, a multinational pharmaceutical company, with manufacturing plants in Europe, Africa, Australasia and in Canada, where its Head Office was located. The UK company was part of the European Division and European Headquarters were in Geneva. The general manager for the UK was a member of the European division board, and was accountable for the profitability of the UK company, within the European corporate plan.

A new general manager had recently been appointed to the UK from the French company, with a brief to improve the profitability of the UK company, to slim down its operations and to enliven its marketing effort.

Lysander had been trading on the reputation it had gained for forty years from the success of a pain-reliever, which had been a market leader, but which was now showing signs of a downturn in its life cycle as a product.

There had been attempts to improve the product range in prescribed drugs (ethical pharmaceuticals), where there was an active research base. However, it was mainly in the 'over the counter' products that most of the growth had come (for example indigestion tablets, throat lozenges etc.). Some new product ideas had failed miserably – notably a special chewing gum, and a brand of boiled sweets. There was anticipated to be a growth of only 1–2 per cent in sales turnover in the three years from 1982 to 1985.

Location and organization

The UK company had its offices and factory on one site 25 miles west of London. The organization's charts which follow (see Appendices 3–9) show the detailed structure. The research centre was about 3 miles away, and there were several small distribution depots throughout the UK. There were about 160 managers employed, together with approximately 300 clerical and other monthly staff and 900 hourly rated personnel. The hourly rated personnel were mostly members of trade unions. There were thought to be around 20 per cent of managerial and other monthly staff with membership of ASTMS.

Personnel Department

During 1982 a new personnel manager was appointed. He was a thirty-two-year-old recently graduated MBA, with three years experience of personnel. The new French general manager appointed him from a well known British business school. He found himself facing a number of run down 'systems' with rather a weak Personnel Department to support him (weak in skills and weak in positive ideas). There were three separate grading systems for each of the groupings mentioned above (managerial, monthly/clerical and hourly rated). There were a number of problems with the managerial group.

Problem areas

1 In the past managers had been appointed outside the salary bands. The reasons had long since been forgotten but the consequences were that anomalies had arisen, and this was a source of constant grumbles.
2 Managers complained that there was no incentive because increments were arbitrary, not based on understood criteria, or within scales that were realistic.
3 A number of managers (the younger ones) were threatening to leave because they said they were underpaid.
4 According to some senior managers, there were a number of managers who were overpaid.
5 There was constant pressure from 'Grade F' managers for regrading to 'E' where they would automatically receive a company car.

6 No one seemed to understand the current grading scheme – it had lost face validity. Some higher grade managers were reporting to managers of equivalent grades, for example, due to reorganizations which had taken place.

The job evaluation scheme

The existing job evaluation scheme was of a type known as a 'classification' or grading system. It was an 'in-house' scheme, which required the examination of jobs in the light of predetermined definitions of grades, where the level of work was described in terms of responsibility. New jobs were compared with the predefined grade description to indicate the placing of the job in a relationship with other graded jobs.

The grade of managers in 1982 is shown in brackets on the organization charts, and a list of grade definitions is attached.

Salary administration

There was no salary administration guide, but there were written rules concerning the benefits which applied at each grade. The actual salary scales were not published, however, although the grade definitions were. Pay for all grades (monthly and hourly rates) were reviewed every 1st July when new salary brackets were agreed by the UK company, board and for the grades B and above by the European division. Managers could make recommendations for increments, at the time of the review. Strictly according to the rules, these increments were supposed to be within the scale, however, there were many occasions when due to pressure from managers threatening to leave, increments beyond the grade scale had been granted.

Actions required

The personnel manager examined the existing salaries by grade (see Appendix 2), and discussed the problems with the general manager. His response was that he wanted the problems solved quickly, within the next six months (i.e., before the next pay review), but he was anxious not to raise expectations for more money at the review. He was proposing only a modest rise (possibly even zero for some people!). The general manager indicated his intention to reduce the number of people employed by Lysander Products over the next two years, as part of his drive for greater efficiency. He asked the personnel manager to try and include in his plan for salary administration provision for a reduced head count. The personnel manager took this to mean that there would be some flexibility in the salary budget, but also realized that the existing jobs would be changing. In the past, a number of 'one-off' attempts had been made to improve the job evaluation scheme, without long-term success. The time and effort management had expended on these had led to a degree of scepticism about job evaluation, which may be one of the reasons the old scheme fell into disuse, and the problems abounded.

Question

1 What actions should the new personnel manager take, and what should he recommend to the general manager and the UK board?

Appendix 1   Grade definitions

Grade A Chief Executive of the major units in the group.

Grade B Those people reporting to the Chief Executive, who have a corporate responsibility beyond the function of which they are head. In common with the Chief Executive they are responsible for planning the corporate growth and policy of the unit.

Grade C Those people who do not report directly to the Chief Executive but who head up a function or a large, significant subfunction. They may *advise* on policy formation.

Grade D These people will report to those in Grade B or C; they will head up a subfunction and/or possess specialized knowledge and expertise. They may be specialists (e.g., sales manager) or generalists (e.g., general manager). They will have clear responsibilities for the implementation of policy at the operational level, and may advise on policy formation also.

Grade E This is the bottom level of manager who is expected to be accountable for improving the profitability of the company. They will either be budget controllers, managing others who may also be budget controllers, or top specialists, where the emphasis is on individual contribution rather than the control of others. They will be closely involved in the day-to-day running of a division or function.

Grade F This is the most senior level of manager whose job it is to manage a department or unit without necessarily being regarded as accountable for taking profit-effective initiatives. This level of supporting management may include specialists as well as managers with some years of experience and/or seniority.

Grade G Junior managers and senior supervisors: in the former case they will be starting up the management ladder, in the latter they will be experienced, senior or less able than those in Grade F. This grade also includes the secretary to the Chief Executive. All are engaged in *supportive* roles.

Grade H Supervisors and others whose responsibilities place them in this lowest management grade. They may or may not have responsibility for others. Secretaries working full-time for those who report to the Chief Executive are on this grade also.

Appendix 2   Existing salaries by grade

Grades	Number in post	Average salary	Comparative ratio	Minimum/ maximum of range of scale	Actual range of salaries paid
B	2	£21,000	93.6	£17,825–27,000	£20,000–22,000
C	9	£18,017	106.6	£13,900–19,875	£15,000–25,000
D	10	£13,470	98.5	£11,200–16,150	£10,500–16,000
E	27	£10,527	91.5	£9,325–13,675	£9,000–14,500
F	28	£9,523	98.6	£8,100–11,200	£7,300–13,700
G	45	£7,724	97.3	£6,550– 9,315	£6,300– 9,600
H	34	£5,814	93.5	£4,975– 7,450	£4,700– 7,500

Appendix 3

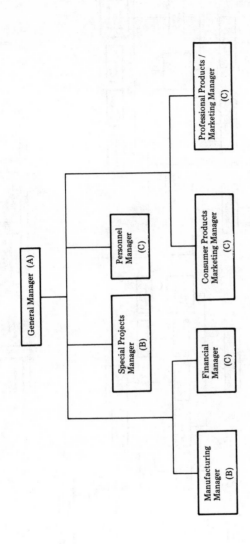

```
                    General Manager (A)
                           |
        ┌──────────────────┼──────────────────┐
        |                   |                  |
  Special Projects      Personnel      Professional Products /
     Manager            Manager         Marketing Manager
       (B)                (C)                  (C)
        |
   ┌────┴────┐
   |         |
Manufacturing  Financial      Consumer Products
  Manager      Manager        Marketing Manager
    (B)          (C)                (C)
```

Appendix 4

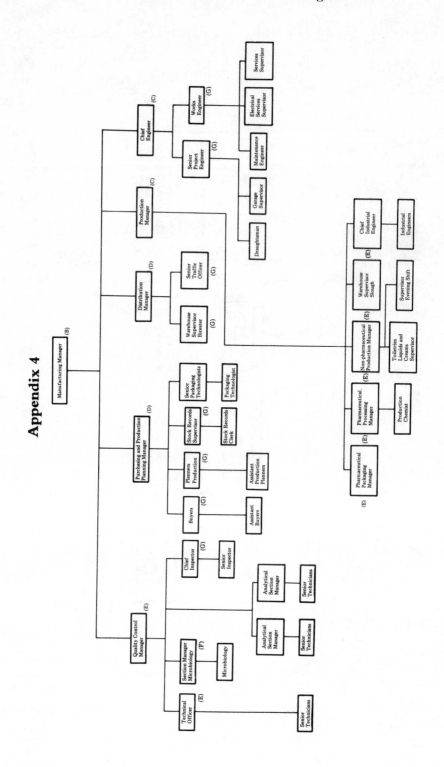

Appendix 5

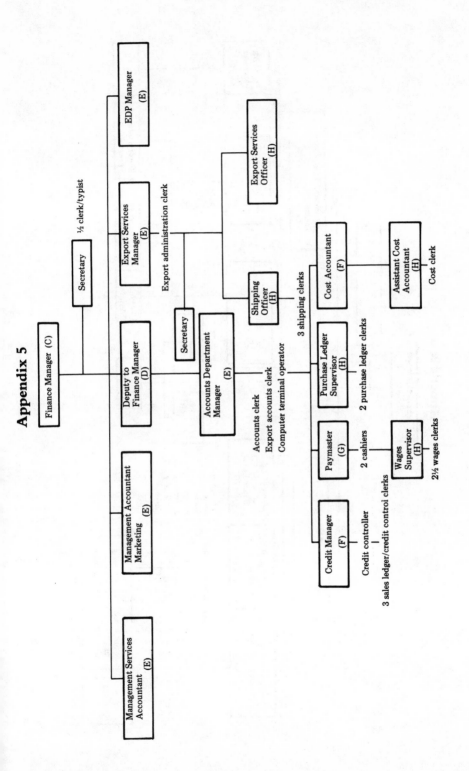

Appendix 6

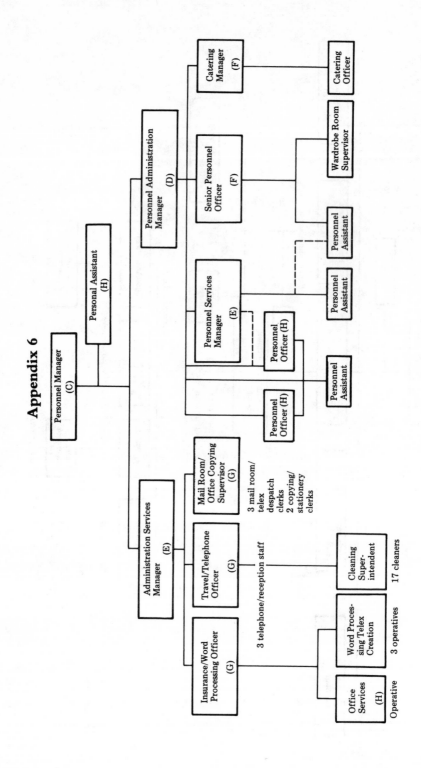

Appendix 7

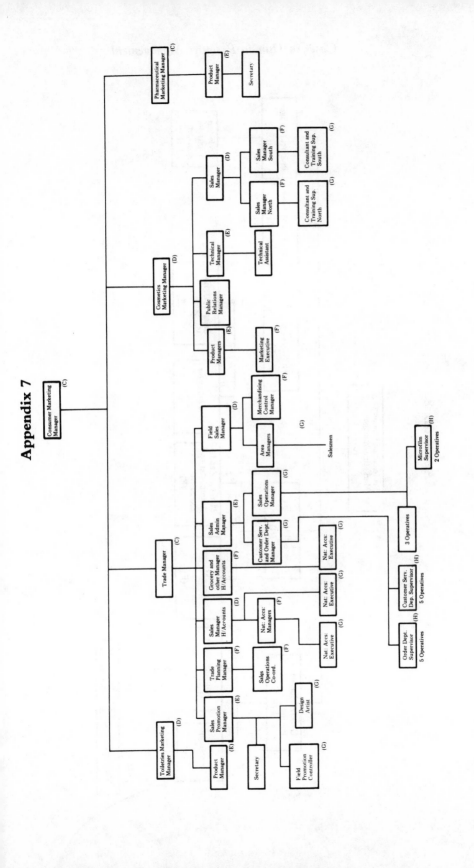

Appendix 8

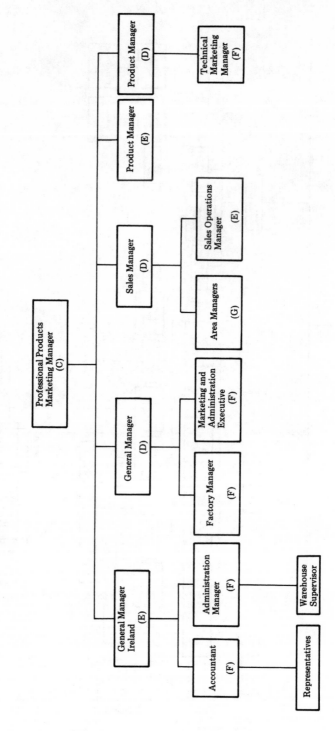

Appendix 9

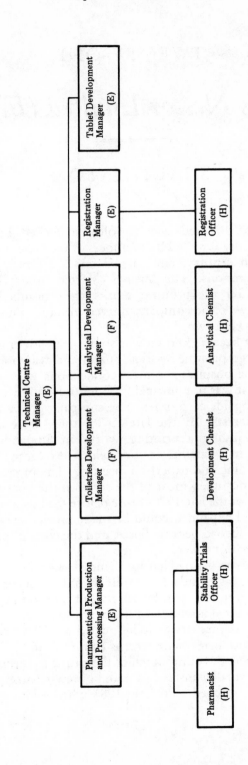

TWENTY-ONE

Thomas Nestor Limited (Printers)

SHAUN TYSON

Thomas Nestor Limited was an old established book printing business, originally founded by members of the Nestor family in the early nineteenth century, and carried on as a family business by successive generations. The business started in the East End of London, but after the printing works were bombed during the Second World War, the company moved into the countryside, near to a coastal market town.

'Nestors' as it became known was soon the major employer in the area, with a large printing works, offices and warehousing. In the expansion of the business the local connections were enhanced by family ties, and it was not unusual for husbands, wives and fathers to be working alongside each other. The company grew, and began to diversify its interests. By the late 1970s, there were a number of subsidiaries, including a printing works in Singapore, a colour printing works in a satellite factory which produced 'coffee table' books, bookbinding and paperback printing. The Nestor family still up to this time occupied most of the seats on the board.

The recession of the late 1970s came before the business into which the company had expanded could be made profitable. Competition from home and abroad became fierce, and the costs of production in Nestor's organizations were too high.

The technology in use had hardly changed since the war, and at the same time, high wages and a large staff with the costs of maintaining the sprawling premises combined to put Nestors in a difficult position. The original intention of the board had been to diversify its business as a response to growing demand. The company was overstretched, with inadequate returns coming from its investments, and with managers devoting much of their time to businesses which were becoming smaller instead of gaining new customers

The problems reached a crisis in 1981 when a loss of £1 million was announced. This change in fortunes led to a drastic change in the board's approach to the business. The older members of the board, including several members of the Nestor family retired. A younger board of directors was appointed, retaining only one of the Nestor family. A corporate plan was formed. The subsidiaries were sold or closed (and the work transferred to the main plant), and new techniques were introduced for the production of paperback books on long runs. The working arrangements had to be changed to make this possible, and new computer-based printing methods had to be introduced, in place of the old hot metal methods. The production facility became more flexible, and soft cover books began to be produced at competitive prices.

The changes resulted in redundancy for 600 people, reducing the headcount to around 1200. The redundancies had included managers, and the remaining managers were made accountable for their own units which were regarded as profit centres, the costs and transfer pricing being controlled through a new system of computerized management accounts.

These far-reaching changes were negotiated with the trade unions. The workforce was totally unionized (NGA, Sogat 82, etc.), and although the unions were not prepared to give management carte blanche, the degree of cooperation achieved between the two sides was remarkable. The credit for the agreement to change was due to both the Personnel Director, and the dynamic young Managing Director.

The personnel function of management

Up to the time of the crisis, the role of personnel management had been defined as a support function, with no capacity to advise senior management or to instigate new policies. The policies that did exist were drawn from the industrial relations traditions of the printing industry, and were only amended marginally to meet changing conditions. The members of the department were a personnel officer, and a training officer. Apart from running a routine administrative function, their activities centred on health and safety, and the organization of the apprenticeship scheme. Both men were close to retirement.

During the reorganization of the board, a Personnel Director was appointed, who redefined the role of the Personnel Department as a major player in the management of change. The training officer was retired early, and the remaining personnel officer was retained to carry all the routine administration of personnel. This left the Personnel Director free to work with the Managing Director on the development of a change strategy.

Gradually, a personnel change 'philosophy' emerged, agreed between the Personnel Director, the Managing Director and the board. Essential elements in the personnel philosophy were a high level of trust between work people and management, a cooperative but firm approach to the trade unions, employee involvement in the management of their own working practices, and strong leadership from front line supervisors and middle managers. From their long history, Nestors had acquired a style of management at once paternalistic and respectful of their union representatives. The management of change at Nestors built on this tradition. Trust could not have been created where management or unions had acted deceitfully before. The Fathers of the Chapel (employee representatives) were persuaded to give their support to a plan in which cooperation at the introduction of new technology, and more redundancies of their fellow members were essential parts.

There was a need to do more than just negotiate the changes, management action was needed in order to support and sustain the new approach. Employee involvement was institutionalized, through a parallel communication route, with briefing groups and large scale meetings which were regularly addressed by the directors. Each accountable profit centre was reported on to the employees by the responsible manager.

With the new structure, came new roles, and new challenges for management. It was the Managing Director's intention that there should be a 'new' open style. During discussions between the Managing Director and the Personnel Director, the question of how the management team could be supported and developed was raised.

The management

There were forty-four managers other than directors in the company, the majority being employed in production functions.

The organization chart (Appendix 2) shows the main areas of accountability.

Educational background and previous training

Apart from the more senior members of the management team, most of the managers at Thomas Nestor's were not graduates. They were untrained in management. They relied on their knowledge of the products, and of the processes. The prevailing management style at the time was a form of benevolent paternalism. The general impression gained by the Personnel Director was of scepticism about the idea of 'learning' management. There had been a short course on communication run by the Industrial Society, which had been well attended at the time the new briefing system was introduced.

No data was available on the managers' training needs. There was no formal appraisal scheme. Following the reorganization, some managers had been promoted to new positions, and there were few established facts about managerial performance. It was clear, however, that managerial behaviour was going to be regarded as one of the keys to success for the company in the future.

The financial position

The previous year (1981) the company produced poor financial results because it was overcoming its difficulties. A statement was sent to employees showing what happened to the revenue, and showing some of the costs of the reorganization. Sales for 1981 were up, at £18.9 million, as compared to £18.2 million in 1980; however, the extra costs of wage increases, interest charges and redundancy pay, plus the cost of new equipment led to a loss of £1.7 million.

However, 1982 has proved to be a good year. The order book is full – and costs have now been brought under control. The new book press is being utilized to maximum efficiency on long runs of paperbacks, and the profit forecast for 1982 shows prospects of nearly £1m net profit.

Question

1 As the Personnel Director, you are asked to prepare a management development strategy.

In your answer, give precise details of what steps you would take, and of the development activities you would arrange, including particular training objectives.

Appendix 1 Managers' age distribution

Age range in years	*Number of managers*
Aged over 25 under 30	2
Aged over 30 under 35	4
Aged over 35 under 40	8
Aged over 40 under 45	14
Aged over 45 under 50	7
Aged over 50 under 55	4
Aged over 55 under 60	2
Aged over 60 under 65	3
	44 Total

Managers' length of service

Service in years

Under 5 years	2
Over 5 under 10	3
Over 10 under 15	17
Over 15 under 20	7
Over 20 under 25	8
Over 25 under 30	3
Over 30 under 35	2
Over 35 under 40	—
Over 40 under 45	1
Over 45 under 50	1
	44 Total

Managerial split by function

Personnel	4
Finance	8
Production	21
Sales/Marketing	8
Technical	3

Appendix 2 Thomas Nestor Limited (Printers) organization chart

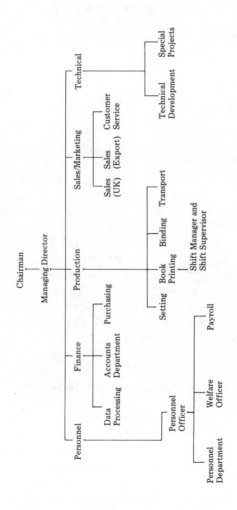

TWENTY-TWO

Recruiting a national sales force

FERGUS PANTON

Background

The case is concerned with the entry into the UK market of a giant international company which dealt mainly in fast moving consumer goods (FMCG). Students of 'business policy' might find the historical and legal circumstances which led up to the situation, of absorbing interest, but they do not materially affect the issues involved and they will, therefore, be dealt with in a summary fashion. Suffice it to say, the company concerned, which we will call International Consumer Goods (ICG) had been prohibited from trading in the UK since 1902, owing to the terms of an agreement reached with a major competitor who is a household name in the UK. Both companies in fact flourished as a result of this agreement, ICG particularly so, as it was given freedom to trade anywhere in the world, provided it kept out of Great Britain and Ireland. The world became a very profitable oyster for ICG.

The requirements of the Treaty of Rome 1972, in anticipation of the UK joining the Common Market, led to the cancellation of the agreement by mutual consent. This left ICG free to enter the UK market, if it so wished.

In the seventy intervening years, 1902–72, several other companies, not circumscribed in the same way, also became established in the same industrial field. Understandably, therefore, ICG, in the face of well-established competition approached the whole question of entry into the UK market with considerable circumspection; but there were quite clearly commercial opportunities in the offing. Britain's entry into the EEC heralded a range of taxation changes, the principal effect of which was to cause a dramatic shift in consumer demand for the products made and sold by ICG.

In a classically 'good' marketing approach, ICG researched the market thoroughly, initiated test markets successfully in 1976 and 1977, and as a result decided to go full steam ahead and make a total company entry into the UK.

The task

Complex and critical decisions on investment, production and marketing had been made, but the success of the initial operation was clearly going to be greatly dependent on whether the 'people' resources could be procured on time, at the right quality and in the numbers required. Virtually a whole sales force had to be recruited, together with marketing staff and support services. Some 250 bodies had to be found and be operative within 7 or 8 months.

A number of factors combined to complicate the issue. ICG was not well known in the UK, apart from two locations, one in the south and one in the north, where it had factories which manufactured for export. It had a high blue-chip rating in the city but it was jokingly known as the 'whispering giant'. Its products and brands were not known to the UK consumer and it had no established reputation for marketing expertise in the UK and little knowledge of local conditions.

On the credit side, there was a wealth of experience on tap of recruiting and training sales staff all over the world. It was an opportunity to put this knowledge to the test and one of the first illustrations was the decision to recruit the sales force from the UK, it being a commonly held belief in ICG circles that it was sound practice to employ nationals of the country in which one was operating.

Other considerable potential advantages were freedom to choose their own organizational structure, freedom to offer attractive salaries and conditions at a time of pay restraint and substantial financial support for the whole project.

Reputations both collectively and individually were at stake and much hinged on the acquisition of talent to do the job. The need for commercial security was paramount and conflicted with the need for 'selling' the company to establish a PR image and to attract applicants. Everyone was working under considerable pressure, time was in short supply and the need to devise a recruitment system which was economic of effort yet thorough in application was critical.

The main job of the sales force was to sell, promote and merchandize the company's products in order to achieve agreed sales volume and distribution targets. This entailed the establishment of a widespread distribution network through which the company's products would flow from the factory to wholesalers, agents or distributors down to a mass of retail outlets varying in size from supermarkets to corner shops and encompassing pubs, wine stores, newsagents and confectioners.

The overall plan envisaged a phased recruitment programme, but by far the largest number had to be taken on in the first phase so as to obtain comprehensive distribution and coverage of urban outlets. Significant differences in organization structure from those adopted by the competitors were in higher ratios of managers to sales representatives, with a view to developing small, compact work teams. Untypically, the area manager was to have three to four reps in his team and he was himself to make calls, estimates varying from 20 per cent to 30 per cent of his time. Equally, the next level of manager, called regional, was to have no more than four area managers reporting to him and in some cases initially only three or two.

The first phase saw an expansion of the existing sales force of eighteen (three managers and fifteen reps) to 150. This figure comprised an establishment under the national sales manager of two divisional managers, nine regional managers, twenty-eight area managers and 114 sales reps. In addition, there was to be a central sales training department.

In numbers alone, this was going to entail a sizeable problem of sequencing through the principal elements of the recruitment and selection process – planning, specifying requirements, advertising, screening/short listing, interviewing, selecting and appointing. How many people might apply was anybody's guess – one estimate was as high as fifty per post which would have meant 7500 applications and interviewing perhaps 1500 applicants!

Obviously, additional resources were going to be required if the recruitment task was to be achieved in seven months. Both the Marketing and Personnel Departments were deeply involved and there was a need for coordination so that any systems that were designed by either function were compatible. The sheer volume of work meant extra pairs of hands would be needed.

A senior marketing manager was appointed project coordinator, an experienced sales training manager was seconded from another part of ICG group, personnel staff were reallocated to special duties and a recruitment consultant employed on a short-term (six months) contract. A key figure in the project was the national sales manager who had run the test markets in the UK and been appointed as a result of his success.

The problem

At the first meeting of the project team in September, some immediate decisions were made. Target dates for the recruitment of the three principal levels; regional managers, area managers and sales representatives, were set as follows: nine regional managers to join by mid-December; twenty-eight area managers by mid-January and 114 sales reps by the end of March. This was to be the first phase.

The consultant pointed out that this was an uncomfortably tight schedule, allowing only half the time normally budgeted for management selection. He felt it was a pity that when the financial and commercial decisions were being made, the short- and long-term manpower implications had not been considered. The answer he received was that these were the requirements of the business plan and they had to be met.

The other significant decision made was to make use of recruitment agencies for the preliminary screening of area managers and sales representatives. Two were appointed, one based in Manchester for coverage of the north; the other in Guildford to cover the south. But personnel was none too happy about the way the agents had been selected, partly because they had not been involved. It was evident that there was friction between the sales and personnel managers: both functions saw themselves as having prime responsibility for the successful implementation of the project.

Questions

1 Who was going to brief the agencies? In what way?
2 No survey had been carried out of the employment market, which contrasted interestingly with all the money and effort expended on the test market. Where were these bodies going to come from? What was going to attract them to apply – and join? Competitive companies? Similar industries? Others?
3 If the company was, virtually simultaneously, recruiting three levels of management, what career prospects could they offer to applicants?
4 There was clearly no time to follow the conventional personnel route of job analysis – job description – person specification for most of the thirty different jobs. How accurate a specification could be produced without the preliminaries?
5 The twenty-eight 'areas' were determined geographically. How important was it that managers/reps should 'know' the area and/

or be identified with it? Did Scots have to be recruited for Scotland, Welsh for Wales, Brummies for Birmingham? Or what?

6 What about product knowledge? Should people be wooed from competition, or was sales expertise more important?

7 Was there any policy about employing women? Should there be?

8 What should the remuneration policy be? Same as the competition or better?

9 How important were status of car, allowances etc?

10 If first interviews were going to be conducted by the agencies, who should do the second and how?

11 Experience was vital, but so was motivation and people skill. Should tests be used? If so, what? What about using an assessment centre approach? If so, what and for whom?

12 What relationship, if any, should there be between the person specifications at different levels?

13 Was there a requirement for a balanced force and if so should people be selected because they had *different* qualifications?

14 How important was it that people should have managerial experience if they were to be recruited for managerial jobs? Would eight years as a senior representative in a competitive company be worth more or less than four years as a manager in ladies' support garments?

15 If you were a recruiter, how would you react to the attached person specification? Identify what you consider to be essential and desirable qualities for the job.

Appendix 1   Person specification, sales representative

Profile	Essential	Desirable
Physique, health, appearance		
Height	Slightly above average for region	5ft 8in to 6ft
Build	In proportion to height	Well proportioned
Hearing	Normal	Perfect
Eyesight	Normal	Perfect
General health	Good	Excellent, physically active
Looks	Presentable	Acceptable to all levels
Grooming	Smart	Acceptable to all levels
Dress	Business–like, presentable	Takes care in appearance
Voice	Clear, concise	Interesting and commanding manner; acceptable accent
Attainments		
General education	O-level English language, Maths and 1 other O-level	HND or equivalent
Job training		Courses in selling and appreciation of business methods
Job experience	Two years direct sales fast moving consumer goods with major UK company	Two years experience first line sales management
Special aptitudes		
Verbal	Communicates well in all media	Communicates well in all media

Profile	Essential	Desirable
Numerical	Familiar with basic arithmetic	Read and interpret management accounts, apply statistical techniques and use software
Interests		
Physically active		Participates in active pastimes
Aesthetic		Appreciates design tastes as applied to packaging, advertising etc.
Disposition		
Acceptability	Ambassador of	Can influence others
Leadership	company	to accept his/her recommendations
Stability	Self-control under normal circumstances	
Self reliance	Working without supervision and handling company's and customers' money	
Circumstances		
Age	22–35	
Mobility	Car driver – valid licence – no pending charges	No more than one endorsement
Domicile	Controls own movements during working week Prepared to work in any location Ready to work irregular hours	
Others	Takes pride in professional selling	
Notice	Not more than one calendar month from offer	

PART FOUR

Employee Relations

The 1980s has seen a new approach towards what used to be called 'industrial relations'. The study of industrial relations tended to be the study of the institutions, the trade unions, employers and state bodies which controlled the structures, agreements, procedures, and processes by which the behaviour of people at work was judged to be conditioned.

With the advent of the recession, high unemployment, reduced trade union power, greater local control of trade unions, and more company level bargaining, the industrial relations game is no longer played by the old rules. The term 'employee relations' is used here to signify that relationships at work are covered here, in the widest sense, including all employees, the strategic initiatives of management and trade unionists, and the relationships within the workplace.

In practice, it has always been important to explain relationships in the workplace where employers and employees negotiate over the frontiers of control. In the case of *East Midland Electronic* the way that control systems operate is questioned, and a disjunction is apparent between what management believe happens and what actually occurs. Similarly, in *A case of piecework bargaining* the manipulation of payment systems throws doubt on managerial claims to motivate through piecework bonus schemes.

The impact of new technology, and the growth of white collar unionism are two of the trends which are addressed in the *BIFU* case, where the reader has the opportunity to reflect on the direction of trade unionism as the century draws to a close. *The Greenfield Industrial* case looks at management strategies towards employee relations by asking the reader to set out the rules for the new industrial relations game.

In the *Alcan Plate Limited* case, there is an opportunity to examine employee involvement. The new emphasis on quality has led many large organizations to try to build a concern for quality into jobs and working practices through such devices as quality circles, which are discussed here.

TWENTY-THREE

East Midland Electronic

ROGER JONES

Introduction

Before the First World War what is now East Midland Electronic manufactured cars. In the 1920s car manufacture was phased out and the company began to specialize in the production of cranes and electrical magnets. Today the company specializes in electrical control equipment for the steel, chemical and oil industries as well as for public utilities. In addition, many standard components such as transformers, contactors and circuits are manufactured.

At the time of this study (late 1960s and early 1970s) the company had about 1000 employees.

Each department had a character which was, to some extent, different from that of other departments. In part, this was due to the fact that each department had its own somewhat distinctive technology. The company as a whole operated a unified control and information system, but this was often manipulated in different ways in various departments. The operation of formal controls will, therefore, be analysed departmentally.

The machine shop

Time keeping

Checking in and out of work and on and off jobs was here, as elsewhere in the company, part of the formal system for controlling the behaviour of hourly paid employees. The latter part of this provision, clocking on and off jobs, had fallen into disuse in the machine shop and was replaced with a different system. Before the Second World War, operators risked dismissal if they earned more than a certain amount of bonus. They would not, for this reason, record less than a given number of actual hours on each job card. Operators were, therefore, forced to 'cross-book'. That is to say, they attempted to maintain a consistent bonus rate by working in good and bad jobs together. The rate might have been consistent, but it was very low. In fact, the upper limit to earnings was set at the guarantee of twenty-seven per cent over base rates as specified by the 1931 Agreement between Federated Employers and the Engineering Joint Trades Movement. Even in the harsh pre-war labout market, it was difficult for supervisors to maintain the surveillance necessary to ensure wholly accurate clocking. The variegated nature of work combined with short job cycles and small batches created a great deal of clocking and this complicated supervision. Long serving operators were able to recall incidents which demonstrated that some foremen and chargehands had been overzealous in enforcing formal clocking provisions. In the war and immediate post-war years, many operators spun jobs out into overtime rather than risk the displeasure of supervisors and ratefixers by recording lower actual times on job cards.

This had become embarrassing to senior management and, as a result, a new system was introduced. In each week the amount of bonus or standard hours for all jobs completed by an operator were added, and from this total actual or clock-hours were subtracted to give bonus earnings. This system, because it concealed the times taken on specific jobs, enabled operators to exceed the piecework guarantee over a week without fear of reprisals. Much to the chagrin of ratefixers it seemed as though this result was intended by management. The new system was, of course, an open invitation to cross-book.

Quality control: the formal system

The formal control system specified a certain distribution of responsibility for the quality of work. Some operators were responsible for setting and others for machining. Appropriate instructions were written on job cards. Operators who had difficulty in interpreting these were supposed to seek clarification from supervisors.

Inspectors were responsible for seeing that work conformed to instructions. Operators were relieved of responsibility for their work after it had been passed by inspection. If machined parts were found defective in the assembly shops, then machine shop inspection was formally responsible.

Interdependency and the inter-play of quality and budget control

When parts were rejected during assembly, machine shop inspectors would usually recheck them for correspondence to drawings. This might show that specifications on the drawings were inappropriate to the functions which parts fulfilled in assemblies. If this was so, machine shop inspection would be able to shift the blame and issue rejection notes so that fault correction was costed against the drawing office budget. Draughtsmen would, if possible, object to this. They might, for instance, be able to argue that the machine shop and inspection had interpreted tolerances too laxly. Again, they often maintained that draughtsmen and designers could not foresee everything and that it was unfair to blame them for the failure to use common sense on the shop floor. Often, the drawing office was able to make much of the fact that the defect was not found until assembly. Such counter-assertions were much more persuasive to inspectors and others if they implied that culpability was widely distributed. This enabled correction costs to be shared among several departmental budgets. Paradoxically, if everybody was at fault then nobody was to blame. When one department refused to play the 'game', then the other departments would combine against it.

In the absence of opportunities to transfer responsibility to the drawing office, machine shop inspectors employed other means to avoid the painful experience of costing faults against their own budget. The partial nature of inspection provided them with an important resource. Inspection consisted of a first-off check supplemented by further checks made by 'walking inspectors'. Because of alleged staff shortages, these supplementary checks were not made as frequently as might be desired. They might also be omitted because of the rapidity with which some small batches were completed. In addition, first-off parts were sometimes machined by setters so that they might have a further check on the corrections of their tool and machine adjustments. A subsequent error by an operator could result in defective parts even though the first-off check was satisfactory. Quite often, these faults were the result of operators increasing cutting speeds in an attempt to earn more bonus. Of course, further faults could result from machine defects and variations in materials. Inspectors would, therefore, usually be able to find reasons for attributing blame largely or wholly to the machine shop itself even though they had passed the parts subsequently rejected in the assembly shops.

Several years earlier, first-off checks were supplemented by last-off checks. This system afforded inspectors less opportunities for escaping blame and, for this reason, it fell into disuse. Last-off checks were not now a formal requirement.

Even when supervisors had to admit that a fault was the responsibility of the machine shop, they were often able to prevent inspectors from issuing rejection notes against their shop budget.

Machine shop supervisors had bargained so as to obtain a quite generous provision concerning waste. The budget allowed a wastage of 10 per cent of the materials used, and this normally allowed faults to be corrected without the provision of new material. Generally, such provision would only be sanctioned if a rejection note was issued. In most cases supervisors were able to 'lose' correction notes because of surplus materials, and this ensured that many cost penalties were avoided.

Demarcation

Formally, the job responsibilities of setters and operators were clearly separated. In practice, matters were not so clear cut. Operators, because they were on bonus, often set their own work rather than wait for a setter. This saving of time did not jeopardize the allowance which operators received for setting delays. Setters were paid a bonus related to average earnings in the shop and, for this reason, they did not mind if reasonably competent operators set the simpler sorts of work. Supervisors did not attempt to enforce a rigid formal distinction between setters and operators as this would undermine efficiency. They spent much time in setting and inspecting the work of poorer operators, and they would try to ensure that these men were given only the simplest tasks. If such an operator's work was faulted, a supervisor might be criticized – at least if the job was difficult.

Supervisors often felt obliged to argue with ratefixers for extra allowances so that an operator's earnings would not be reduced because of time spent on fault correction. Sometimes supervisors avoided this obligation by doing corrections themselves or by getting setters to do them on an unpaid basis. Naturally, both supervisors and setters resented doing this, and they would make operators keenly aware of their displeasure.

Training and the role of shop stewards

Supervisors were not just protecting operators when they gave them simple work and extra attention; they were also training them. In this shop, as in others, stewards often helped supervisors to train operators. Stewards regularly clocked off their jobs on to what were called 'training officer' cards. They had an advantage over supervisors as trainers; their help did not carry unpleasant evaluative and disciplinary implications.

Supervisors were appointed by management while stewards were selected by workers. Supervisors were 'in charge' but, unlike stewards, they could not 'lead'. The ill-defined position which stewards occupied outside the formal chain of command also enabled them to act as conciliators between supervisors and inspectors.

The large assembly shops

Inspection

In the large assembly shops inspection was administered by two sections: mechanical inspection and the test room.

The work of mechanical inspection was simple: it consisted of such tasks as seeing that wires were securely fastened and that nuts were tight. In spite of formal job specification which implied that this work was rather skilled, mechanical inspectors were known in the factory vernacular as 'nut-tighteners'. Officially, they were supposed to report all faults to relevant supervisors but, because of their low status, they would correct mistakes themselves unless these were both bad and numerous. Unofficially, they acted as duplicate fitters who tidied up rushed piecework jobs.

Test room staff, especially those called 'test engineers', were highly skilled. Their work consisted, typically, in the following sequence of operations on large units of electrical control equipment:

- Analysis of key diagrams (schematic presentations of circuits).
- Seeing that drawings corresponded to key diagrams.
- Checking that designs conformed to safety requirements.
- Inspecting the work of fitters and mechanical inspectors.
- Applying electrical tests.
- Simulation testing.
- The modification of specifications.
- Commissioning plant on site.

This work was vital to the operation of the factory as a whole.

Testers: autonomy and functional importance

The formal status of test engineers and the more senior test engineers was much lower than one would have expected in view of their functional importance. This was, in all probability, attributable to the fact that they spent most of their time on the shop floor.

The work of testers involved checking the output and competence of persons who enjoyed higher earnings and greater status than themselves. In spite of their formal inferiority testers had a great deal of autonomy. They would, usually, obtain prompt attention from many people, and only on the rarest occasions had they to invoke the formal authority of the test room head in their relations with other departments.

The independence of test room staff compensated to some extent for their relatively low pay. In the long-term several of them were able to look forward to promotional compensations. A surprisingly large number of senior managers within the company had served their 'apprenticeship' in the test room.

One result was that culture of senior management embodied the belief that the company was in the business of making equipment to specific requirements of individual customers. The company which had acquired East Midland Electronic made television sets, washing machines, and other electrical appliances for the mass market. The Chairman of this company liked to see quickly moving assembly lines and he tried, unsuccessfully, to convert East Midland Electronic so that it conformed to this image. This failure was the main reason why he eventually sold the company to an American corporation.

The department of Research and Development was not studied. However, the work of the test room was, in a sense, research and development. The rigid separation of this function from production is characteristic of mass production; it was inconsistent with the nature of activities within East Midland Electronic.

Conflict between production and quality controls

Delivery dates tended to assume an increasing importance with each successive step in production. Unforeseen last minute hitches and delays accumulated in the earlier stages of production combined to create an atmosphere of almost perpetual crisis in the large assembly shops. The fact that piecework prices tended to become tighter as jobs increased in complexity made it especially difficult for supervisors to get work done in time and maintain a satisfactory standard.

Seniority

Supervisors tried to reserve the more complex assemblies for the most skilled men or, at least, those who were prepared to put pride in work before high piecework earnings. The less interesting, more repetitive and more standarized jobs were greedily sought by those who put earnings first.

Further constraints were imposed on supervisors by the shop culture which emphasized seniority. Naturally, skill is related to experience, but this was exaggerated by a tradition based on long service. Operators were asked the question: How long would it take a skilled fitter from outside to get the measure of the work here? There was a marked tendency for the period quoted to increase in line with length of service. Even those with several years service were called 'greenbacks'. Supervisors as well as operators tended to believe that these were by definition somewhat deficient in skill and reliability. The seniority culture was further reinforced by a wage system in which seniority played an important part in the determination of merit rates. This seniority culture distorted perceptions. There was reason to believe that relative newcomers were in fact, often much more skilled than was generally admitted.

The seniority culture was also evident in the organization of work groups. Much of the work was single-handed, but even so, most men habitually worked in pairs and in groups of three or four. It was not surprising that they should work in groups on the largest assemblies, but it was somewhat unexpected that they should continue to do so on the smallest assemblies. Group membership was the result of choices made by the men themselves, and the composition of all groups was remarkably stable. Several had existed for a dozen or even more years.

Group membership had a number of advantages. One was that groups could bargain more effectively than individuals over the distribution of jobs and overtime. Large groups also provided much scope for the development of a labour-saving practice. This could be very advantageous on a long run of similar or identical jobs. Another advantage was confirmed by group membership in relation to fault correction. One man could correct faults while his mates worked a bit harder on the current job so as to maintain collective earnings.

In spite of advantages of this kind the more self-reliant and individualistic fitters often choose to work on their own. If they did not have time in hand, they would have to ask ratefixers for an allowance to cover time spent on fault correction. The concession usually demanded by ratefixers was that they should earn on corrections a bonus percentage lower than their average. Group members were, normally, able to avoid this indignity.

Bonus earnings were uneven and relatively low in the large assembly shops. The main purpose of payment system manipulation was, in fact, to maximize opportunities for overtime. Testers could afford to leave the task of disciplining fitters for bad work to supervisors; their main concern was that someone should be on hand to correct faults immediately. This operational requirement encouraged overtime.

The joint manipulation of budgetary control and the payment system

The budgetary control system related shop running costs to the total number of bonus or standard hours issued by ratefixers in each shop. An increase in standard hours entailed a consequential increase in budget allowances. The interplay of piecework and budgetary control resulted in a situation where both supervisors and operators gained through the relaxation of job times. It was not surprising that supervisors tended to support claims for extra time to cover fault correction or for other reasons.

Uncontrolled cost centre

The budget of the main assembly shops was vulnerable to certain pressures because the value of work in progress was high and because this department was at the end of a production process. This vulnerability was greatest when complex assemblies had to be made quickly if the firm was to avoid cost penalties for failing to meet contractual delivery dates. In this circumstance, supervisors were often obliged to put as many men as possible on such jobs. Not surprisingly, these jobs often had numerous fitting faults, some of which could only be detected by time-consuming procedures in the test room. In such cases, embarrassingly large correction costs could be charged against the large assembly budget. This would, normally, be unfair as the large assembly shops were often trying to make up time lost in the earlier stages of production. In such circumstances, senior management could use its discretion and transfer charges to an uncontrolled cost centre.

The sheet metal and welding shop

Work groups and the payment system

The formal quality control system required that operators booked individually on job cards. It also made the payment of bonus conditional on work being passed as satisfactory by inspection.

Almost all of the men, with the exception of spot welders, worked in small gangs. Gang members pooled their job cards, and they distributed actual hours on them so that each card showed an identical, or almost identical, bonus percentage. Jobs varied greatly in size, and it was not, therefore, possible to ensure an even distribution of bonus among gang workers in each week, but debits and credits were carried forward for subsequent correction. A calculation which the present writer made of one gang over a ten week period showed that bonus percentages varied among its members by only 3 points from a high of 300 to a low of 297. The earnings of other gangs were at a similar level and showed strictly comparable consistencies over the same period.

Staff in the work study department attributed this consistency to the accuracy of work measurement. They were, however, unaware of both the existence of informal work groups and of the spurious nature of actual times recorded on job cards.

Conflict between quality and output controls

Formal procedures required that operators gave job cards to

inspectors on the completion of work. A refusal of an inspector to sign these cards, until faults were corrected, would delay the payment of bonus. Inspectors were presented with bunches of job cards on Mondays and Tuesdays so that they could be signed for payments to be made the following week. Jobs did not accompany cards and, as a consequence of the informal system of gang work, it did not necessarily follow that the operator whose number was on a particular card had done the job. Smaller completed jobs were left by operators on the floor near the inspectors' benches. Inspectors had to find large jobs in the shop itself. Operators drew attention to these by attaching to them route cards and drawings. These arrangements served to deny inspectors the sanction of delaying bonus payments; they had, instead, to rely on persuasion to get faults corrected.

Only when work was very bad could they get the backing of supervisors; the latter were more interested in output than quality. Sometimes inspectors reacted by issuing rejection notes costed against the sheet metal shop's budget. Such resorts to formality put a great strain on relations between them and the supervisors. Here, as elsewhere in the organization, supervisors had a vested interest in the 'piecework fiddle'; relaxations in job times were used by them to manipulate the system of budgetary control.

Conflict between the payment system and quality control

In this shop the bonus system, undoubtedly, accentuated inconsistencies between output and quality control. Some operators neglected to give drawings proper scrutiny. Although moving housings – the metal frames and coverings which would contain electrical equipment – were standard, they were often modified in certain detail. Less conscientious operators saved time by assuming that particular housings were entirely standard. They relied on inspectors to point out modifications after jobs were completed. These operators were rewarded for saving themselves time and effort even though this created additional work for others. Such occurrences were, of course, not unique to the sheet metal shop.

The long-term consequences of payment system manipulation

General observations

Over the last two decades there had been a tendency for bonus earnings, expressed in percentage terms, to rise. This tendency had been particularly pronounced in the sheet metal shop and in some sections of the machine shop. The rise in bonus earnings was not even and gradual; it tended to consist of fairly sharp increases followed by periods of relative stability. It was hard to devise an adequate explanation of why these revisions had been abrupt rather than gradual. There certainly had not been any sudden relaxations in job times which would account for steep increases in bonus earnings. There had been gradual relaxation in job times but these were insufficient in magnitude to explain the increase.

The sheet metal shop

Some of the increase in bonus earnings seemed due to operators working harder. This seemed to be especially true in respect of the sheet metal shop. Here, increases in bonus earnings had been accompanied by decreases in overtime. This is highly indicative of rising effort standards. At the time of the study, the culture of the sheet metal shop had, except for the spot welding section, become hostile to overtime. Significantly, spot welders had much lower bonus earnings than other workers in the shop.

The large assembly shops

The rise in bonus earnings had been less marked in the large assembly shops. Here tighter times and lower bonus earnings produced a situation in which many operators found it expedient to 'hang out' jobs into overtime.

The machine shop

In the machine shop earnings were higher on capstan lathes than on general lathes, and they were still higher on milling machines. They were highest of all on numerically controlled machines. These particularly high bonuses were the price which management had to pay to get technical changes accepted when workers exploited their bargaining power.

The winding room

In the winding room, where women were employed in assembling small transformers and contactors, new machines and methods had resulted in a slight fall in bonus earnings. The women, even though they were all union members, bargained less strongly than their male counterparts elsewhere in the organization.

Managerial policy

Management had gone some way to rationalize and consolidate the general rise in bonus earnings by agreeing with the shop stewards to incorporate piecework guarantees larger than those laid down in national agreements, into the factory's wage structure. Some managerial decisions had facilitated the rise in bonus earnings. In particular, management had adopted a policy whereby each shop was paid an 'efficiency bonus' related to its average piecework earnings. Managers assumed that standard or bonus hours were uniform units so the proportion of such time saved was a reliable indicator of efficiency. The sheet metal shop which had the highest bonus earnings of all departments, also enjoyed the largest efficiency bonus. This not only reflected high standards of effort, it also reflected the fact that sheet metal work, and gas and arc welding are notoriously difficult to price.

In the long run, it was clear that the system of payment had contributed to the development of undesirable working practices and to the establishment of anomalous pay differentials.

The small assembly shop and other activities

Women's work and the transfer of intelligence

In the small assembly shops work was light and most of it was done by women. Production engineers took pride in the fact that they had, through method improvement, eliminated the need for operators to think. Work had become so simple that the possibility of operators making mistakes had been reduced to a minimum. Inevitably, a certain proportion of small components would be found defective for reasons unconnected with their actual assembly. Consequently, the budgetary control system allowed for a rejection of a proportion of assemblies before there was any question of costing these against the departmental budget. Only in exceptional cases would the rejection of assemblies endanger operators' bonuses. The quality of output was, for all practical purposes, outside their control.

The discretion to resolve conflict between production and quality had been removed from the shop floor and transferred to the office. The price of this 'transfer of intelligence' was high; it consisted in a substantial increase in the number of production engineers and their ancillary staff. Those who plan and organize the sort of work undertaken by the small assembly shops try to anticipate all sorts of things which could go wrong, and this activity is extremely costly in terms of manpower and other resources. In the firm as a whole 'indirects' outnumbered those directly engaged on production, and a trend towards more product standardization was increasing this disparity.

Certain problems are removed from the shop floor, but they reappear elsewhere in the organization in a different form. Meanwhile, new problems associated with monotony and low job satisfaction are created on the shop floor. It seemed as though operators in the small assembly shops had to get used to, rather than get interested in, their work.

It would be pointless to try to reduce the monotony of work by rotating jobs, but supervisors (male) did this so as to ensure reasonable equality of earnings among operators. Job times varied enormously in their tightness and looseness. This was, on the face of it, surprising. Professionalized industrial engineering techniques were used. The work was very simple and standardized and job cycles were measured in seconds rather than minutes. The inconsistency of job times was largely attributable to the failure of the women to bargain.

Product control

None of the supervisors in these shops bothered to look at production schedules. Irregularities in the supply and quality of components, particularly from outside suppliers, made any adherence to schedules impossible.

One section of the winding room employed men who worked on the larger transformers and brakes. This section had been very busy for a long time. The culture of the section was summed up by its shop steward with the slogan 'one in, all in'. One operator who refused to do overtime was regarded by the supervisor and men as very unsociable. Production schedules were drawn up for 'standard products'. Often, however, customer specials and repairs constituted the bulk of the work. This made nonsense of production schedules.

Quality control and skilled work

In a few shops which did highly specialized and often very skilled work, quality control was either nominal or non-existent. In one, quality control was nominal because most of the assemblies could not be inspected unless they were dismantled. Even as a sample method of checking work this was ineffective because finer adjustments were upset by dismantling. In another section, elaborate testing and inspection procedures were carried out by operators who were, incidentally, not on bonus. Paradoxically, in these shops where inspectors played a minimal role, the quality of work was exceptionally high.

Stores

The formal system

The main stores stocked well over 20,000 standard parts as well as numerous non-standard items and materials of various kinds. The computerized system of stock control assigned a number to each of the standard parts. The parts themselves were not numbered, but they were placed in numbered boxes and bins. Many parts were hard to distinguish from each other visually. Many errors could have been avoided if parts were labelled and if verbal descriptions had supplemented numerical ones. Another elementary precaution would have been to improve the lighting in the stores which was often very poor. Storemen were required to record the number of parts in each container and this information was fed into the computer. The computer then 'printed' shortage lists which were attached to job cards and sent to the assembly shops.

The informal system

These shortage lists were hopelessly inaccurate, and operators spent much time 'chasing' missing parts in the stores. Fitters in the large assembly shops had adopted the practice of labelling surplus parts and returning them to the stores. Rate fixers refused to give them allowances for this time-consuming work and, consequently, the men decided collectively to discontinue it.

Those in charge of stock control attributed shortcomings of the formal system, so far as they were aware of them, to human errors in the stores; they stressed, especially, the need for greater diligence among the storemen in relation to paper work. They also tried, unsuccessfully, to exclude operators from the stores.

The storemen devised 'rules of thumb' which enabled the stores to function, after a fashion, in spite of the handicaps imposed by the formal system. Storemen specialized in certain parts of the stores and they had their own way of deciding whether to accept or reject over and under consignments from outside suppliers. The formal system failed to give clear instructions to storemen in the goods inward section on this matter. 'Rules of thumb' were augmented by an unofficial modification of the function of the spares department. In theory, this department kept spares under contract or to please important customers. This formal function had been supplemented by another: spares acted as a source of parts when the main stores ran out! Those in charge of the stock control system were unaware of this adaptation.

The design of the formal system also reflected a lack of appreciation of the function of stock control in the context of the organization as a whole. Great importance was attached by senior management to limiting the size of production batches as a means of economizing on circulating capital. This policy interfered with production by artificially creating shortages. It also undermined efficiency more indirectly. In the machine shop and winding room, it caused the proportion of time spent in setting to rise relative to that spent in machining. More generally, it reduced the efficiency of operators by shortening production runs.

The commitment of those in charge of stock control to the formal system was part of a wider one to computerization. Further examples of the uneconomic consequence of computer applications within the company could be given. Computerization had acquired great symbolic importance for several powerful members of senior management. This commitment was further intensified by pressure from the large organization which had acquired the firm through a take-over bid. The Chairman of this organization believed that computerization promoted efficiency and was an indispensible part of modern management. Shortly after this study was completed a new and much more expensive computer was installed at the factory.

Office work

Some research problems

On the shop floor it was often possible to take advantage of machines, assemblies, barriers and other objectives to give interviews some privacy. Workshop noise also helped; it made conversation inaudible to all except immediate participants. The openness and quietness of the main offices detracted from the effectiveness of interviews as a method of research. The protocol of offices tended to be much more extensive and rigid than that of the shop floor, and this served to reduce the accessibility of staff. It was possible for the present writer to observe and interview some staff by more indirect means, however.

Demarcations

Clerks and administrators tried to establish monopolies over this or that bit of paper work. Often they would ensure the inaccessibility of paper work to other members of staff by developing their own filing and record systems. As long as these demarcations did not interfere seriously with the work of others, they would be respected by colleagues and sanctioned by superiors. One result of the demarcations was that staff often had only vague and general ideas about the work of many of their desk neighbours. A further consequence was that office chiefs did not have anything like a detailed grasp of the work of many of their subordinates. The artificial differential of work helped to establish the belief that jobs were unique and not

readily transferable from one clerk or administrator to another. All
but the lowest office staff tried to develop so as to preserve such
fictions which would, in the case of the most successful, be reinforced
and be given a certain tangibility through the occupation of private
offices. A clerk or administrator who proclaimed that jobs were more
interchangeable than was commonly supposed, would encounter the
disapproval of superiors as well as of colleagues and subordinates.

In workshops, tasks were concrete and often related to each other.
Workshop culture emphasized interdependency and the sharing of
responsibilities. Office culture emphasized the separateness and non
dependency. Demarcations gave individuals areas of privacy and they
curtailed scope for individuals to interfere with the work of others.

Standardized work

Staff who did routine and readily transferable work had low status.
The effort standards of these staff were conspicuously less than those
who enjoyed at least some autonomy. The turnover rate among them
was also relatively high. Even when their departments were visited by
senior managers, they could not hide their intense apathy and bore-
dom.

Management

Bargaining

Many departmental chiefs spent at least as much time on inter-
departmental politics as they did on the administration of their own
sections. Meetings about budgets were almost continuously in progress. The way budget performances were presented was conditioned
by political rather than operational requirements. A department's
budget might be reduced because it had kept down costs to a figure
below that allowed. This encouraged expenditures which were, from
an operational point of view, quite unnecessary. A more serious view
was taken by senior management of failures to meet some budget
requirements rather than others. Departmental chiefs doctored
accounts to accommodate these predilections.

Production schedules were also influenced by bargaining requirements. Had this not been so, schedules would have had to be ignored
even more frequently than was the case.

Budgetary controls were taken more seriously than production
schedules. The former had purely abstract reference points; they were
related to the intangibilities of notional cost. The latter were subject to
tangible things like awkward customers, the unreliability of bought in

components and the difficulties of product development. Myths about accurate planning of the composition and quantity of production where too often upset by harsh intrusions of reality to be taken over-seriously. The world of notional cost is much more self-contained. Budgetary control is for this reason a potent device for exerting pressure on people. In the language of office politics, the statement 'you have an adverse variance' is equivalent to 'I don't like you'.

Job descriptions

Superiors often described the responsibilities of their subordinates in obviously unrealistic terms. A head of a staff department, for instance, described to the present writer, the supposed responsibilities of his immediate subordinates. Among other things they were supposed to hire and fire those under them; they were alleged to make decisions about pay increases, promotions and overtime. They were also said to have complete freedom to authorize expenditures within certain budget limits. In fact, these subordinates had to refer everything, except the most routine questions, to their superior. This, admittedly extreme case, was different in degree rather than in kind from most other responses obtained from departmental chiefs.

Inaccurate descriptions, by departmental chiefs, of the responsibilities of those reporting to them were frequently combined with acute observations about the obscurity of responsibilities elsewhere in the organization. Among other things, this showed how involvement undermines objectivity.

The belief that responsibilities were well defined among their subordinates was a source of comfort to departmental chiefs; it gave them the impression that they controlled their behaviour to a much greater extent than was the case. It also enabled them to draw flattering comparisons between the order of their own departments and the disorder elsewhere.

It was apparent that they were, perhaps unconsciously in some instances, talking about themselves when they were allegedly talking about their subordinates. The responsibilities which they imputed to subordinates were often those which they themselves lacked and desired. Inaccurate descriptions contained also hidden defensive implications. As heads of departments they were, in the formal sense, accountable for everything that might be done in them. They were aware that their control over their departments did not match this accountability. Inaccurate job descriptions enabled them to claim when things went wrong, i.e. that they were accountable but not culpable. The phoney delegation of responsibility by means of inaccurate job descriptions was potentially a device for locating culpability as distinct from accountability.

Summary

A report closely resembling this case study was presented to the Managing Director. It is scarcely an exaggeration to say that it induced in him something approaching a state of shock. Neither he nor any of the senior managers had had any inkling of the extent and nature of the failure of formal control and information systems. The Managing Director and several senior managers spent two months in an attempt to find factual errors in the report. They were wholly unsuccessful in this endeavour.

Questions

1 Why do the formal controls fail to work as planned?
2 Are all manipulations of formal controls detrimental to organizational efficiency?
3 Is the organization in question typical or atypical?
4 What requirements must formal controls meet if they are to work effectively?

TWENTY-FOUR

A case of piecework bargaining

ROGER JONES

Ginger and Stan were mates. They worked in the Fuselage Department of a large aircraft factory in Southern England. Ginger was in his middle thirties and had been in the company since his demobilization in 1946. Stan was in his early twenties and had spent about two years in the company all of it in the fuselage shop. These two were put to work together when Stan's previous mate, George, left to take up a job as a sales representative. George was attracted by the sales job because of the opportunities it afforded for amorous adventure. George had an extrovert personality and had a casual attitude regarding work. Stan was introspective and serious minded but shared George's dislike of work; he, too, had a strong preference for non-work activities. One of the reasons why they had got on well together was the fact that they never worked overtime. Most of those in the department worked some overtime and several a great deal. Almost all of the work required two men and it would be inconvenient if mates had opposing requirements concerning overtime. Ginger was selected by the chargehand, Cyril, to work with Stan because, among other things, Ginger disapproved of overtime working. In their shared attitude toward overtime Ginger and Stan deviated from the prevailing norm of the department. Ginger was influenced not only by his preference for leisure work but also by his Marxist beliefs. He argued that overtime artificially increased the supply of labour and had the effect of lowering wage rates. Stan found this argument completely convincing, if only because it fitted in with his leisure preferences.

The Fuselage Department was erecting the bodies of a four engined jet bomber. 104 production models of this aircraft had been ordered and, as yet, only a half dozen or so fuselages were in a state of near completion. Stan had inherited three main jobs: the fitting of refuelling points in the sides of the fuselage, the fixing of steel

206

brackets around wing apertures, and the positioning of two front panels or skins just behind the cockpit. None of these were good jobs; it was hard to earn 150 per cent (1½ hours bonus per hour worked) on any of them even if they worked flat out. At that time 150 per cent was generally accepted by operators in the shop as an appropriate level of earnings. It was believed that if an operator exceeded this level ratefixers would take retaliatory action. Once a job price was agreed between an operator and a ratefixer it could not be altered. This, in practice, was the way the piecework guarantee in the engineering agreements was interpreted. The retaliatory action would consist not in the alteration of existing prices but in the adoption of a more stringent attitude towards the determination of prices on new jobs. In extreme cases, it would also be possible to redefine a job or modify it and claim, as a result, that it ought to have a lower price. It could be that earnings would have to exceed 150 per cent by a great margin before retaliation occurred, but it was undoubtedly true that there was a certain level which if exceeded would cause managerial concern. In the course of time (about five years) the average level of bonus earnings expressed in percentage terms rose by gradual stages to 250 per cent. At this stage the problem tends to be diagnosed by management not in terms of individual errors by ratefixers on particular jobs but as a 'decay' of the whole incentive system.

The tactics used by ratefixers were quite simple. They knew who among the workers could be browbeaten and who could not resist the opportunity to earn a lot in the short term by really sweating on the job. This behaviour would be encouraged by the ratefixer with the offer of really generous 'provisional times'. The task of hoodwinking the more gullible was one in which supervisors often cooperated with ratefixers. One of the peculiarities of the payment system was that the time apprentices devoted to a job was not recorded. The foreman of the fuselage was in the habit of putting several apprentices with two mates who were known to be 'teararses' on riveting jobs. At one stage he put no fewer than ten apprentices on the one job card. The ratefixer could then argue that the job was actually done in the time ostensibly taken by the two operators. This incident prompted a walk out of the shop.

The rates of pay had two elements. On the one hand there were flat rate components like base rates, merit allowances, and shift and overtime premia and on the other hand there were bonus rates which varied according to the base rates of particular operators.

An operator got one third of the time he saved on a job. For instance, if he did a four hour job in one he would obtain a single hour's bonus. If an operator was unable to earn bonus on a job his card wold be plussed up to the piecework guarantee under national agreements which, at that time, meant that he would earn his flat rates plus 25 per cent of base rate. Times were set by ratefixers from synthetic data: the unions in the factory objected to the use of stop watches and there had been walk outs in various parts of the factory after attempts by ratefixers to use them. The usual engineering agreements applied in the factory concerning the mutuality of piecework prices. In other words, these prices could only be applied after they had been agreed between a representative of management and an operator. Once one operator agreed a price it applied to any other operator who might be required to do the job. In some shops, like the sheet metal, where union organization was 100 per cent, a procedure had evolved whereby all operators obtained the sanction of the senior shop steward in the department before agreeing to any particular price. This was considered rational by the unions because piecework prices were a matter of collective as well as individual concern.

Trade union organization was less well established in the fuselage shop at the time of the case study. About 60 per cent of the men in the shop, whose total labour force was about 700, were in the union. The most important union in the shop was the Amalgamated Union of Engineering Workers but the Transport and General and the National Union of Vehicle Builders were also represented. In this shop, as in most others throughout the factory, what was important was whether one was a card holder. The particular union to which one belonged was of lesser importance. The shop stewards of the various unions in the plant formed a joint committee which negotiated with management on more important issues, especially those of importance to the plant as a whole. Issues of concern to particular individuals of departments were taken up by the shop stewards in the relevant sections, in the first case with supervisors and, subsequently, with representatives of management should an agreement not be reached on the shop floor. In some of these cases the convenor or deputy convenor of the Joint Shop Stewards' Committee would assist the departmental stewards in meetings with management.

In the fuselage shop most men worked Saturday and Sunday mornings and several evenings in the week as well. Shops with higher average levels of bonus earnings tended to work significantly less overtime. The two were obviously related. If men cannot obtain their expected level of earnings through bonus earnings they will often try to make it up through overtime. They will forego certain bonus earnings and hang their jobs out into overtime. Often or always supervisors will cooperate in this, especially when their pay itself is related to the hours they actually work. One of the favours which Jack, the foreman of the fuselage shop, used to dispense was to allow men who had completed the day shift to work until a quarter past midnight. These men could then clock off at that time and be paid under the shift work agreement. This meant that they would be paid as though they had worked to seven in the morning. The more thoughtful operators and most of the shop stewards disapproved of this overtime because among other things it reduced interest in piecework prices and base rates. Supervisors were often under some pressure from management to maintain and increase overtime working. This was seen as the only possible way of meeting production schedules. Even when a supervisor was not paid by the hour there were strong pressures on him apart from supposed production requirements to work long hours. Among other things, it demonstrated in the most tangible possible way his commitment and interest in work and thus prepared the way for his possible promotion. Those operators like Ginger and Stan in the fuselage shop who never worked over, were called somewhat disparagingly 'part-timers'.

Union organization was, as has just been mentioned, weak in the Fuselage Department, but just before Ginger and Stan became mates an increasing number of men were joining. A year or two later Stan became a shop steward in spite of Ginger's advice that the men were not worth 'sticking your neck out for'. When Stan eventually left the shop there was only one person in the shop who was not a member. He was regarded as a religious maniac as he used to quote passages from the Bible which, he maintained, made it a mortal sin to join a union. Stan spent some time in arguing with Paddy, but he failed to make any impression; he said that he had the greatest respect for Paddy's religious convictions but could not see what these had to do with unions. Stan argued that unions were not in existence when the events described in the Bible took place and he, therefore, could not see how the scriptures could possibly proscribe such organizations. Paddy was given up as a hopeless case but as his behaviour was quite acceptable to others except for his strange aversion to unions he was tolerated with good humour.

At the time trade union control in the shop was weak. In those shops where trade unionism was well established average earnings were much higher than in weakly organized shops like the fuselage. Especially significant was the fact that the wing shop which did exactly the same sort of work as the fuselage had an average bonus level of 200 per cent at the time when the latter's was less than 150 per cent. The wing shop was a closed shop and walk outs were always occurring among its various sections over prices and allowances. In well organized shops both the norms and the actual earnings were higher than in the less organized ones and this tended to confirm the rationality of collective action.

Collective controls over piecework earnings and bargaining processes were weak in the Fuselage Department, except that sentiments about the appropriate level of bonus were exerting some kind of general influence over the behaviour of individual operators.

It was mentioned earlier that Stan had inherited three main jobs from his previous mate George. Both Ginger and Stan were among the more careful and skilled workers in the shop and, as a result, Cyril used to give them the modifications to completed work and the faults in fitting discovered by inspectors after the work had left the Fuselage Department. This work commanded 150 per cent however long it actually took. Shortly after they were put together Cyril also gave them a new job, the fitting of anchor nuts for the attachment of racks to the bomb bay on which the actual bomb doors articulated. This addition to their work enabled them to discard their hardest and worst priced job, the positioning of front panels.

The necessity for anchor nuts had, seemingly, been overlooked by the Planning Department and the job was not originally scheduled. As a result the jig locating the positions of anchor nuts had not been made and this meant that over 4000 holes had to be drilled from blue print dimensions. In the first production model especially the job was made more difficult by the amount of wiring and components that had been fitted. This reduced accessibility and entailed some dismantling. It was these difficulties which prompted Cyril to give this job to Ginger and Stan.

These operators knew that the ratefixer would expect them to increase their efficiency on a job as they became more familiar with it. They, therefore, formed some rough and ready judgement about the time it would take to do the job under standard production conditions. They came to the opinion that it could be done in about a day if they got stuck into it, and they set themselves the object of obtaining a price that would enable both of them to stay on the card for a week at a bonus rate of 150 per cent. They decided to take a month over the first job and to gradually decrease the time taken over the next few aircraft to something just under three weeks. Cyril considered that Ginger and Stan were doing him a favour in tackling this job and he readily agreed to give Stan all the available job cards (those for the first ten aircraft). The chargehand told the ratefixer that they were doing a good job and backed Ginger and Stan up in their contention that the provisional times on these cards should be made up to 150 per cent. Ginger and Stan continually got the ratefixer down on the job so that he could see all the difficulties of the job. The ratefixer soon got tired of this and took the easy way out by accepting their opinion that the job was exceedingly difficult.

At that time in the contract the production line was moving slowly so there was no pressure on Ginger and Stan from their chargehand to get on with it. When the jig arrived Ginger hid it in a special locker. He also made sure that all the available drawings were in his possession. The job demanded a certain number of specially designed anchor nuts and the mates ensured that they drew out of stores all the available supply of these. These tactics were directed at other operators so as to make it impossible for them to poach the job. Ginger and Stan knew that their strategy would be rendered useless if some fool got cracking on the job. Later when the production line started to move somewhat faster Ginger and Stan were careful to see that there were no hold-ups on other jobs because of incompleted bomb bays. This ensured that Cyril was not under pressure to get the job done quicker and thus had no excuse to put extra men to work on the bomb bay.

In their arguments with the ratefixer Ginger and Stan insisted that the formal procedures for doing the job were the only proper ones and that errors would result from attempts to improvise. They told the ratefixer that if he had any bright ideas about how the job ought to be done he should take it up with production planning. Fortunately for them the ratefixer was unable to make any specific proposals about job method.

On the first few aircraft Ginger and Stan spent some of their time on making their own jigs which enabled them to eliminate some of the operations for which the ratefixer had to make allowances. The use of these jigs meant that anchor nuts only had to be fitted once instead of twice and this in turn eliminated the need for deswarfing. Another advantage of these jigs was that they enabled many thousands of holes to be drilled by a straight drill from within the bomb bay rather than with small angle drills from inside the narrow passage between the bay and the external skin. Riveting was scheduled, quite naturally, as a two handed job, but by using small guns at reduced pressure and by leaning through apertures in the sides of the bays it was perfectly possible for this task to be accomplished solo. Ginger and Stan found that the vibration caused by the gun did not cause loose rivets to fall out if they were first dipped into an anti-corrosion compound. This greatly increased the speed of solo riveting. By these methods the time taken for this part of the job could be reduced by at least 40 per cent. One of the major difficulties of the job arose out of the fact that many of the nuts which were to hold electrical controls near the door racks could not be positioned without modifications because of existing rivets and assemblies. Ginger and Stan found out from an inspector in electrical assembly that the precise positioning of these controls was not important. If they were an inch or two either way this could be accommodated by lengthening or shortening connecting wires. Ginger and Stan then cleared it with production planning that certain jig drillings need not be made. This, and the consequent saving in working time were not, of course, reported to the Ratefixing Department.

In the bargaining between the ratefixer and Ginger and Stan certain ritualized arguments were used. The ratefixer maintained that he was being very generous and that he simply could not find any more time. When he was asked where he got his time from he replied that he got it from synthetics which were scientifically arrived at. The operators replied he was just about as synthetic as his times and that their knowledge of the job, on the contrary, was not derived from some crackpot theory but was based on experience of actually doing the job. The ratefixer would reply that he wished he was allowed to roll up his sleeves so that he could demonstrate the adequacy of his suggested times. (The Amalgamated Engineering Union was not a party to the piecework demonstrators agreement and there would have been a mass walk out of the factory if a ratefixer had attempted to demonstrate a job.)

Both Ginger and Stan argued that they did not come to work for fun, and that they had wives and children to keep. Both men were, incidentally, single. Many of the arguments they used were highly abusive of the ratefixer as a person. They would laugh in an uncontrolled manner at his suggested prices. The ratefixer would invite them to look at his calculations. He would suggest with an air of false reasonableness that if he had made any arithmetical errors he would be only too pleased to rectify them. The mates would reply that these calculations were obviously mad and that the ratefixer must be out of his mind even to think of them. Other standard arguments used by the operators related to the meanness of the ratefixer; a meanness that was all the more reprehensible because it was not even his own money that he was looking after. At all stages these operators would claim extra allowances to cover shortages, modifications and other contingencies. Stan especially used to argue that there was no logical connection between the time taken to do the job and the time allowed for it. He used to say: 'Suppose we agree that it will take me or anyone else about half an hour to do that. You might say it is a two-hour job and I could say it was a six-hour job. I value my time and my effort at a higher standard than you do. Any job time must make some assumption about what is the appropriate level of earnings for an operator at given levels of performance. Just tell me what level of bonus you think I ought to be able to earn on this job.' These logical type arguments were reinforced by a splendid abusive vocabulary that Ginger had acquired as a result of his army experience in India.

After about three months of hard bargaining Ginger and Stan obtained the price that they originally had thought of when they did the first aircraft. How did they use it? Apart from the fact that it enabled them to enjoy some welcome leisure at work it had many other uses. Most importantly, it enabled them to build up time in hand to use on other jobs. As was mentioned earlier Stan had inherited some pretty bad jobs from George. Ginger and Stan used to do these jobs while they were booked on the bomb bay. In this way they could return all their jobs at the highest bonus rate set by the normal standards of the shop. Fault correction jobs were also extremely useful in building up time in hand. It should be pointed out that the price they negotiated on the bomb bay was the main reason why they were able to sustain this rate of earning for a period of over four years.

Questions

1 Can work standards be accurately set by time study methods?
2 What are the psychological assumptions on which payment by results is based?
3 What are the advantages and disadvantages of payment by results?
4 How typical or atypical is the case study in terms of payment systems?

TWENTY-FIVE

BIFU: A problem of union structure and democracy

PAUL WILLMAN

Background

The Banking, Insurance and Finance Union (BIFU) is a medium-sized, TUC affiliated union organizing manual, clerical and managerial staff in the finance sector. It had approximately 150,000 members in 1984 and, unlike many UK unions, it has continued to grow since 1979, on average by about 4 per cent per year. This reflects the continued expansion of employment in the sector. It is recognized for the purposes of collective bargaining by most of the main retail banks, as well as by a number of insurance companies, finance houses and building societies (see Appendix 1).

Traditionally, the union's centre of gravity was the clearing banks, mainly Lloyds, Barclays, Midland and NatWest. BIFU waged a long battle for recognition in these banks, which did not have a wholly satisfactory outcome. While resisting BIFU demands, the major clearers established in-house staff associations to process staff grievances. When recognition was finally conceded, BIFU had to share the negotiating table with the staff associations in dealings with the Federation of London Clearing Banks. After recognition, failure to remove the associations led to financial difficulties (Appendix 2). Conflict between the different staff bodies caused BIFU to withdraw from joint negotiations for a time in the 1970s. In addition, several fruitless attempts to merge with the staff associations were made; one of the main stumbling blocks was BIFU's affiliation to the TUC. Competition for membership and for influence is thus a central issue in BIFU operations.

Because of this competition, BIFU has never managed to achieve high membership density in the clearers. The proportion of clearing bank employees in the union has fluctuated around 35 per cent since 1975. During the 1970s the union sought to compensate for this failure by organizing outside the clearers. As a result, the percentage of members employed in the clearing banks has fallen sharply; BIFU was still a clearing bank union in 1972, with 73 per cent of members employed there, but by 1984 this had fallen to 48 per cent.

The strategy of diversification has secured steady growth for the last fifteen years (Appendix 3). The union is relatively small, and has few assets in comparison with its larger competitors, so the generation of new subscription income is vital (Appendices 2 and 4). It is also important for the union's status within the TUC; the general secretary has recently become a member of the General Council.

Issues

The pattern of growth has presented problems; the main ones are as follows:

The clearing banks

The expansion of membership outside the clearers makes it more difficult to negotiate a merger with the clearing bank staff associations. They stress the distinctiveness of their own institutions and the importance of in-house organization. The wider the span of BIFU membership, the more difficult the exercise of convincing them becomes. Since the clearers remain the biggest employment concentrations in the sector, these mergers are crucial for BIFU's growth.

Competition

BIFU has grown outside the banking area primarily by absorbing staff associations in mergers ('transfers of engagements'). This has caused conflict between the union and ASTMS in the insurance sector, which ASTMS had previously regarded as its own. The two unions now compete to offer the best terms to likely staff associations, one consequence of which has been discontent among the union's own employees about the pay levels offered to staff association heads on merger. Another consequence has been the involvement of the TUC in membership disputes between the two affiliates.

Structure and democracy

Pressures have arisen over the accommodation of members in new sectors. Traditionally, BIFU has been organized regionally, branches electing to area councils and thus to the executive committee.

However, 'minorities' in the union, such as in foreign banks, find their votes swamped by clearing bank members who still predominate in most areas. The union has created 'sections' based on institutions to cope with this; so, for example, there is a foreign banks Section Council with some independent decision-making power (Appendix 5). But the executive committee is still elected on a regional basis and is clearer-dominated; it is the central decision-making body and controls finances and the right to call strikes.

The clearer membership will resist further 'sectionalization'. But there are two powerful pressures for its further development. The first is that it makes it easier to attract staff associations outside the clearing banks into membership; staff in insurance and building societies do not want to be ruled by the clearing bank membership. The second is that the full-time officials of the union, who are appointed by the general secretary rather than elected by the membership are very much in favour of sections, since it organizes the union along the lines on which collective bargaining actually occurs. The major obstacle remains the current electoral system, which allows clearing bank membership through Area Councils and the Annual Delegate Conference to block change. In practice, some sections such as technical and services which control maintenance work in the bank computer centres are sufficiently powerful to go their own way.

Ownership and control

BIFU would probably have had to organize outside the banking sector sooner or later in order to retain control over employment in a substantial proportion of the financial services market. Increased levels of competition, particularly between banks and building societies, would have required extension of the membership base to preserve bargaining power. But the present sectional structure does not map that of ownership. The clearers actually own most of the finance houses and a number of other employing institutions outside the clearing bank section. The problems this can cause were shown recently in the Barclays–BBI merger when the International Banks Section lost a third of its membership to the Clearing Bank Section. The union may be diversifying at the wrong time (Appendix 6).

Technical change

The use of electronics affects the union in a number of ways. It leads to a growth in the numbers of part-time staff. It threatens to erode the power of computer centre staff. The distinctiveness of bank work is also eroded when technical changes such as counter automation and point-of-sale terminals cloud the distinction between banking and retailing where terms and conditions of employment are generally much poorer. There has been no widespread job loss as yet, but messengers in the city are a particularly vulnerable group given the advent of automated payment systems; they are all BIFU members. The union's membership is good in 'new technology' areas, but the banks generally will not discuss their future plans.

Question

1 How should the general secretary try to reform union structure and government in order to deal with these problems over the next five years?

Appendix 1

Procedural agreements

The union has a large number of procedural agreements with banks and other financial institutions and new agreements continue to be signed at a steady rate. The list of banks and companies below will give some idea of the wide scope of BIFU negotiations.

National agreements
English clearing banks   The Union negotiates directly with the Federation of London Clearing Bank Employers covering the five major banks. These negotiations deal with conditions of service at a national level. New procedural agreement signed in 1982.

  Non-clerical staff, England   The Joint Negotiating Council for Non-Clerical Banking Staff, 1970. Re-negotiated 1981.

  Scottish Clearing Banks   The Scottish Banking Staff Council negotiates direct with The Federation of Scottish Bank Employers at the national level on major terms and conditions of employment in the three clearing banks. The SBSC is composed entirely of BIFU members and officials.

  Clerical staff, Scotland   The Joint Negotiating Council of the Scottish Banking Industry, 1970.

  Non-clerical staff, Scotland   The Joint Negotiating Council for the Scottish Non-clerical Banking Staff, 1971.

Other national agreements
Trustee Savings Bank, 1947 Extended 1982.

Domestic Agreements, English Clearing Banks
Those conditions of service not negotiated at national level are negotiated

between the union and the individual banks under domestic procedural agreements.

Other banks
Airdrie Savings Bank, 1974.
Co-operative Bank Limited, 1938 Extended 1972.
Greenock Provident Bank, 1953.
Lloyds Bank In-store Division, 1973.
Yorkshire Bank, 1968 Extended 1972.

Procedural Agreements
Non-clerical staff, English Clearing Banks
Lloyds Bank Limited, 1970.
National Westminster Bank Limited, 1970. Re-negotiated 1981.

Scottish Clearing Banks
Bank of Scotland, 1971.
Clydeside Bank plc, 1972
Royal Bank of Scotland plc, 1971.

Foreign and Commonwealth Banks
Bank of Cyprus, 1976.
Bank of New South Wales (T & S), 1981.
Bank of Tokyo, 1972.
Bank of Tokyo Trust Company, 1972.
Bank of Baroda, 1976.
Central Bank of India, 1972.
National Commercial Banking Corporation of Australia Ltd, 1982.
Commercial Bank of Australia, 1980.
Commonwealth Banking Corporation, 1973.
Credit Lyonnais, 1978.
Bank of India, 1975.
Banco di Roma, 1975.
Banca Commerciale Italiana, 1979.
Banca Nazionale del Lavoro, 1979.
Bank fur Gemeinwirtschaft, 1983.
Habib Bank, 1975.
Ghana Commercial Bank, 1975.
Muslim Commercial, 1980.
National Bank of Greece, 1972.
National Bank of Pakistan, 1975.
National Bank of New Zealand, 1972.
Nedbank Limited, 1972.
Sonali Bank, 1976.
State Bank of India, 1975.
United Bank, 1980.

United Commercial Bank, 1972.
Zivnostenska Banka, 1973.

British Overseas Banks
Barclays Bank International, 1969. New Agreement, 1982.
Lloyds Bank International, 1972.
Moscow Narodny Bank Limited, 1975.
Standard Chartered Bank, 1973.
Grindlays Bank, 1979.

Finance Houses and Credit Card Companies
Credit Factoring International Ltd., 1976.
Joint Credit Card Company, 1972.
Lloyds & Scottish Finance Ltd., 1974.
Lombard North Central, 1974.
St Margaret's Trust, 1975.
United Dominions Trust, 1972.
First Co-operative Finance Ltd., 1979.

Procedural Agreements
Building Societies
Barnsley, 1972.
Birmingham and Bridgwater. New Agreement signed, 1982.
Blackheath, 1976.
Chatham Reliance, 1974.
Furness, 1974.
Hanley Economic, 1976.
Monmouth, 1974.
Newcastle, 1976.
Principality, 1976.
Ramsbury B. Soc., 1982.
Yorkshire, 1972.

Insurance Companies
Ecclesiastical Insurance Office, 1972.
Guardian Royal Exchange Assurance Company, 1978.
Methodist, 1978.
Phoenix, 1979.
TSB Trust Co. HQ, 1979.
TSB Trust Co. Sales Force, 1979.
Eagle Star, 1981. New Agreement signed in 1984.
Hearts of Oak Benefit Society, 1981.
United Kingdom Civil Service Benefit Society, 1983.
Royal Liver & Composite, 1982.

Other Institutions
Bankers Automated Clearing Services Limited, 1972.

Bankers Clearing House (Technical & Services), 1973.
Centre File Limited & Centre File Northern Limited, 1972.
Eurocom Data, 1974.
Stock Exchange, Engineering Staff, 1972.
Stock Exchange, Waiters, 1975.
Johnson Mathey, Messengers, 1979.

Appendix 2   Real subscription income per member 1965–84 (income per member)

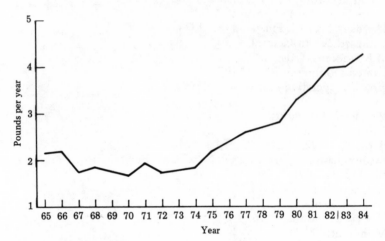

Note: At 1965 prices.
Source: BIFU

Appendix 3   BIFU membership growth 1945–83

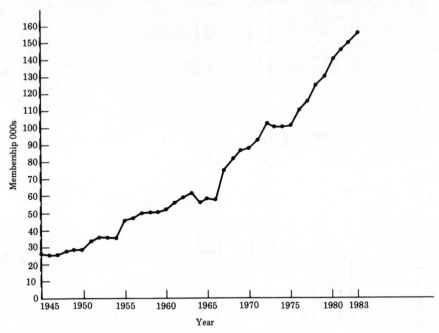

Source Union Records.

Appendix 4   Income, expenditure and assets, 1965–84

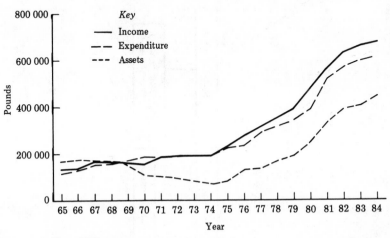

Note: 1965 prices.

Appendix 5 Organization and structure

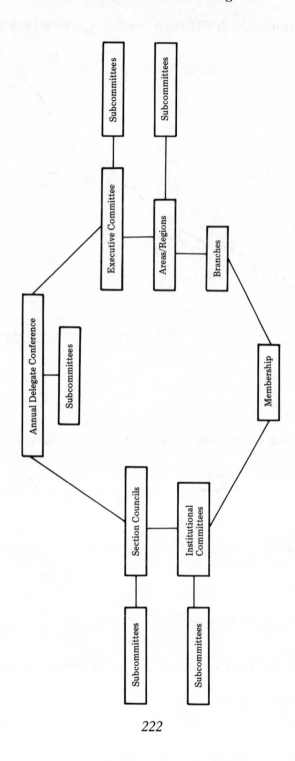

Appendix 6   Ownership and recognition; BIFU and clearance bank

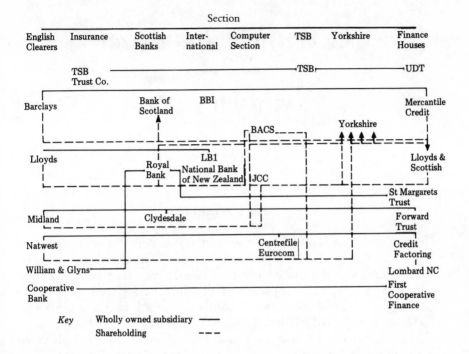

Section

| English Clearers | Insurance | Scottish Banks | Inter-national | Computer Section | TSB | Yorkshire | Finance Houses |

Key   Wholly owned subsidiary ——
        Shareholding   ---

TWENTY-SIX

Greenfield Industrial

PAUL WILLMAN

Background

Greenfield Industrial is a large multinational concern with its Head Office in the USA. It is primarily involved in the production of components for the motor vehicle industry where it has a technological lead in the development of fuel injection systems for diesel engines. Greenfield operates in a number of locations in the USA and Canada, as well as Brazil and South-East Asia.

In the USA and Canada, Greenfield has a long history of collective bargaining involvement with the United Auto Workers. The company's original Mid-Western operations have been unionized for a generation. Its newer parts in the south became unionized in the 1970s through an agreement which guaranteed union control over work transferred out of the mid-western plants. The UAW is recognized in Canada but the Brazilian and South-East Asian operations are non-union.

Greenfield has no overall corporate view on union recognition: its prevailing strategy has always been to bargain only when pressured to do so, and in general it seeks to adapt to local conditions. When production began in the Southern states union-free operation was seen as an advantage in terms of higher productivity and greater efficiency but unionization has not appeared to have the adverse effect on plant performance which many managers feared. In particular, the success of concession bargaining in the early 1980s, in which the company tended to follow the approach of Ford (see Appendix 1), has tended to change the view of union activity held within the company.

Investment in Europe

Greenfield are seeking to produce within the EEC: in particular, there is seen to be a growing market for the company's fuel injection system, and it is hoped to sell both to Ford Europe and to Opel/Vauxhall. In the first instance, the company intends to produce on only one site, where it will employ about 800 people. As yet, it has made no firm decision about location: the product has a high value-to-weight ratio but ease of access to good transport facilities is seen as important.

Preliminary analysis of the latest labour cost and strike data has already occurred (Appendix 3). Since the two major operations to which Greenfield hopes to sell are in the UK and West Germany, the company sees advantages in location in one or other, although alternative locations have not necessarily been ruled out. The company is attracted to the UK by labour cost considerations and by the prospect of regional grants. West Germany, though involving higher wages, has lower levels of conflict and, possibly as a consequence, slightly better unit labour costs (Appendix 4). In Germany higher levels of redundancy payment, statutory restrictions on overtime working (maximum two hours per day) and the requirement to offer board level representation to Works Councillors are also seen as disincentives. In addition, it is feared that there will be further conflicts over the thirty-five hour week.

A proportion of the board thus favour UK investment, particularly since the venture is regarded as slightly risky given the state of the European car market: it is felt that it would be easier to disinvest from the UK at low cost should something go wrong. However, the Managing Director has formed a very negative view of the 'union problem' in the UK, and will not go ahead unless he can be convinced that industrial relations problems can be avoided: a friend from Ford has recently shown figures on the Halewood–Saarlouis comparison and he feels that this is typical of labour relations problems in the UK.

Question

1 Your firm of consultants has been asked to produce a brief for the Managing Director outlining the main industrial relations problems likely to be faced by inwardly investing firms in the UK, and suggesting ways in which they can be avoided. In addition to the above, the following has been provided:

(a) The manual workforce will be relatively highly skilled, and predominantly male.
(b) Because of property prices, the company would probably locate away from the London area.
(c) The plants will have facilities for computer-aided design, and many assembly operations will be automated.
(d) The company is prepared to pay high wages by UK standards, but places a high premium on continuity of production.
(e) In the first instance, senior and middle managers will be imported from the USA.
(f) If the venture succeeds, a second European plant of approximately the same size and capacity will open.

Appendix 1   UAW-Ford report

Highlights of the revised contract

Following are some highlights from the proposed new contract negotiated between the UAW and Ford Motor Co. Summaries of the major points of the agreement are contained in this special report.

• **Plant closings** – A 24-month moratorium on out-sourcing-related plant closings.
• **Outsourcing** – Commitments by Ford aimed at maintaining job opportunities equivalent to those now encompassed by the total UAW-Ford national bargaining unit. Efforts will be made to manage work force reductions by attrition.
• **Guaranteed income** – A guaranteed-income-stream programme for high seniority Ford workers, which is a disincentive for the company to lay off workers.
• **Profit sharing** – A plan in which Ford workers will share in company profits.
• **Sub plan** – A strengthened Supplemental Unemployment Benefit programme, with prompt resumption of payments to eligible laid-off workers.
• **Training** – A new jointly-governed programme for training and retraining of current and displaced workers.
• **Equality of sacrifice** – A pledge that Ford managerial employees will share in any economic adjustments.
• **COLA** – Principle and formula of COLA (indexed cost of living allowance) is maintained. COLA deferral for three quarters will be fully restored.
• **Economic reopeners** – An economic reopener in the event of an unexpected major upturn in Ford sales.
• **Time off** – Paid Personal Holidays and bonus Sunday payments eliminated; full maintenance of Excused Absence Allowance Days and vacation entitlements unchanged from the 1979 agreement.

Breakthrough in job security

After more than a month of bargaining, UAW negotiators have won a new contract from Ford Motor Co. which provides major job-protection programmes for US Ford workers.

Under the proposed 2½-year agreement, which is subject to ratification, Ford would impose a 24-month moratorium on plant closings that would have occurred as a result of outsourcing the product manufactured in the facility (beyond those for which announcements already have been made).

The union also won a Guaranteed Income Stream (GIS) programme under which eligible Ford employees with 15 or more years seniority will receive 50% or more of gross pay until retirement or age 62; obtained new preferential placement opportunities for workers affected by plant closings; and secured the establishment of a new programme for training and retraining of current and displaced Ford employees. The union won a pilot programme in which lifetime job security will be guaranteed for 80% of the workforce in two locations.

In another key provision, UAW won – for the first time at Ford – a profit-sharing programme under which employees will receive a share of the company's earnings as sales of cars and trucks return to higher levels.

UAW also gained a pledge for immediate resumption of SUB payments for eligible workers who currently are laid off but not receiving SUB, due to a fall off of fund assets.

These – and many other gains – are summarized in this special UAW-Ford Report. In exchange for the breakthroughs in job security negotiated under the new agreement, Ford workers will make some adjustments. For example, there will be a deferral of three COLA payments, but they will be restored by the end of the contract.

'We have achieved an agreement which will preserve the jobs of thousands of Ford workers, and bring many of our unemployed brothers and sisters back to work.' UAW President Douglas Fraser and Vice-President Don Ephlin said. 'By negotiating now, instead of waiting until summer, when economic conditions likely will be worse, we were in a stronger position to bargain.'

Appendix 2   From *The New York Times*, Tuesday, February 16, 1982

Ford's New Contract: Who May Win, Who May Lose

By JOHN HOLUSHA
Special to the New York Times

Detroit, Feb. 15 – A tentative contract between the United Automobile Workers and the Ford Motor Company trades immediate wage and benefit concessions by workers for assurances of job security that may only prove their value over time, if at all.

News analysis

Under the terms of the agreement, which must be approved by local union leaders and ratified by Ford's workers, union members will give up annual pay increases, defer cost-of-living adjustments for nine months and lose six paid days off. In return, Ford has agreed to a profit-sharing plan, a 'guaranteed' income for workers with more than 15 years' seniority if they are laid off and a two-year moratorium on closing any plants because of decisions to buy components from outside suppliers.

The benefits to Ford are clear. According to James Harbour, an auto industry manufacturing consultant, the new contract will trim about $2 an hour from the company's labor costs over the life of the contract. Since it takes about 95 hours of direct labor to build a Ford compact car, the savings will be about $190 a car.

Unlike a plan developed at the General Motors Corporation earlier this year, Ford is under no obligation to pass this savings on to customers in the form of lower prices. Douglas A. Fraser, president of the UAW., said today that Ford would be 'hard-pressed to reduce prices' in its current money-losing condition.

The benefits to the union

The benefits to the union are less clear and less immediate, except for those currently unemployed workers who will again get supplemental unemployment benefits as a result of a $70 million advance to the benefits fund by Ford.

Among the cornerstones of the agreement are the moratorium on plant closings and a provision pledging the company to 'use every effort' to maintain current employment levels.

'A lot of that language is very vague to me, and it clearly gives Ford a great deal of flexibility,' said Maryann Keller, an auto industry analyst with Paine Webber Mitchell Hutchins Inc. 'Suppose a plant is building transmissions for rear-wheel-drive cars, and the company switches to a front-wheel-drive model. It seems to me the company could close that plant without violating the contract.'

Similarly, the guaranteed income plan may not cost Ford much during the agreement, which is to run until September 1984. 'Ford had 197,000 production workers at one point,' Mr. Harbour said. 'They're down to 105,000 now; they probably won't go below that, and if sales improve, it will probably go up. So that doesn't look like too much of a burden.' Regardless of what happens, Mr. Fraser said today, the new agreement puts a $45 million limit on total payments under the income plan.

Union dissidents at GM and Ford have argued against these concessions, saying that the company would simply use such savings to invest in automated machinery that would reduce jobs.

How to use the money saved

'This danger is real', said Harley Shaiken, a labor relations specialist at Massachusetts Institute of Technology.

'There are two ways to reduce costs: You can outsource or you can automate,' said Mr. Shaiken. While the contract puts limits on 'outsourcing,' or shifting production to outside suppliers, there are no limits on automation. 'The familiar danger is Ford moving an operation to Mexico,' Mr. Shaiken observed. 'Now the danger is that the plant stays where it is, but the new technology goes in and decimates the work force.'

The union retreated on some of its long-held bargaining goals, while establishing some new principles.

The loss of the remaining six paid personal holidays in the old contract represents a retreat from the goal of a four-day workweek. When the extra paid time off was first won in 1973, it was presented as the first step toward that goal.

And, Mr Shaiken notes, the absence of any inflation protection for retired union members in the new contract means that the key goal of the 1979 negotiations was quietly dropped.

The principle of profit-sharing

But the contract does establish the principles that Ford will share profits with its production workers, and will guarantee incomes as long as the funds last.

Though modest in scope now, these programs could become a problem for Ford in later years, Mrs Keller cautions. 'Principles have a way of becoming enriched as time goes on,' she said. Both cost-of-living adjustments and paid days off began in modest fashion, but became major costs in successive contracts.

Whatever its ultimate costs and benefit, the Ford contract appears to have been carefully drawn to assure ratification. Most of those still working in Ford plants have over 15 years' seniority and stand to benefit from the job-security provisions. And some of the sacrifices, such as reduced benefits for new employees, are to come from people not yet on the payroll, and thus will not be difficult for those already on the job to accept.

Copyright © 1982 by The New York Times Company. Reprinted by permission.

Appendix 3

Hourly Compensation in Motor Vehicles and Equipment Industry etc.

	Hourly compensation in motor vehicles and equipment industry[1] (USA=100)	Working days lost per 1000 workers (whole economy)[2] (USA=404)
Canada	69	860
Brazil	18	—
Korea	12	—
Japan	50	85
Belgium	95	219
France	65	181
Germany	102	24
Italy	58	1197
Netherlands	87	22
UK	46	448
Spain	43	770

[1]*Source* US Department of Labor, 1983.
[2]*Source DE Gazette*, 1984. Figures are the average of the decade 1973–83.

Annual per cent changes in hourly compensation and unit labour costs in manufacturing, 12 countries. 1960–82

Year	United States	Canada	Japan	France	Germany	Italy	UK	Belgium	Denmark	Netherlands	Norway	Sweden	Eleven foreign countries (weighted)*
Hourly compensation													
1960–82	7·0	9·0	14·4	12·5	10·0	16·5	13·4	12·3	13·2	12·7	11·7	11·9	12·1
1960–73	5·0	6·4	14·6	9·6	9·6	12·3	8·7	10·5	11·8	12·8	9·8	10·4	12·1
1973–82	9·5	11·8	9·1	15·4	8·5	19·6	17·8	11·1	12·2	9·1	12·1	12·3	12·3
1973–79	9·3	12·2	11·4	16·0	9·2	20·5	19·0	13·5	13·5	11·4	13·8	14·4	13·4
1980	11·7	10·4	7·9	14·1	8·9	18·9	21·6	9·6	10·9	5·2	11·0	11·1	11·7
1981	9·9	14·8	6·3	16·0	7·6	22·1	17·2	8·9	10·6	5·0	12·1	10·8	12·0
1982	8·5	12·2	3·4	16·7	5·5	18·1	9·1	5·3	9·8	6·5	10·2	7·2	9·3
Unit labour costs													
1960–82	4·3	5·2	4·8	6·3	4·7	10·2	9·5	4·7	6·8	5·3	7·7	6·8	6·1
1960–73	1·9	1·8	3·5	2·7	3·7	5·1	4·1	3·3	5·1	4·8	5·1	3·5	3·4
1973–82	7·7	10·0	1·8	10·4	4·7	15·4	15·7	4·9	7·8	4·1	9·8	10·0	8·1
1973–79	7·2	9·6	4·3	10·1	4·6	16·9	17·1	6·3	8·6	5·3	11·8	12·1	8·9
1980	11·5	12·9	1·5	12·4	7·3	12·4	22·9	6·8	9·4	3·0	8·2	9·3	9·3
1981	6·1	12·1	0·5	13·4	5·1	18·0	9·9	3·1	3·3	2·5	10·1	10·4	8·1
1982	7·2	15·3	0·7	11·3	3·8	16·5	5·1	0·2	8·7	3·2	10·4	5·8	7·1
Unit labour costs in US dollars													
1960–82	4·3	4·7	7·6	6·3	8·8	7·4	7·3	7·0	7·5	8·3	9·6	7·4	7·1
1960–73	1·9	1·9	4·9	2·4	6·1	5·4	2·6	4·4	5·0	6·1	6·0	4·3	4·0
1973–82	7·7	7·0	5·1	7·8	7·5	6·8	13·5	5·5	5·6	6·0	9·3	7·1	7·5
1973–79	7·2	6·4	9·7	10·5	11·0	9·2	12·7	11·3	10·8	10·9	13·7	12·0	9·9
1980	11·5	13·1	4·7	13·3	8·3	9·2	34·6	7·3	2·2	4·0	11·0	10·9	10·0
1981	6·1	9·3	3·1	-11·6	5·3	-10·8	-4·4	-18·7	-18·1	-18·2	-5·4	-7·3	-5·8
1982	7·2	12·0	-12·2	8·5	-3·7	-2·6	-9·2	-19·0	-7·5	-3·9	-1·8	-15·2	-4·6

*A trade-weighted average of the 11 foreign countries.
Note: Rates of change computed from the least squares trend of the logarithms of the index numbers.
Source NIER.

231

Appendix 4 Total labour costs, productivity and unit labour costs in manufacturing: UK, USA and Germany, 1971–83

| | UK | | | | USA | | | | Germany | | | |
	1971	1976	1981	1983	1971	1976	1981	1983	1971	1976	1981	1983
1 Total labour costs	100	100	100	100	236	209	146	186	151	208	145	160
2 Labour productivity	100	100	100	100	294	284	302	298	133	147	157	153
3 Unit labour costs	100	100	100	100	80	74	48	62	114	141	92	105

Source NIER.

TWENTY-SEVEN

Suspending quality circles: Alcan Plate Limited

JOHN BANK

Preparing for a £11.5 million expansion, while many other firms in the Midlands were contracting, put Alcan Metal in an enviable position in the spring of 1981. It seemed a very good time to launch quality circles.

Background

Alcan Plate Limited is a subsidiary of British Alcan Aluminium. Alcan is the short name for Alcan Aluminium Limited of Canada, a multinational based in Montreal, whose main business is aluminium, from the mining of ore to the production and sales of numerous finished products. It has gross assets of over $US6.4 billion. British Alcan Aluminium employs over 7000 people in Britain and operates one of the only two major aluminium smelters left in the UK.

Alcan Plate Limited's works and offices are in Kitts Green (Birmingham). It now employs about 700 people, who are engaged in the manufacture and sales of plate products and the rolling of special sheet products. At the time of the quality circle launch the workforce numbered 1000.

Production of aluminium has continued at Alcan Plate since 1938, when the company operated the plant to meet the needs of aircraft production during the Second World War. Throughout the years, the works have been continually modernized and the company has invested many millions of pounds in major plant and equipment since the late 1950s and early 1960s. Alcan Plate is the only source of aluminium plate in Britain and one of three large plants in Europe.

The works receive aluminium ingot and coil from other companies and convert this into a variety of semi-finished products by rolling and other methods. In recent years the company has been associated with, and supplied the metal for, a number of prestige products.

Almost all the major British aircraft – including the Anglo-French Concorde – have incorporated Alcan metal in their structure. The company currently provides material for the Trident, European Airbus, RAF Nimrod, the multirole combat aircraft Tornado, the Jaguar and the Harrier, as well as many others. The Scorpion aluminium tank uses plate from Alcan. The European spacelab also required Alcan's aluminium plate.

A wide variety of high-technology plate produced by Alcan is also utilized in the shipbuilding industries. Ironically, Alcan aluminium plate was used both in HMS *Coventry* and HMS *Sheffield* and in the Exocet missiles that sank both ships during the Falklands war. Alcan produces coated strip aluminium for engineering markets and for cladding mobile homes and for use as architectural building sheets. For the domestic market, Alcan supplies circles from which saucepans and kettles can be pressed and spun. This domestic side of the business and the market for coated strip aluminium was very depressed in the spring of 1981. The backbone of Alcan Plate, the military and aircraft market, was buoyant but becoming more fiercely competitive.

Convergences

The thrust to set up quality circles came from two separate sources. On the technical side, both Graham Johnson, quality supervisor, and his immediate superior, Brian Simons, quality manager, had read about quality circles and Johnson attended a half-day conference about them. They were keen to start pilot circles.

Quite independently, Colin Siddle, training–manager, and David Gregson, personnel manager, had initiated a training intervention for middle managers which dealt primarily with superintendents. The management development programme was undertaken in parallel with the extensive investment programme coming on stream. One of the concerns of senior management on site was to ensure that managers at all levels operated fully and consistently with their positions. It was observed that managers tended to drift to tasks and roles below their levels. A modular course was designed at the Cranfield School of Management to re-focus the superintendents and to counter the downward drift of managerial activity. Projects undertaken at the plant were linked to the learning modules at the business school. One of these projects was for the superintendents to help Graham Johnson launch a pilot programme of quality circles.

The decision to launch the quality circles was taken at board level just before Easter in 1981. Early in April, the superintendents attended a five-day management development module at Cranfield. Quality circles was one of the topics discussed. At the end of the module the men selected the introduction of quality circles at Alcan Plate as their project to be effected between 9th April and their next module at Cranfield on 20th September. The quality circles project seemed a perfect choice, as it encompassed many ideas of effective employee participation and good industrial relations.

By late June the preparation for the launch of quality circles was well under way. The superintendents working with Graham Johnson had selected a strategy for introducing the concept of quality circles. They used the 'portakabin' communication centre, affectionately called 'the Wendy House' to reach the workforce in small groups with a showing of a film on quality circles from British Leyland. No outside quality circle consultancies were employed. No formal training in quality circles was given to either foreman or circle members. The company was intent on growing its own circles using only its own resources, and this later proved to be a weakness in the programme.

Avoiding a crisis

Although it is desirable to 'grow your own' quality circles, there are certain core principles that emerge from the data on successful circles programmes, for example, voluntariness and the *training* of circle members, which are ignored at a company's peril. Alcan kept the programme voluntary, but the superintendents were on the verge of violating several other key principles.

The superintendents had no expert input, nor had they been to visit quality circles in other companies. Not surprisingly, the plan the superintendents produced contained three fundamental errors.

1 They wanted to hand down the initial problems for the circles to solve, rather than let the circles select the problems themselves. This would affect the 'ownership' of the problems. It also affected the level of trust in the circle members, particularly when linked with the desire of superintendents to attend circle meetings happening on their 'patch'.
2 They had decided to give some 'chairmanship' training to the

foreman, and *no* quality circles training to the foreman or to circle members.

3 They were over-reacting to an initial rebuff from the craft trade unions.

The trade union issue was by far the most immediate. At short notice, the superintendents had invited six representatives from the craft trade unions to an introductory session on quality circles at the plant communications centre. The short session was to consist of the showing of a film on quality circle introduction at British Leyland. The initial response of the trade unionists to the face-to-face invitations was positive. They all said they would be there. But at the appointed time, not one trade union leader came. 'Well, they've had their bite of the cherry,' one superintendent said, 'they'll not get another. We'll do it without them.' Fortunately, cooler heads prevailed and the trade union representatives were approached again.

Industrial relations at Alcan Plate were running smoothly in 1981. The main unions on site were the Transport and General Workers Union with two-fifths of the blue-collar workforce, and the balance divided among the Amalgamated Union of Engineering Workers, the Electrical, Electronic, Telecommunications and Plumbing Union and the National Union of Sheet Metal Workers, Coppersmiths, Heating and Domestic Engineers. Staff belonged to the Association of Scientific, Technical, Managerial and Supervisory Staffs or the Association of Clerical, Technical and Supervisory Staffs.

The introduction of continuous shiftworking (the continental shift) had earlier met trade union opposition, but management had prevailed without building up a legacy of hostility. A renegotiation of the bonus system in the winter of 1981 to bring it into line with the company's profits rather than tonnage of production went surprisingly well. The main union involved in the quality circle installation was the T&GWU.

Start-up

The two pilot quality circles were begun in the Plate Finishing Department and in the paint line section in late August. Because Alcan Plate works a continuous shift system, the meetings were held every twelve days at the start of the day shift for the circle members.

Ken Smith, general foreman in the Plate Finishing Department, became the first QC leader. He summed up the launch. 'Initial reactions were the same as in the past: "Well it's another meeting and it will die a death." We got volunteers which included the shop steward who came to only one meeting but continued to give his support.' The QC in the Plate Finishing Department decided, as its first problem, to improve the surface quality of magnesium (non-heat-treatable) plate. Alcan had a bad reputation for surface quality in the marketplace for customers looking for scratch-free, decorative finish on magnesium plate. The company's plate tended to be pitted and scratched, which was all right for machining or forming, but unsatisfactory if the customer planned to leave it as it came from the factory.

The QC produced a dozen solutions to the problem of surface scratches. These included using vacuum beans to handle the large wide plates, the use of foil to protect overlaps at annealing, and the use of card as protection when getting shoes across plate. The QC instigated the use of 2ft × 2ft wooden spacers (offcuts from cases that are used in another department) between the large sheets of metal at the stacking on the stretcher and did other practical things such as putting felt on rest plates and fitting more air wipes to blow swarf more successfully off the plate; all in an attempt to eliminate or reduce surface scratches. The basketful of ideas produced a 25 per cent lower rejection rate for surface defects as compared to the preceding six months, saving 3.36 tonnes of plate. In a period when customers were driving up inspection standards, this produced a direct saving (in six months) of $1,200 and an unquantifiable advantage in the market as the quality of Alcan magnesium plate began to rival that of its competitors.

Graham Johnson credits the QC with a 'dramatic improvement' in the surface quality of the magnesium plate. 'We went from horrible surfaces for non-heat treatable magnesium to quite presentable surfaces as good as any in Europe and our salesmen felt the improvement immediately. This was directly attributable to the quality circle' He explained, 'the circles enabled us to get closer to the guys, to feed them information about the problems and the implication. They came up with ideas and ways of solving the problems. They asked for more information and this increased their overall interest in the job.'

The second pilot quality circle was started in the paint line with K. Rider as leader. Its first project was to improve the Tannoy system to effect speedier line communications. This proved to be an important project because a five-minute delay can cost up to 400 kg of scrap. During its first meeting the circle also decided to improve on line viewing facilities which helped to spot paint defects.

Two further circles were started: another in plate finishing and one in the foundry. The foundry circle was the most dramatic first project. It registered savings of £15,000 per year.

The project was aimed at reducing melt loss. In the foundry casting furnaces, process scrap, raw ingots of aluminium and the necessary alloying elements are combined together and melted in one of three large casting furnaces. After the molten metal has been fluxed and cleansed it is cast into slabs or ingots by the semi-continuous direct chill method. At all stages in the process, samples are taken for quality control purposes to ensure that the metal is of the correct alloy composition and of the highest quality.

During the melting process the dross rises to the top and is dragged off with rakes. Alcan Plate used to pay an outside firm to take away the dross, reclaim good aluminium metal and then sell the metal back to Alcan. The quality circle in the foundry took on this problem of melt loss, solved it, and was able to dispense with the services of the outside firm. The circle then began to look at ways of improving draining and preserving spillage scrap as a usable commodity. The suggestions they came up with and implemented included:

1 Designing small dross pans with holes to drain holder dross after fixing it with a flux. (The flux makes the dross cling to it, and when the flux is raked into an atmosphere with more oxygen it flares up again, releasing the aluminium.)
2 Developing spillage pans for scrap.
3 Using serrated rakes (instead of straight-edge ones) to reduce the amount of metal being skimmed off along with the dross.
4 New procedures for charging pellets.

The use of the small pans alone is saving about 28 kg of metal every time a furnace is charged. This is worth over £15,000 per annum.

Fighting for survival

Despite the initial success, circumstances at Alcan Plate conspired against QCs. There were the problems of installing the new furnace and computer systems. Furthermore, a sharp downturn in the market forced about 300 redundancies on the already small work-force. The redundancies took away the attention of management which was necessary for quality circles to thrive. As Graham Johnson explained in the autumn of 1983, 'When you go through a large redundancy programme you tend not to adjust immediately. You don't gear straight away, you try to carry on providing the information and services you did before. We now must learn to adjust. During the last nine months, we've not had the time for circles, so they've been suspended. But we are now planning a relaunch. We want one in each department on each shift.' The excessive dependency of the circles on the two managers, Graham Johnson and Ken Smith, meant they could not operate without the men in attendance.

Questions

1 Should Alcan re-instate quality circles? Provide reasons for your answer.
2 If you consider that quality circles should be re-instated in Alcan how should they be structured so as to function effectively?
3 What are the advantages of introducing quality circles into an organization?
4 Identify the possible reasons for quality circles failure in an organization.